Historical Thinking and Other Unnatural Acts

In the series

Critical Perspectives on the Past

edited by Susan Porter Benson, Stephen Brier, and Roy Rosenzweig

Historical Thinking
and Other
Unnatural Acts

**CHARTING THE FUTURE
OF TEACHING
THE PAST**

Sam Wineburg

 Temple University Press
PHILADELPHIA

Temple University Press, Philadelphia 19122
Copyright © 2001 by Temple University
Published 2001
Printed in the United States of America

∞ The paper used in this publication meets the requirements of the American National Standard for Information Sciences—Permanence of Paper for Printed Library Materials, ANSI Z39.48–1984.

Library of Congress Cataloging-in-Publication Data

Wineburg, Samuel S.
  Historical thinking and other unnatural acts : charting the future of teaching the past / Sam Wineburg.
     p. cm. — (Critical perspectives on the past)
     Includes bibliographical references.
     ISBN 1-56639-855-X (cloth : alk. paper) — ISBN 1-56639-856-8 (pbk. : alk. paper)
     1. History—Study and teaching—Philosophy. 2. United States—History—Study and teaching. 3. Historiography. 4. Culture conflict—United States. I. Title. II. Series.

D16.2.W56 2001
907 21; aa05 11-06—dc00   00–053214
ISBN 13: 978-1-56639-856-5

Contents

Part IV
HISTORY AS NATIONAL MEMORY

Introduction

Understanding Historical Understanding

dentify the source of the following statement:

> Surely a grade of 33 in 100 on the simplest and most obvious facts of American history is not a record in which any high school can take pride.

The above characterization of high school students' historical knowledge comes from:

(a) Ravitch and Finn's report on the 1987 National Assessment of Educational Progress, in which they argued that students' test scores place them "at risk of being gravely handicapped by . . . ignorance upon entry into adulthood, citizenship, and parenthood."

(b) The 1976 *New York Times* test of American youth, published under the banner *"Times* Test Shows Knowledge of American History Limited."

(c) Reports on the 1942 *New York Times* history exam that prompted Allan Nevins to write that high school students are "all too ignorant of American history."

(d) None of the above.

The correct answer is (d), none of the above.[1] This quotation comes neither from the 1987 National Assessment nor from any of the earlier reports. To find its source we have to go back to 1917, long before television, the social studies lobby, the teaching of "thinking skills," the breakup of the family, the growth of the Internet, or any of the other factors we use to explain low test scores. Yet the conclusions of

J. Carleton Bell and David McCollum, who in 1917 tested 668 Texas high school students and published their findings in the fledgling *Journal of Educational Psychology*, differ little from those of subsequent commentators. Considering the vast differences between those who attended high school in 1917 and the near-universal enrollments of today, the stability of students' ignorance is amazing. The whole world has turned on its head, but one thing has stayed the same: Kids don't know history.

Or so the conventional story goes. But it is a story that rests on shaky foundations.[2] It may be that we have spent so much time discovering (only to rediscover over and over and over . . .) what students *don't* know that we have neglected more useful questions about young people's historical knowledge. For example, what *do* students know about the past? What sources beyond teachers and textbooks contribute to their understanding? How do they make meaning from complex historical documents? How do they navigate between images of the past learned in the home and those encountered in school? How do they situate their own personal histories in the context of national and world history?

These questions have rarely been asked. From Bell and McCollum's 1917 survey to the latest national assessments, efforts to understand children's historical knowledge have followed a well-beaten path. Adults come together to determine what facts kids should know. They administer a test. When results come back showing that students did poorly, they seldom ask what youngsters might have been thinking or how students might have interpreted the task before them. Deliberations about children's minds resemble those of an entomologist peering at an ant: the ant (or child) is viewed as a species not only smaller but vastly inferior to ourselves.[3] We look at it from the outside, measure it, and assign it a number. And, with reference to young people, we quickly forget the leap of faith between the statement that students don't know what we want them to know and the conclusion that they don't know anything at all.

The strategy of labeling, rather than trying to understand, students' historical knowledge has led to arid discussions of pedagogy. Students would know more history, according to one common explanation, if teachers taught content rather than "skills." For commentators like Arthur Bestor, writing in 1953, or Sean Wilentz, writing in 1996, the bogeyman is the "social studies lobby" (one wonders what kind of lobby worked Texas backrooms in 1917, something neither Bestor nor Wilentz happened to mention).[4] Other aspects of the discussion focus on how to periodize the U.S. history course or assign the proper sequence to topics in the curriculum. The 1987 Bradley Commission noted that, with respect to pedagogy, variety is the spice of learning, and it encouraged teachers to select from a mix of teaching methods and techniques. But skilled history teaching is no more a matter of selecting the right mix of methods than historical interpretation is a matter of selecting the right mix of documents. The common factor in all these discussions is a blurry image of the learner and what that learner brings to instruction. To be sure, historical knowledge, as Michael Schudson put it, "seeps into the cultural pores" even if such knowledge is not "readily retrievable by seventeen-year-olds answering a quiz." Large-scale tests may tell us something about what young people know, but to assume that they constitute the alpha and omega of historical knowledge thwarts any serious investigation of American intellectual life and culture.[5]

Beyond the lurid headlines and hand-wringing lies a more basic question: What does the teaching of history contribute to a democratic society? Or, as my colleague Gaea Leinhardt puts it, What does history contribute to social literacy? What ways of thinking, writing, and questioning would be lost if we eliminated history from the curriculum?

This is not a new question, of course. Woodrow Wilson addressed it when he claimed that history endows us with the "invaluable mental power we call judgment," and similar sentiments echo whenever the American Historical Association commissions a study on the state of the undergraduate major.[6] But the role of history as a tool for changing how we think, for promoting a literacy not of names and dates but of discernment, judgment, and caution, does not receive prime billing in the public sphere.

The essays in this book begin with the basic assumption that history teaches us a way to make choices, to balance opinions, to tell stories, and to become uneasy—when necessary—about the stories we tell. This history is worlds apart from Rush Limbaugh's version: "History is real simple. You know what history is? It's what happened."[7]

Limbaugh's history served me well in high school. History was figuring out what topics were on the test and how to psyche out Frances T. Peritano, *Miss* Peritano, in crafting an essay response. I flourished in this system. It wasn't until my freshman year at Brown University, in Jacob Neusner's history of religion course, that I began to worry about my ability as a history student. Neusner ("an experience not to be missed," said the unofficial course guide) began the course at the beginning, literally. "What is the text *doing*," he asked about Genesis 1, as a hundred students or so collectively quaked in their seats. One after another, baffled freshmen summarized the text, only to have Neusner strike his fist on the podium: "*Doing*, not saying. What is the text *doing*?"

When I found myself teaching history to middle and high school students some years later, I realized that I too could exhort students to examine the "polemic" of the text (a term Neusner imprinted on my consciousness). But apart from the tried-and-true pedagogic strategy of "read it again" (or, alternatively, "read it slowly" or "read it to your partner" or "read it in groups"), I had no clue why some students could, and others could not, arrive at interpretations that seemed to me self-evident.

Books on teaching provided few clues. Textbooks on the psychology of learning, as well as how-to books like McKeachie's *Teaching Tips*[8] were concerned mostly with "technique"—when to insert an example into a lecture, how to do group work, or how to ask questions at different levels of Bloom's Taxonomy. But generic issues were not what irked me. I wanted to know about the specific challenges that historical texts posed to young people, and what prevented them from reading these texts more critically.

My arrival at graduate school coincided with the ascendance of the "cognitive revolution" in psychology and education. Behaviorism's decades-old hegemony came crashing down during the early 1980s, as psychologists and educators realized the folly of trying to understand memory by examining nonsense syllables or plumbing the nature of reasoning by using abstract logic problems. Holding a bachelor's degree in the history of religion, and never having taken a psychology course in my life, I was a fish out of water in Stanford's Ph.D. program in "Psychological Studies in Education." But somehow my application ended up on the desk of Lee Shulman, who wagered that what I brought to the program would outweigh what I lacked.

In my first semester, I took a course that symbolized the changes brewing in the field. "Cognitive Science and Education" was filled with the new research on the "naïve epistemologies" of physics students, the "mal-rules" that led math students into systematic and correctable errors, and the Lamarckian and instruction-resistant beliefs of biology students. The requirement for the course was a literature review on one of the disciplines in the school curriculum. When I informed the professor that I would review the literature on history learning, I met a chilly response. "Can't," she said matter-of-factly, "there's no literature to review. Start with the literature on reading."

Ever dutiful, I spent the next two weeks slogging through studies of phonemic awareness, whole language, and issues of dyslexia and other disabilities. In my darkest moments, I rummaged my drawers in search of the law school applications that I had packed away the year before. Finally, I made an appointment with my advisor. "No literature," smiled Shulman, unmoved by my end-of-the-world expression. "You'll start one."

The essays in this book represent my response to this challenge. Since my first acquaintance with the cognitive sciences, I have been concerned with the question of understanding historical understanding, to use Suzanne Wilson's apt expression. Lest I convey the impression that I discovered this question only by ignoring the vast historiographic literature on this topic, let me assure readers that I have benefited immeasurably from the likes of Collingwood, Hexter, Bloch, Gottschalk, Woodward, Becker, Bailyn, Novick, Ginzburg, and others. This body of literature, often autobiographical and self-reflective on the writer's career as researcher, lecturer, and teacher, contains bountiful insights. But, by and large, it trains its gaze on skilled historical practice, and focuses on the endpoints, the termini, of historical cognition. As a researcher into historical cognition, I am most interested in what goes on in the middle: the way stations of skilled historical practice, the false starts, the half-baked ideas, the wild goose chases that are edited out of historians' monographs, as well as their methods books for novices.

To reveal historical cognition before it gets tidied up for public presentation, I could not rely on the traditional arsenal of research techniques. Multiple choice tests tell us only that the correct bubble was blackened, but not what thinking processes led to the choice. In search of historical understanding, I have ventured into hundreds of classrooms—sometimes for months on end—listening, observing, recording, talking to students and teachers alike. At other times, to get a closer look at historical thinking as it unfolded, I have taught historians and students, teachers and parents to articulate their thoughts and "read aloud" the documents I gave them, a technique that provides access to historical cognition in "real time."

I have taken historians out of their natural habitat (their favored research specializations) to study how historical cognition unfolds and to assess the "value added" of historical training when a medievalist is thrown into the documentary literature of the American Revolution or a specialist in the growth of American cities confronts Lincoln's views on slavery. Deprived of their knowledge of the monographic literature and confronting these documents with a paltry knowledge base, these historians faced essentially the same task as undergraduates in survey courses or high school students staring down the Document-Based Question on an Advanced Placement exam. What remains of historical training when someone who has written three books on the Ming Dynasty (and last took a course in U.S. history as a college junior) tries to understand what happened on Lexington Green on April 19, 1775? To say that historians did better on this task than students because they are historians merely substitutes ascription for explanation. What is it, exactly, that historians do when they "read historically"? What concrete acts of cognition lead to sophisticated historical interpretations?

The first two chapters in this book provide an overview of its themes. The first is set in the context of the "History Wars" of the late 1980s and 1990s, when the movement to erect national history standards thrust dusty issues of the curriculum onto the op-ed pages of major newspapers. The debate over *which* history to teach so dominated the debate (falling out along predictable political lines) that the more important question of *why* teach history in the first place was lost. Relying on my research with students, teachers, and historians I take up the latter issue. Chapter 2 places my own research program in the background as I survey the broader field of research on teaching and learning history. This research has been conducted mostly by psychologists but is increasingly carried out by teachers and historians.

Part II focuses on the challenges faced by novices in learning history. Chapter 3 compares the readings of high school students with those of professional historians, while Chapter 4 is a case study of two college students, both preparing to become teachers. Chapter 5 focuses on how fifth and seventh graders "pictured the past" by making drawings of Pilgrims, Western Settlers, and Hippies. Their responses show the resilience, in the face of curriculum interventions designed to overcome them, of traditional assumptions about gender.

The chapters in Part III take up history teaching. These three essays grew out of my experience with Lee Shulman's Teacher Assessment Project at Stanford. Each was co-written with Suzanne Wilson, who has shared with me over the past decade a passionate drive to understand history teaching as a complex intellectual act.

The final duet of essays in Part IV seeks a broader context for history instruction by considering it alongside other "memory sites" in society.

While the setting for the first essay is the classroom, it is clear that high school students bring to their lessons deeply entrenched narratives from the home. The final chapter describes my attempt to reach beyond both the classroom and the school as research sites to embrace the home, the community, the church, and the "cultural history curriculum" of the larger society.

Discerning readers will detect differences in style, tone, and genre in the pieces assembled here. Some chapters began as research reports written for psychologists, others as case studies used in training new teachers, and others as informal talks or academic colloquia. I have reworked some of these essays for a wider audience; others have been only lightly retouched. A brief explanatory note at the end of each chapter describes its origin and provides pointers to more recent work.

Over the years intellectual debts pile up. The hand of Lee Shulman is easily discerned in the chapters on teaching, but his hidden hand is present throughout. Suzanne Wilson and Peter Seixas read every essay that appears here more times than either would like to remember. The University of Washington has provided a supportive environment in which to do this work. I have learned much from my colleagues in the history department, in particular Tom Pressly and John Findlay, both of whom were sufficiently intrigued by what a cognitive psychologist might say about learning history that they invited me into their midst. In the College of Education, my friendship with Pam Grossman has been a rock of support. Likewise, Debby Kerdeman has been a patient friend and colleague. Susan Monas has read every one of these essays as well, showing me where my prose faltered and teaching me more about writing than she will ever realize. I thank them all.

In 1991, after publishing a summary of some of this research in the American Historical Association's *Perspectives,* I received an unsolicited note from Roy Rosenzweig cheering me on. It was Roy's prodding that eventually led to this volume. Without his encouragement and that of Janet Francendese at Temple, this book would not exist.

Beginning with my Ph.D. assistantship, continuing through pre- and post-doctoral fellowships, and extending to grant support for the Historical Sense-Making project (see Chapter 10), my work has been generously supported by the Spencer Foundation. Patricia Albjerg Graham, past president of the foundation, took a special interest in this work and gambled that this "unconventional" line of inquiry would ultimately bear fruit. For the ongoing support of the Spencer Foundation, I am very grateful.

NOTES

1. See Diane Ravitch and Chester Finn, Jr., *What Do Our 17-Year-Olds Know? A Report on the First National Assessment of History and Literature* (New York, 1987), 201; *New York Times*, May 2, 1976; Allan Nevins, "American History for Americans," *New York Times Magazine* (May 3, 1942), 6, 28–29; J. Carleton Bell and David F. McCollum, "A Study of the Attainments of Pupils in United States History," *Journal of Educational Psychology* 8 (1917), 257–74.

2. The psychometrican Dale Whittington has challenged claims of depreciation in historical knowledge based on results of large-scale tests. See her "What Have 17-Year-Olds Known in the Past?" *American Educational Research Journal* 28 (1991), 759–80.

3. The analogy is David Olson's. See his introduction in David R. Olson and Nancy Torrance, *Handbook of Education and Development* (Cambridge, Mass., 1996).

4. Arthur Bestor, *Educational Wastelands: The Retreat from Learning in Public Schools* (Urbana, 1953); Sean Wilentz, "The Past Is Not a Process," *New York Times*, April 20, 1996. Wilentz predicted that the "historical illiteracy of today's student will only worsen in the generation to come," without reference to similar baleful predictions from 1917, 1942, or 1987.

5. On this point, see Michael Schudson, *Watergate in American Memory: How We Remember, Forget, and Reconstruct the Past* (New York, 1992), 64.

6. See Chapters 1 and 3.

7. Rush Limbaugh III, October 4, 1994, cited in Gary Nash, Charlotte Crabtree, and Ross Dunn, *History on Trial: Culture Wars and the Teaching of the Past* (New York, 1997), 6.

8. Wilbert James McKeachie, *McKeachie's Teaching Tips: Strategies, Research, and Theory for College and University Teachers* (Boston, 1999).

WHY STUDY HISTORY?

1

Historical Thinking and Other Unnatural Acts

T he choice between the two seemed absurd but this was exactly what the debate about national history standards had become. "George Washington or Bart Simpson," asked Senator Slade Gorton (R-Wash.) during the 1995 Congressional debates on this subject: Which figure represents a "more important part of our Nation's history for our children to study?"[1] To Gorton, the proposed national standards represented a frontal attack on American civilization, an "ideologically driven anti-Western monument to politically correct caricature."[2] The Senate, in apparent agreement, rejected the standards 99–1.

The standards' architects did not take this rejection lying down. Gary Nash, Charlotte Crabtree, and Ross Dunn, the team largely responsible for collating the reports of many panels and committees, issued a 318-page rebuttal packed with refutations of Gorton, his chief sponsor, Lynne Cheney, then chair of the National Endowment for the Humanities, and their various conservative allies—many of them op-ed columnists and radio talk show hosts. Gorton was right, Nash and his colleagues admitted, in claiming that no standard *explicitly* named George Washington as the first president. But this was a mere technicality. The standards asked students "to examine major issues confronting the young country during [Washington's] presidency," and there was more material on

Washington as the "father of our country" in the standards for grades K–4.[3] To counter Cheney's claim that Americans such as Robert E. Lee or the Wright Brothers were expunged because they had the misfortune of being dead, white, and male, Nash and colleagues added up the names of people fitting this description—more than 700 in all—and announced that this was "many times the grand total of all women, African-Americans, Latinos, and Indians individually named."[4]

Similar exercises in tit for tat quickly became standard in the debate over standards. But just below the surface, name counts took on an uglier face: Each side felt it necessary to impute to the other the basest of motives. So, to Bob Dole, the Republican presidential candidate in 1996, the national standards were the handiwork of people "worse than external enemies."[5] To Nash's team, critics of the proposed standards were driven by latent fears over a diverse America in which the "new faces [that] crowd[ed] onto the stage of history ruin the symmetry and security of older versions of the past."[6] In the barroom terms befitting such a brawl, those who wrote the standards were traitors; those who opposed them, racists.

The rancor of this debate was rich soil for dichotomous thinking. Take, for example, the forum organized by the journal *American Scholar*, the official publication of the national honorary society Phi Beta Kappa. *American Scholar* asked eleven prominent historians to write a thousand words in response to the question, "What history should our children learn?" Should children learn "the patriotism, heroism, and ideals of the nation" or "the injustices, defeats, and hypocrisies of its leaders and dominant classes"? In case panelists didn't get the point, they were also asked whether the United States represented "one of the great historical success stories" or "the story of one opportunity after another lost"?[7] Fortunately, sanity prevailed. Yale's Edmund Morgan, author of the *Stamp Act Crisis* and thus no newcomer to the topic of propaganda, noted that any answer would necessarily "look more like slogans than any reasoned approach to history," adding, wryly, that he didn't need "a thousand words to say it."[8]

Given the tenor of the debate, some might wonder why history was ever considered a part of the humanities, one of those disciplines that are supposed to teach us to spurn sloganeering, tolerate complexity, and cherish nuance. Writing at the turn of the century, Woodrow Wilson and other members of the Committee of Ten noted that history went well beyond particular stories and names to achieve its highest aim by endowing us with "the invaluable mental power which we call judgment."9 Sadly, the present debate has become so fixated on the question of "which history" that we have forgotten a more basic question: Why study history at all?

The answer to this neglected question is hardly self-evident. Americans have never been fully convinced of history's place in the curriculum. History education may be riding a momentary crest of interest, but its roots do not run deep. Many states set minimal requirements for the study of history. Schools of education offer future teachers courses in the teaching of mathematics, the teaching of science, and the teaching of literature, but we would be hard-pressed to find more than a handful of courses in the *entire* nation devoted to the teaching of history. History is getting a lot of airtime in national policy debates, but in the places that matter most—the schools where kids learn and the colleges where teachers are taught—history's status is anything but secure.

In this chapter my focus is not on which history is better—that of the victors, the vanquished, or some Solomonic combination of both. Rather, I take several steps back from the current History Wars to ponder another question: What is history good for? Why even teach it in schools? My claim in a nutshell is that history holds the potential, only partly realized, of humanizing us in ways offered by few other areas in the school curriculum. I make no claim of originality in arguing this point of view. But each generation must ask itself anew why studying the past is important, and remind itself why history can bring us together rather than—as we have seen most recently—tear us apart.

The argument I make pivots on a tension that underlies every encounter with the past: the tension between the familiar and the strange, between feelings of proximity and feelings of distance in relation to the people we seek to understand. Neither of these extremes does justice to history's complexity, and veering to one side or the other dulls history's jagged edges and leaves us with cliché and caricature. Achieving mature historical thought depends precisely on our ability to navigate the uneven landscape of history, to traverse the rugged terrain that lies between the poles of familiarity and distance from the past.

The pole of familiarity pulls most strongly. The familiar past entices us with the promise that we can locate our own place in the stream of time and solidify our identity in the present. By tying our own stories to those who have come before us, the past becomes a useful resource in our everyday life, an endless storehouse of raw materials to be shaped or bent to meet our present needs. Situating ourselves in time is a basic human need. Indeed, it is impossible to conceptualize life on the planet without doing so.

But in viewing the past as usable, something that speaks to us without intermediary or translation, we end up turning it into yet another commodity for instant consumption. We discard or just ignore vast regions of the past that either contradict our current needs or fail to align tidily with them. The usable past retains a certain fascination, but it is the fascination of the flea market, with its endless array of gaudy trinkets and antique baubles. Because we more or less know what we are looking for before we enter this past, our encounter is unlikely to change us or cause us to rethink who we are. The past becomes clay in our hands. We are not called upon to stretch our understanding to learn from the past. Instead, we contort the past to fit the predetermined meanings we have already assigned it.

The other pole in this tension, the strangeness of the past, offers the possibility of surprise and amazement, of encountering people, places, and times that spur us to reconsider how we conceptualize ourselves as human beings. An encounter with this past can be mind-expanding in the best sense of the term. Yet, taken to extremes, this approach carries its own problems. The past "on its own terms," detached from the circumstances, concerns, and needs of the present, too often results in a kind of esoteric exoticism, precisely the impression one comes to after a tour through the monographic literature that defines contemporary historical practice. Much of this specialized literature may engage the attention of a small coterie of professionals, but it fails to engage the interest of anyone else.[10]

There is no easy way around the tension between the familiar past, which seems so relevant to our present needs, and the strange and inaccessible past, whose applicability is not immediately manifest. The tension exists because both aspects of history are essential and irreducible. On the one hand, we need to feel kinship with the people we study, for this is exactly what engages our interest and makes us feel connected. We come to see ourselves as inheritors of a tradition that provides mooring and security against the transience of the modern world.

But this is only half the story. To realize history's humanizing qualities fully, to draw on history's ability to, in the words of Carl Degler, "expand our conception and understanding of what it means to be human,"[11] we need to encounter the distant past—a past less distant from us in time than in its modes of thought and social organization. It is this past, one that initially leaves us befuddled or, worse, just plain bored, that we need most if we are to achieve the understanding that each of us is more than the handful of labels ascribed to us at birth. The sustained encounter with this less-familiar past teaches us the limitations of our brief sojourn on the planet and allows us to take membership in the entire human race. Paradoxically, the relevance of the past may lie precisely in what strikes us as its initial irrelevance.

I approach these issues not as a historian, someone who spends time using documents to reconstruct the past, but as a psychologist, someone who designs tasks and interviews that shed light on how we come to know who we are. Similarly, my data are not found in archives but are created when I sit down to interview people from all walks of life— teachers, practicing historians, high school kids, and parents. In the following three vignettes, I offer glimpses from this program of research. The first comes from a high school student's encounter with primary documents from the Revolutionary War; the second, from an elementary school principal's reactions after reading the diary of a midwife from the turn of the nineteenth century; and the third, from a historian's encounter with documents that shed light on Abraham Lincoln's views on race.

In these vignettes, I try to show that historical thinking, in its deepest forms, is neither a natural process nor something that springs automatically from psychological development. Its achievement, I argue, actually goes against the grain of how we ordinarily think, one of the reasons why it is much easier to learn names, dates, and stories than it is to change the basic mental structures we use to grasp the meaning of the past. The odds of achieving mature historical understanding are stacked against us in a world in which Disney and MTV call the shots. But it is precisely the uses to which the past is put that endow these other aims with even greater importance.

THE UNBRIDGEABLE RUBICON

Let me begin with Derek, a seventeen-year-old Advanced Placement history student (and later the salutatorian of his senior class), who participated in one of my earliest studies. I remember Derek clearly because it was in working with him that the questions I take up here first came into view.[12]

Derek participated in a study in which high school students (as well as professional historians) read a series of primary sources about the Battle of Lexington. Derek read that British forces encountered the minutemen standing in their way on Lexington Green. He remarked on the unequal numbers of the combatants—something on the order of hundreds of British regulars opposed seventy or so colonists, according to the documents. He noted that when the encounter was over, eight colonists lay dead, while there was only one casualty on the British side. This suggested to him that the engagement might have been more one-sided than the term "battle" suggests. These were astute observations that reflected Derek's keen intelligence and made him stand out among his peers. However, when asked to select the picture that best reflected the written evidence he had reviewed, Derek did not choose the one that showed the colonists in disarray, which would have been the logical choice given his earlier observations. Instead, he chose the picture that showed the colonists hiding behind walls, reloading their muskets, and taking aim at the Redcoats. Derek believed that this depiction was the most accurate because

> it gives [the minutemen] sort of . . . an advantageous position, where they are sort of on a hill and I presume somewhere over here is a wall I guess. . . . The minutemen are going to be all scrambled, going to be hiding behind the poles and everything, rather than staying out here facing [the British]. . . . You know there's got to be like a hill, and they're thinking they got to hide behind something, get at a place where they can't be shot besides being on low ground, and being ready to kill. Their mentalities would be ludicrous if they were going to stand, like, here in [the depiction showing the minutemen in disarray], ready to be shot.[13]

Judged by conventional definitions of what we want kids to do in history classrooms, Derek's reading is exemplary. In the words of the Bradley Commission, the report that launched the current reform movement in history education, students should enter "into a world of drama—suspending [their] knowledge of the ending in order to gain a sense of another era—a sense of empathy that allows the student to see through the eyes of the people who were there."[14] Derek has not only tried to see through others' eyes; he has attempted a reconstruction of their world views, their *"mentalités."* However, Derek's reconstruction holds true only if these people shared his own modern notions of battlefield propriety: the idea that in the face of a stronger adversary, you flee behind walls and wage guerrilla warfare. Derek's reading poses a striking irony. What seemed to guide his view of this event is a set of assumptions about how normal people behave. These assumptions, in turn, overshadowed his very own observations, made during the review of the written testimony. Ironically, what Derek perceived as natural was perceived as beastly by the Puritans when they first encountered this form of combat. By the sixteenth century, European warfare had evolved into a highly complex form of gentlemanly encounter: It was not unheard of for combatants to wage war during the day and dine together at night. Battlefield engagements conformed to an elaborate etiquette, in part the result of the cumbersome sequence of actions—up to forty-two separate steps—involved in firing and reloading a musket.[15]

The culture of large-scale warfare clashed with the mores of the indigenous peoples the Puritans encountered along the New England coast. Among the Pequots, for example, a military culture of symbolic acts prevailed. The norm was not face-to-face encounters with massive bloodshed, but small-scale raids that settled feuds by exacting symbolic tribute. This clash in traditions led to ruinous confrontations, as when the Puritans encircled the entire Indian village at the Mystic River in 1637 and burned it to the ground. Solomon Stoddard, writing to Joseph Dudley in 1703, explained:

> If the Indians were as other people are, and did manage their warr fairly after the manner of other nations, it might be looked upon as inhumane to persue them in a manner contrary to Christian practice. . . . But they are to be looked upon as thieves and murderers. . . they don't appeare openly in the field to bid us battle, they use those cruelly that fall into their hands. . . . They act like wolves and are to be dealt with as wolves.[16]

It is not that Derek was a careless reader. On the contrary, his reading was fluent, and his skill at monitoring his own cognition (what psychologists call "metacognition") was enviable. But when all was said and done, Derek's encounter with these eighteenth-century documents left him unfazed. The colonists' behavior did not cause him to stand back and say, "Wow, what a strange group of people. What on earth would make them act this way?" Such a reaction might lead him to contemplate codes of behavior—duty, honor, dying for a cause—foreign to his world. These documents did not spur Derek to ask himself new questions or consider new dimensions of human experience. Instead, his existing beliefs shaped the information he encountered so that the new conformed to the shape of the already known. Derek read these documents but he learned little from them.

Derek's reading raises questions that lie at the heart of historical understanding. Given what we know about the entrenched nature of beliefs, how, exactly, do we bracket what we know in order to understand the thinking of people in the past? This is no easy task. The notion that we can strip ourselves of what we know, that we can stop the "spread of activation" set off when we read certain words, recalls Allan Megill's notion of hermeneutic naiveté, or the belief in "immaculate perception."[17] Among philosophers, Hans-Georg Gadamer has been the most instructive about the problems this position entails. How can we overcome established modes of thought, Gadamer asks, when it is these modes that permit understanding in the first place?[18] We, no less than the people we study, are historical beings. Trying to shed what we know in order to glimpse the "real" past is like trying to examine microbes with the naked eye: The instruments we abandon are the ones that enable us to see.

This position differs considerably from the classic historicist stance one finds in Robin Collingwood and others. For Collingwood, "all history is the history of thought," the ability of the historian to put him- or herself in Julius Caesar's mind, "envisioning . . . the situation in which Caesar stood, and thinking for himself what Caesar thought about the situation and the possible ways of dealing with it."[19] Collingwood believed that we can somehow "know Caesar" because human ways of thought, in some deep and essential way, transcend time and space.

Not so fast, say contemporary historians. Consider the words of Carlo Ginzburg, the eminent Italian historian and author of the best-selling *The Cheese and the Worms:*

> The historian's task is just the opposite of what most of us were taught to believe. He must destroy our false sense of proximity to people of the past because they come from societies very different from our own. The more we discover about these people's mental universes, the more we should be shocked by the cultural distance that separates us from them.[20]

Or these words from Robert Darnton, award-winning author of *The Great Cat Massacre:*

> Other people are other. They do not think the way we do. And if we want to understand their way of thinking we should set out with the idea of capturing otherness. . . . We constantly need to be shaken out of a false sense of familiarity with the past, to be administered doses of culture shock.[21]

Or these from Richard White, historian of the West:

Any good history begins in strangeness. The past should not be comfortable. The past should not be a familiar echo of the present, for if it is familiar why revisit it? The past should be so strange that you wonder how you and people you know and love could come from such a time.[22]

In coming to understand how we differ from Caesar, can we ever "know" him in the way he knew himself or in the way contemporaries knew him? Even if we were convinced of the possibility, how would we know we had succeeded, short of appealing to necromancy? In other words, the point made by these contemporary historians seems to be the opposite of the one cited earlier—that the goal of historical understanding should be to "see through the eyes of the people who were there." If Ginzburg and others are right, the goal of historical study should be to teach us what we *cannot* see, to acquaint us with the congenital blurriness of our vision.

Even the notion that historical knowledge should serve as a bank of examples for contemplating present problems has come under challenge. The more we know about the past, claimed the philosopher of history Louis O. Mink, the more cautious we should be before drawing analogies to it. Historical knowledge in Mink's view can sever our connection to the past, making us see ourselves as discontinuous with the people we study. John Locke, for example, is no longer our contemporary by virtue of his seemingly "modern" understanding of government and human motivation. Instead, our awareness of discontinuity with Locke forces us to reconcile two contradictory forces: intellectual proximity with the Locke of the *Second Treatise on Government* and intellectual estrangement from the anti-empiricist Locke, author of the rarely read *Essay on the Reasonableness of Christianity*. In studying the Locke who fits our image as well as the Locke who complicates it, we can come to know a more nuanced personality. Locke becomes more than a projection of our own views. "The new Locke," writes Mink, "is accessible in his remoteness and strangeness; it is precisely his crotchety Calvinism which changes our understanding of all his views although it destroys the illusion that in political and philosophical discussion we are communing with Locke as with a contemporary."[23] Put differently, when we think about Egyptian drawing and representation of perspective, we can no longer "assume that the Egyptians saw as we see, but could not draw as we can."[24] Rather, we must consider the possibility that they drew differently because they *saw* differently, and that there is something about this way of seeing that is irretrievably lost. Much as we try, then, we can never fully cross the Rubicon that flows between our mind and Caesar's.

CONTINUITY AND CHANGE

How willing are we to press this point? Exactly when in the flow of human experience does last month become strange, last year remote? Indeed, when pushed to its extreme, the consequence of thinking that there is no continuity with the past is as grave an error as thinking that the past directly mirrors the present. David Lowenthal reminds us that the past is a "foreign country."[25] A foreign country, not a foreign planet. To replace naive historicism with a rigid sense of disconnection is to play mental musical chairs, to give up one reductionism only to adopt another.

Historical thinking requires us to reconcile two contradictory positions: first, that our established modes of thinking are an inheritance that cannot be sloughed off, and, second, that if we make no attempt to slough them off, we are doomed to a mind-numbing presentism that reads the present onto the past. It was precisely this paradox that drew me to Laurel Thatcher Ulrich's *A Midwife's Tale*, which narrates the story of Martha Ballard, a midwife who lived between 1735 and 1812. As Carl Degler wrote in his review of the book, Ulrich "unravels the fascinating life of a community that is so foreign, and yet so similar to our own."[26]

About the time I was reading this book, I was asked by a group of educators in Minnesota to develop a workshop on history as a "way of knowing," something beyond the compendia of names and dates that history had become in the course of that state's affair with "outcome-based education."[27] In the two days of this workshop, I chose to contrast learning history from books like Ulrich's with the approach most familiar to participants: learning history from history textbooks.

As vehicles for creating historical understanding, textbooks present intriguing challenges and create a set of problems all their own. Textbooks pivot on what Roland Barthes called the "referential illusion," the notion that the way things are told is simply the way things were.[28] To achieve this illusion, textbooks exploit various linguistic conventions. First, textbooks eliminate "metadiscourse," or the existence of places in the text where the author intrudes to indicate positionality and stance. Metadiscourse is common in the writing historians do for one another, but it is edited out of the writing they do for schoolchildren.[29] In addition, traces of how the text came to be are hidden or erased: Textbooks rarely cite the documentary record; if primary material appears, it is typically set off in "sidebars" so as not to interfere with the main text. Finally, the textbook speaks in the omniscient third-person. No visible author confronts the reader; instead, a corporate author speaks from a position of transcendence, a position of knowing from on high.

I began the Minnesota seminar by giving the twenty-two participants a selection from Winthrop Jordan's *The Americans*, a widely used U.S. history textbook for the eleventh grade.[30] In describing the colonial economy during roughly the same period as Ballard's diary, Jordan focuses on "triangular trade," the nexus of routes involved in the exchange of slaves, sugar cane, and rum between the colonies, the West Indies, and Africa. The story is organized under the boldfaced heading "The North Develops Commerce and Cities—Molasses and Rumbullion," with women appearing in the story only in the section entitled "Family Farms." The following paragraph about the role of women in economic life became, for the next two days, the touchstone against which we assayed our own developing understanding and the text that, in the final hours of the workshop, we attempted to rewrite.

> Anyone who has ever lived on a family farm knows that such a life involves long hours and hard work for everyone. Children worked at least part time from the age when they could be shown how to shell peas, shuck corn, or fetch firewood. Women performed an unending round of tasks. They cooked in metal pots that were hung over the open fireplace. They baked in a hollow compartment in the chimney that served as an oven. They spun rough cloth and sewed it into clothing for the family. They washed clothes and bedding in wooden tubs with soap they made themselves.[31]

After examining this passage and the surrounding narrative, we turned to Ulrich's book. As a text for exploring historical thinking, this work offers multiple points of entry. Each chapter starts with several pages from Martha's diary, with eighteenth-century spelling and grammatical conventions intact. Only after giving the reader a feeling for the kinds of evidence she reviewed does Ulrich go on to explore themes and trends that spring from Martha's life. The following diary excerpt is representative of the kinds of materials participants studied:

November   15   6 At Mr Parkers. Mrs Holdman here.
    Cloudy & Cold. Mrs Holdman here to have a gown made. Mrs Benjamin to have a Cloak Cut. Polly Rust after work. I was Calld to Mr Parkers aftern. Mr Ballard is better. . . .
    17 F   At ditoes & Mr Poores. Birth 47th a daughter. At Capt Meloys
allso   Rainy. I was called from Mr Parkers at 2 hour morn to Mr Poores.

Doct Page was Calld before my arival. I Extracted the Child, a dagt. He Chose to Close the Loin. I returnd home at 8 hour morning. Receivd 6/ as a reward. Mr Ballard & Ephm attend worship, Dolly & Sally aftern. Charls and John Coks supt here. I was calld to Capt meloys at 11 hour Evening. Raind. Birth Mr Poores daughter X X[32]

Such excerpts formed one part of our inquiry. We also examined tables of delivery data compiled by Ulrich from Martha's diary, and compared these with statistics from Dr. James Farrington (1824–59), born a generation after Martha, when midwifery had fallen into disfavor and doctors had turned to bloodletting and the use of opium derivatives such as laudanum during delivery.[33] We puzzled over what seemed to be dramatic changes in how midwives were viewed, from the turn of the eighteenth century, when Martha stood beside doctors at an autopsy, to less than twenty years later, when a Harvard professor wrote that "we cannot instruct women as we do men in the science of medicine; we cannot carry them into the dissecting room . . . without destroying those moral qualities of character which are essential to the office" of midwife and woman.[34]

From correcting and expanding the initial textbook account, we ventured on to question the rarely articulated assumptions that guide the writing of textbooks. Such assumptions were thrown into relief when we placed the textbook alongside Ulrich's narrative. Laurel Thatcher Ulrich is present in the story she tells, sharing how she pieced together the labyrinthine social relationships of colonial New England from the haziest of references; how she immersed herself in the world of herbal medicine to decode cryptic allusions to traditional remedies; how, in order to understand the work of Martha's husband, Ephraim, she had to learn about the operation of sawmills in the eighteenth and nineteenth centuries.

As we dove deeper into Martha's world and work, we could not help thinking about the world and work of the historian. We marveled at the author's steely resolve in the face of the persistent question: "When will the book be finished?"[35] We found it impossible to learn about Martha Ballard without learning about Laurel Thatcher Ulrich. It helped that the historian made no attempt to hide. In fact, Ulrich placed herself squarely in the text, as, for example, when she described how other historians found Martha's diary "trivial and unimportant." That such a view could come from men writing in the nineteenth century was, perhaps, understandable, but when a feminist history written in the 1970s characterized the diary as "filled with trivia," it was too much for Ulrich.

It is in the very dailiness, the exhaustive, repetitious dailiness, that the real power of Martha Ballard's book lies. To extract the river crossing without noting the cold days spent "footing" stockings, to abstract the births without recording the long autumns spent winding quills, pickling meat, and sorting cabbages, is to destroy the sinews of this earnest, steady, gentle, and courageous record. . . . when [Martha] felt overwhelmed or enlivened by the very "trivia" the historians have dismissed, she said so, not in the soul-searching manner of a Puritan nor with the literary self-consciousness of a sentimentalist, but in a plain, matter-of-fact, and in the end unforgettable voice. For more than twenty-seven years, 9,965 days to be exact, she faithfully kept her record. . . . "And now this year is come to a close," she wrote on December 31, 1800, "and happy is it if we have made a wise improvement of the time." For her, living was to be measured in doing. Nothing was trivial.[36]

This short excerpt bears witness to the profound changes in histori-cal writing over the last half-century.[37] Historical narrative is no longer restricted to great acts of statecraft but now encompasses everyday acts like childbirth and the daily routines of ordinary people trying to make ends meet. While this passage reflects the influence of social history and feminism, it also highlights the new, more active role of the historian in narrating the past—something that distinguished Ulrich's writing from the textbook prose that participants knew best. Ulrich the storyteller is in the thick of her story, sharing her anger at previous historians' dis-missal of Martha's diary, identifying with her protagonist's patience and resolve, showing sadness as Martha's life comes to an end. In revealing Martha Ballard the midwife, Laurel Thatcher Ulrich reveals herself. From the power of Ulrich's voice to the power of Martha's indomitable spirit, this excerpt, when read aloud, moved several participants to tears.

Colleen was one of them. An elementary school principal, Colleen had last studied history when she was a high school student. She signed up for the workshop because her school was moving toward an interdisciplinary curriculum and she wanted to understand how his-tory might be combined with other subjects. At the start of the work-shop, she admitted that she had a "bad memory," a statement of deficiency in the attribute she thought most important to historical study. But Colleen was surprised by the workshop's end. She was immediately drawn into these documents, identifying with Martha's endless cycle of work in and out of the home, and the competing demands of her roles as mother, career woman, wife, and community leader. The chance to work with original sources was new to Colleen, and she found it invigorating. During the two days of the workshop, she was among the most vocal and passionate participants.

At the end of the second day, we asked participants to "rewrite history," to take what they had learned and compose a narrative on the role of women in the economic life of colonial and post-Revolutionary America. We gave them the option of amending the selection from Jordan's textbook or putting it aside and starting from scratch. Colleen chose to put it aside. She took pen in hand and wrote furiously, scribbling a few sentences, muttering under her breath about how angry she was at the textbook, crumpling up the paper, and starting again. She wrote without interruption for thirty-five minutes.

You might predict that Colleen's essay would bear the traces of this passion, giving voice to the range of emotions—from identification and recognition to anger and resentment—that she felt as she worked through the documents. But this was not the case. Colleen's detached writing trudged along like the textbook prose she sought to banish. Narrated in the third person, Colleen's account strove for objectivity, or, as she put it later, to "keep my emotions out of it." Nowhere in her two-page history does the word "I" appear. Absent are indications of emphasis, judgment, and doubt. To be sure, the content had shifted. From Colleen we learn that women like Martha Ballard contributed to the colonial economy as midwives, by engaging in small-scale textile production, by raising poultry, and by myriad other activities. The facts may have changed, but the epistemological stance of the text remained firmly intact.

Like Derek before her, Colleen faced a conflict between two spheres of experience: her immediate experience in reading these texts and her prior experiences, especially her memories from high school. Her frustration boiled over when she put pen to paper and could not find a way of resolving the belief that history had slighted her as a woman and the belief that when writing history one should be cool, dispassionate, scientific, objective. In rewriting history Colleen confronted herself, but rather than engage this self and make it a part of her story, she interpreted her job as one of self-effacement—removing from the story her passion, her anger, and even her own experience as a mother. As a result Colleen was nowhere to be found in her creation.

Unrestrained, passion distorts the story we seek to tell. The balancing of perspectives requires us to step back and see things in other ways, an exceedingly difficult thing to do when anger sears our gut. But Colleen went to the other extreme. Rather than compensating for her subjectivity by sharing it with her reader, she tried to construct a story without a teller—to deal with her deep feelings by pretending that they did not exist. In the end, Martha Ballard, a person brought to life in the primary documents, returned to a still life in the document Colleen herself composed.

Ironically, then, Colleen's text bore a greater resemblance to Jordan's *The Americans* than to Ulrich's *A Midwife's Tale*. The textbook and all that it symbolized became for Colleen, and other workshop participants, not *one* way of transmitting the story of the past, but the *only* way.

THE WEAVING OF CONTEXT

How do we navigate the tension between the familiar and the strange? How do we embrace what we share with the past but remain open to aspects that might startle us into reconsidering what it means to be human? The distant past—the burial practices of ancient Egypt, the medical practices of the Middle Ages, the hanging of witches in Salem: These jar us with their strangeness. But what about the more recent past, a time like ours with televisions, radios, cars, and planes, a time that looks superficially like the present except for old-fashioned clothes and hairstyles? How do we approach this past so that it emerges as something more than a faded version of the present?

These questions came into focus when I visited a Seattle high school to observe a class that had watched the PBS series "Eyes on the Prize." On the day I arrived, students had seen the segment in which Governor Ross Barnett physically bars James Meredith from registering at Ole Miss. In the ensuing discussion, the teacher asked students why Barnett objected to Meredith's enrollment. One boy raised his hand and volunteered, "Prejudice." The teacher nodded and the discussion moved on.

That simple "prejudice" unsettled me. Four hundred years of racial history reduced to a one-word response?[38] This set me to wondering what would it take before we begin to think historically about such concepts as "prejudice," "racism," "tolerance," "fairness," and "equity." At what point do we come to see these abstractions not as transcendent truths soaring above time and place, but as patterns of thought that take root in particular historical moments, develop, grow, and emerge in new forms in successive generations while still bearing traces of their former selves?[39] If Ross Barnett's problem was that he was "prejudiced," how would these students and their teachers regard Abraham Lincoln, variously dubbed the "Great Emancipator" or "White Supremacist" depending on social fashion and current need?[40]

To study this question, I put together a series of documents that combined the words of Abraham Lincoln with the voices of some of his contemporaries: Stephen Douglas, Lincoln's opponent for the 1858 Senate seat from Illinois; John Bell Robinson and John Van Evrie, religious racialists who looked to the Bible for justification of slavery; and William Lloyd Garrison, the abolitionist who worked tirelessly for emancipation.[41] In the same document set I included three documents by Lincoln, each reflecting a different situation in his life: the keen observer traveling up the Mississippi in 1841 and seeing slaves chained together "like so many fish upon a trot-line"; the candidate, debating Stephen Douglas before a largely pro-Douglas crowd in Ottawa, Illinois; and the beleaguered, war-weary president, addressing a group of freed slaves in 1862 about the possibility of founding a freedmen's colony in Central America.

I presented these documents to a group of college history majors and nonmajors, all of whom were enrolled in a fifth-year program to become public school teachers. I asked them to read through these documents and tell me what light they shed on Lincoln's thought. Although there was great variety in participants' responses, two broad trends stood out. One group took Lincoln's words at face value. They saw these words as offering a direct window into Lincoln's mind, unobstructed by either the particular circumstances in which they were uttered or the passage of time between 1860 and today. Lincoln was a racist, pure and simple. Other, more careful, readers recognized that they needed a context for these words. But rather than fashioning a context from the raw materials provided by these documents, they borrowed a context from their contemporary social world.

Faced with seeming incongruities in Lincoln's position, we have at hand an array of contemporary social forms and institutions—press conferences, spin doctors, response dials—which allow us instantly to harmonize discrepant information. Even if we recognize the vast technological changes in the political process between 1860 and today, we often perceive a unity in ways of thinking that span the breach of time. In many readings by college students, Lincoln and Douglas become our contemporaries in top hats, much like characters from a James Michener novel who happen to dress funny but whose behavior and mannerisms are those of our next-door neighbors.

In other words, "presentism"—the act of viewing the past through the lens of the present—is not some bad habit we've fallen into. It is, instead, our psychological condition at rest, a way of thinking that requires little effort and comes quite naturally. If Lincoln seems to be saying two different things, it is because he is speaking to two different audiences, for in our world we know exactly why George W. Bush says one thing to Kansas wheat farmers and another to New York City stockbrokers. In resolving contradictions in Lincoln's words, we turn him into one of us: His goal is to get elected, and he has spin doctors to help.[42]

I broadened my study by asking several working historians to read these same documents. Some of them knew a great deal about Lincoln and had written books about him; others knew little more than what was required to give a few lectures in an undergraduate survey course.[43] Bob Alston, a middle-aged Caucasian Americanist, fit into the latter group. Like most members of his department, he taught undergraduate survey courses spanning all of American history, but the majority of his upper-level and graduate courses were in a different specialization. During graduate school, he had taken examinations that covered the Civil War but had not studied this period extensively since then.

Alston did not have an easy time, and in the beginning his reading is virtually indistinguishable from those of the stronger college students. From Document 1, Douglas's opening statement at Ottawa, Alston stared his lack of knowledge in the face:

> I don't know as much about Lincoln's views as I thought I did. I mean, as I read it and see Douglas perhaps putting words in Lincoln's mouth, I'm not quite sure about what I do and don't know about Lincoln. Douglas makes it sound as if Lincoln believes they're equal, blacks and whites, on virtually every level but I don't know to what extent Lincoln did or did not believe that. I know that he was very practically aware of the concerns of bringing them together as if they were equal in the same society at this point, but I don't know enough about Lincoln's views to make some other judgments I've been making.

In the second document, Lincoln's rebuttal of Douglas, Lincoln states that he has "no purpose to introduce political and social equality" between the races. At this point Alston paused: "Just rereading the sentence again. Again trying to think about how Douglas's statement about Lincoln thinking the two were equal could have some truth if it falls outside the realm of what Lincoln identifies as political and social equality." Seven lines later, Alston stopped again: "I'm going back and rereading the sentence. These nineteenth-century orators spoke in more complicated sentences. They weren't used to sound bites. I'm wondering what he means by 'physical difference' ":

> If blacks have the "natural rights to life, liberty, and the pursuit of happiness" one would assume that liberty and pursuit of happiness would indicate that they cannot be slaves at the same time. Similarly, if blacks have the "right to eat the bread which his own hand earns," that they have the right to the product of their labor, that is the pursuit of happiness or liberty, one form or the other, then if that is a natural right then slavery goes against those natural rights.

When the college students reached this point, they tended to locate this contradiction in Lincoln or created multiple Lincolns who said different things to different people. But Alston responded by calling attention to the contradiction, not dissolving it. Over the next five documents, his reading was a prolonged exercise in the "specification of ignorance." He asked, on average, 4.2 questions per document, and underscored what he did not know with markers such as "I don't have enough to go on" or "This makes no sense to me" a total of fourteen times. Only at the end of the task did Alston come up with something resembling an interpretation. It came in response to the passage in which John Bell Robinson appeals to God as providing a sanction for slavery. At this point Alston made the following comment (asterisks indicate places in the reading where he flipped back to previous documents):

> Lincoln . . . talks about Blacks being endowed with certain things from God, but "usefulness as slaves" or a status of slaves isn't one of the things that he mentions. [I'm going to] look at some of the earlier [documents]. What I'm looking for is his discussion [of] the physical difference between the two and his discussion of natural rights [to] see if he links those at all to God.* It was Douglas* who linked Lincoln to believe about the Negro to God and the Declaration of Independence. But in this,*in Lincoln's reply, he refers—I'm looking here for reference to God—I'm not finding it but I haven't finished yet, he refers to the Declaration of Independence. But in the letter to Mary Speed* he did say "how true it is that God renders the worst of human conditions tolerable." But God didn't render slavery a condition that Blacks ought to find themselves in, according to Lincoln. Lincoln keeps going out of it in these things, he talks about the Declaration of Independence,* he talks about natural rights—I'm not sure where these come from in his mind—and he talks about natural differences. But he does not bring God into it other than to say that God makes, God allows people to make the worst of human conditions tolerable.* And that's a form of mercy, not of any kind of restriction on their status or behavior. What I thought—Douglas* has accused Lincoln of saying that Blacks had equal rights from the

Declaration of Independence and God. Lincoln didn't say that in these
things. [He didn't say] anything about God, just the Declaration of
Independence* and natural rights, wherever those come from.

This is a dense excerpt that itself merits interpretation. John Bell
Robinson's reference to God sparked confusion and sent Alston back to
Lincoln's response to Douglas. There, he searched for Lincoln's invocation of God. Finding only a reference to the Declaration of Independence, the historian returned to Douglas's opening statement. He then
jumped to the letter by Mary Speed, written in 1841, where the word
"God" is found but with very different connotations from Robinson's
invocation. From the Speed letter Alston went back to the second document, Lincoln's response to Douglas, for another look at the reference
to the Declaration of Independence and "natural rights."

In the course of this zigzagging comment, Alston referred to the previous documents eight times. He learned that whereas Robinson appeals
to God to justify slavery as an institution appropriate for a lower form of
manhood, Lincoln appeals to God to connect the races in common
humanity. Through this intertextual weave, Alston learned that Lincoln
justifies the equality of Africans, not by appealing to God, but by appealing to "natural rights," a view of Lincoln that comes remarkably close to
Richard Weaver's "argument by definition" interpretation.[44] Although
Alston started the task confused and full of questions, he ended up with a
nuanced and sophisticated understanding of Lincoln's position.

What Alston did here is misrepresented by notions of "placing" or
"putting" Lincoln into context, verbs that conjure up images of jigsaw
puzzles in which pieces are slotted into pre-existing frames. Contexts
are neither "found" nor "located," and words are not "put" into context.
Context, from the Latin *contexere*, means to weave together, to engage
in an active process of connecting things in a pattern. Alston made
something new here, something that did not exist before he engaged
these documents and confronted his ignorance.

The questions Alston asked are the tools of creation, dwelling in the
space between his present knowledge and the circumstances of the past.
Alston is an expert, to be sure, but not in the sense in which that term
is typically used. His expertise lay not in his sweeping knowledge of this
topic but in his ability to pick himself up after a tumble, to get a fix on
what he does not know, and to generate a road map to guide his new
learning. He was an expert at cultivating puzzlement. It was Alston's
ability to stand back from first impressions, to question his quick leaps

of mind, and to keep track of his questions that together pointed him in the direction of new learning. Such an approach requires skill, technique, and a great deal of know-how. But mature historical cognition is more: It is an act that engages the heart.

So, for example, when Alston encountered the phrase "we have men . . . capable of thinking as White men," uttered by Lincoln in his address to the freed slaves, he was not only confused by the language but also visibly shaken by it. But rather than resolving his discomfort by concluding that Lincoln was a racist, Alston sat with this discomfort over the course of several documents. When he said, shaking his head, "I don't know what Lincoln is saying," he did not mean that he was confused by the words on the page, but something much larger: that he was confused by the world conjured up by these words, a world in which one human being could go to the market to buy others. What could Lincoln's words mean in *that* world?[45] And what did he as a modern historian not know that prevented him from fully entering Lincoln's world?

Alston's reading shows a humility before the narrowness of our contemporary experience and an openness before the expanse of the history of the species. It grants people in the past the benefit of the doubt by casting doubt on our ability to know them as easily as we know ourselves. This does not mean that we cannot judge the past—we cannot help making judgments. But it does mean that we must not rush to judgment. Other readers used these documents to confirm their prior beliefs. They encountered the past here and labeled it. Alston encountered the past and learned from it.

A UNICORN OR A RHINOCEROS?

Several years ago I went to see *Schindler's List*. I had long been acquainted with Steven Spielberg's oeuvre—what parent isn't?—so I was wary. I was drawn into the movie immediately, but what stays with me years later is what happened after the final credits rolled. I watched the man in front of me turn to his wife and say, "I never understood what happened then until now, right now. Now, I know."

I don't want to read too much into this comment, other than to note that it was a fragment of the present, shot on location in Kraków, that gave birth to this man's understanding. As I sat in the theater, my thoughts settled on the puzzle of understanding set by the Italian chemist Primo Levi, whose writings on the Holocaust, lyrical and haunting, always offer insight. "Among the questions that are put to us," wrote Levi, "one question is never absent; indeed, as the years go by, it is formulated with ever increasing persistence and with an ever less hidden accent of accusation."[46] The question Levi refers to actually has three parts:

1. Why did you not escape?
2. Why did you not rebel?
3. Why did you not evade capture before they "got to you"?

Levi describes what happened when he spoke to a group of fifth graders in an elementary school:

> An alert-looking boy, apparently at the head of the class, asked me the obligatory question: "But how come you didn't escape?" I briefly explained to him what I have written here. Not quite convinced, he asked me to draw a sketch of the camp on the blackboard indicating the location of the watch towers, the gates, the barbed wire, and the power station. I did my best, watched by thirty pairs of intent eyes. My interlocutor studied the drawing for a few instants, asked me for a few further clarifications, then he presented to me the plan he had worked out: here, at night, cut the throat of the sentinel; then, put on his clothes; immediately after this, run over there to the power station and cut off the electricity, so the search lights would go out and the high tension fence would be deactivated; after that I could leave without any trouble. He added seriously: "If it should happen to you again, do as I told you. You'll see that you'll be able to do it."[47]

This boy did everything we want from our students. He engaged with the subject matter, he drew on his background knowledge, he formulated questions and offered solutions. Lest we attribute the boy's question to his tender age, we should bear in mind that these same questions have been posed by people far older and far more knowledgeable. For this boy, as for many of us, Levi's experience inspires incredulity: This youngster cannot believe that so many could miss what is, in his mind, so very plain.

In his response, Primo Levi echoes one of the central themes that I have explored here: the seductiveness of coming to know people in the past by relying on the dimensions of our "lived experience." But for Levi the problem is broader than one of historical knowing. Our "inability to perceive the experience of others," as he put it, applies to the present no less than the past.[48] This is why the study of history is so crucial to our present day and age, when issues of diversity dominate the national agenda. Coming to know others, whether they live on the other side of the tracks or the other side of the millennium, requires the education of our sensibilities. This is what history, when taught well, gives us practice in doing. Paradoxically, what allows us to come to know others is our distrust in our capacity to know them, a skepticism about the extraordinary sense-making abilities that allow us to construct the world around us.

A skepticism toward the products of mind can sometimes slide into cynicism or solipsism. But this need not be the case. The awareness that the contradictions we see in others may tell us more about ourselves is the seed of intellectual charity. It is an understanding that counters narcissism. For the narcissist sees the world—both the past and the present—in his own image. Mature historical knowing teaches us to do the opposite: to go beyond our own image, to go beyond our brief life, and to go beyond the fleeting moment in human history into which we have been born. History educates ("leads outward" in the Latin) in the deepest sense. Of the subjects in the secular curriculum, it is the best at teaching those virtues once reserved for theology—humility in the face of our limited ability to know, and awe in the face of the expanse of human history.

On his journey from China to India, the Venetian traveler Marco Polo ventured into Basman, believed to be Sumatra, where he chanced upon a species he had never before seen: the rhinoceros. But Polo did not see it that way. As his diary records, he saw instead

> unicorns, which are scarcely smaller than elephants. They have the hair of a buffalo . . . [and] a single large, black horn in the middle of the forehead. They do not attack with their horn, but only with their tongue and their knees; for their tongues are furnished with long, sharp spines. . . . They are very ugly brutes to look at . . . not at all such as we describe them when . . . they let themselves be captured by virgins.[49]

Our encounter with history presents us with a choice: to learn about rhinoceroses or to learn about unicorns. We naturally incline toward unicorns—they are prettier and more tame. But it is the rhinoceros that can teach us far more than we could ever imagine.

NOTES

This chapter began as a talk given at the annual meeting of the American Historical Association, held in New York in January 1997. It appeared in print in the *Phi Delta Kappan* (March 1999). In writing it, I tried to do two things: to bring conceptual order to the work on historical teaching and learning that I had done since the late eighties, and to weigh in on the "standards war" raging from coast to coast. Previous versions benefited from comments by Peter Seixas, Peter Stearns, Susan Mosborg, Debby Kerdeman, David Lowenthal, Veronica Boix Mansilla, Howard

Gardner, Chris Browning, Kent Jewell, and the perspicacious but gentle members of the "Aspects of Historical Cognition" seminar at the University of Haifa (1997–98). Risë Koben at the *Kappan* provided priceless editorial feedback and encouragement. I thank them all.

1. Cited in Gary B. Nash, Charlotte Crabtree, and Ross E. Dunn, *History on Trial: Culture Wars and the Teaching of the Past* (New York, 1997), 232.

2. Ibid., 234.

3. Ibid., 197.

4. Ibid., 204.

5. Ibid., 245.

6. Ibid., 10–11. As Todd Gitlin points out, the history wars cannot be reduced to a simple left/right political struggle but have manifested as bitter internecine struggles within the left itself. See Gitlin's account of the Oakland, California, textbook adoption process in *The Twilight of Common Dreams: Why America Is Wracked by Culture Wars* (New York, 1995).

7. *American Scholar* 67 (Winter 1998), 91.

8. Ibid., 103.

9. Cited in Paul Gagnon, "History's Role in Civic Education: The Precondition for Political Intelligence," in Walter C. Parker, ed., *Educating the Democratic Mind* (Albany, 1996), 243.

10. See the incisive comments by T. S. Hamerow in *Reflections on History and Historians* (Madison, 1987).

11. Carl N. Degler, "Remaking American History," *Journal of American History* 67 (1980), 24.

12. See Chapter 3. For copies of all the original documents used, see Samuel S. Wineburg, "Historical Problem Solving: A Study of the Cognitive Processes Used in the Evaluation of Documentary and Pictorial Evidence," *Journal of Educational Psychology* 83 (1991), 73–87. "Derek," like other participants' names, is a pseudonym.

13. Ibid., 79.

14. Bradley Commission on History in Schools, *Building a History Curriculum: Guidelines for Teaching History in Schools* (Washington, D.C., 1988).

15. Adam Hirsch, "The Collision of Military Cultures in Seventeenth-Century New England," *Journal of American History* 74 (1988), 1187–1212.

16. Solomon Stoddard writing to Joseph Dudley, October 22, 1703, cited in Hirsch, "Collision," 1208.

17. Allan Megill, "Recounting the Past: 'Description,' Explanation, and Narrative in Historiography," *American Historical Review* 94 (1989), 632.

18. See Hans-Georg Gadamer, "The Problem of Historical Consciousness," in Paul Rabinow and William M. Sullivan, eds., *Interpretative Social Science* (Berkeley, 1979).

19. Robin G. Collingwood, *The Idea of History* (Oxford, 1946), 215.

20. Jonathan Kandell, "Was the World Made Out of Cheese? Carlo Ginzburg Is Fascinated by Questions That Others Ignore," *New York Times Magazine* (November 17, 1991), 47.

21. Robert Darnton, *The Great Cat Massacre* (New York, 1985), 4.

22. Richard White, *Remembering Ahanagran: Storytelling in a Family's Past* (New York, 1998), 13.

23. Louis O. Mink, *Historical Understanding* (Ithaca, 1987), 103.

24. Ibid.

25. David Lowenthal, *The Past Is a Foreign Country* (Cambridge, England, 1985).

26. The quotation from Degler appears on the book jacket: Laurel Thatcher Ulrich, *A Midwife's Tale: The Life of Martha Ballard, Based on Her Diary, 1785–1812* (New York, 1990).

27. This workshop was the brainchild of Randy Schenkat and was taught collaboratively with Professor Kathy Roth of Michigan State University, a specialist in the teaching of biology. The workshop's intent was to model an interdisciplinary approach that joins forces while still maintaining the powerful lenses that two different disciplines bring to a common problem. See Roth's critique of the typical approach to interdisciplinary curricula in K–12 settings: "Second Thoughts about Interdisciplinary Studies," *American Educator* 18 (1994), 44–48.

28. Roland Barthes, "Historical Discourse," in Michael Lane, ed., *Introduction to Structuralism* (New York, 1970), 145–55.

29. Avon Crismore, "The Rhetoric of Textbooks: Metadiscourse," *Journal of Curriculum Studies* 16 (1984), 279–96. See also Richard Paxton, " 'Someone with Like a Life Wrote It': The Effects of a Visible Author on High School History Students," *Journal of Educational Psychology* 89 (1997), 235–50.

30. The book is corporately authored, with Jordan as the main historian and two collaborators: Winthrop D. Jordan, Miriam Greenblatt, and John S. Bowes, *The Americans: The History of a People and a Nation* (Evanston, Ill., 1985).

31. Ibid., 68.

32. Ulrich, *Midwife's Tale*, 162.

33. Ibid., 251.

34. Ibid.

35. Ibid., 41.

36. Ibid., 9.

37. See Peter Novick, *That Noble Dream: The "Objectivity Question" and the American Historical Profession* (Cambridge, England, 1988).

38. English navigators reached the shores of West Africa sometime after 1550. See Winthrop D. Jordan, *White over Black: American Attitudes Toward the Negro, 1550–1812* (New York, 1968), chap. 1.

39. See Chapter 4 of this volume. My framing of these questions is indebted to David Lowenthal's essay, "The Timeless Past: Some Anglo-American Historical Preconceptions," *Journal of American History* 75 (1989), 1263–80. See also Ronald T. Takaki, *A Different Mirror: A History of Multicultural America* (Boston, 1993).

40. For an introduction to the ways Lincoln has been viewed, see Merrill Peterson, *Lincoln in American Memory* (New York, 1994). For a concise statement on Lincoln's views on race see Arthur Zilversmit, *Lincoln and the Problem of Race: A Decade of Interpretations*, Papers of the Abraham Lincoln Association (Springfield, Ill., 1980), 22–45. For an example of how Lincoln was viewed during the height of the Black Power movement of the 1960s, see Lerone Bennett, Jr., "Was Abe Lincoln a White Supremacist?" *Ebony* 23 (February 1968), 35–42.

41. My inspiration for situating Lincoln among his contemporaries in this exercise came from George M. Fredrickson's *The Black Image in the White Mind* (New York, 1971).

42. To be fair, this student is in esteemed company in this reading. In *The American Political Tradition and the Men Who Made it* (New York, 1948), Richard Hofstadter wondered whether Lincoln's mind was "a house divided against itself. In any case it is easy to see in all this the behavior of a professional politician looking for votes" (p. 116).

43. See Chapter 4 for copies of the documents. For a full description of the methodology, see Sam Wineburg, "Reading Abraham Lincoln: An Expert-Expert Study in the Interpretation of Historical Texts," *Cognitive Science* 22 (1998), 319–46.

44. Richard M. Weaver, *The Ethics of Rhetoric* (Chicago, 1953).

45. On this point see, in particular, Quentin Skinner, "Meaning and Understanding in the History of Ideas," *History and Theory* 8 (1969), 3–53.

46. Primo Levi, *The Drowned and the Saved* (New York, 1989), 150–51.

47. Ibid.

48. Ibid., 151.

49. Marco Polo, *The Travels* (Suffolk, England, 1958), 253. Thanks to Mike Bryant for pointing this passage out.

The Psychology of Teaching and Learning History

I t was a politician, not a historian, who offered the most persuasive rationale for studying history. Addressing the Roman Senate nearly a century before the birth of Christ, Cicero proclaimed, "Not to know what happened before one was born is always to be a child." Since the beginning of the twentieth century, scholars have tried to understand the unique features and challenges of learning and teaching history. Too often those who inquire into these questions have little awareness of the efforts of their predecessors, venturing childlike into issues that would benefit from a historical mooring.

My goal here is to redress this predicament by examining the ways in which scholars have studied the learning and teaching of history.[1] Most of this research has been conducted, for better or worse (and often it *is* for worse), by psychologists. Even when historians or historically minded philosophers try their hand at conducting empirical studies, their approach bears the imprint of psychological research and its core assumptions.[2] Future research on learning and teaching history may indeed grow beyond this psychological legacy, but in so doing it will still have to contend with its past. Understanding this legacy thus becomes central in creating a path to future inquiries.

To view the body of psychological work on history as a cohesive undertaking would be to commit the error of novices in a famous study of expertise in physics: the tendency to group elements by surface similarity, not by deep structure.³ In reality, the studies described here are united more by common keywords in data bases than by a shared conceptual focus. Research on history may be thought of as the counterpoint to Shakespeare's rose. Though the word "history" appears in all these reports, it rarely describes the same thing. To researchers, historical understanding can mean anything from memorizing a list of dates to mastering a set of logical relations, from being able to recite an agreed-upon story to contending with ill-defined problems resistant to single interpretations. These histories and the empirical studies done in their name tell as much about the researchers who conducted them as about the children and teachers who participated in them. In this sense, the body of psychological research on history constitutes an intriguing historical record in its own right, a landscape of mixed forms that attests to the multiplicity of ways in which the study of the past can be understood.

My story is organized into three sections. First, I discuss the treatment of history by early psychologists working in the United States. The accomplishments and shortcomings of this work, the goals it achieved or left unfulfilled, disclose much about our present condition. In the second section I examine research conducted in Great Britain. Although this work goes back to the beginning of the twentieth century, I pick up the story with the research programs of British psychologists working in the Piagetian tradition.⁴ In the final section I review contemporary research programs that have arisen with the collapse of behaviorism and the ascension of cognitive approaches to learning.

RESEARCH ON HISTORY: SOME EARLY INVESTIGATIONS

For the founders of educational psychology, history was more a topic of theoretical than empirical concern. In the 442 pages of Edward L. Thorndike's *Educational Psychology—Briefer Course*, history goes unmentioned save for a single reference to sex differences in historical achievement (which favored boys).⁵ Only in *Education: A First Book* does history receive more than fleeting attention. Here Thorndike paused to speculate on the burning question of his day: Should history be taught "backward," that is, beginning with the present and tracing events back in time, or was the traditional chronological treatment better suited to the abilities and dispositions of youngsters? Despite the absence of data, Thorndike was certain of the answer:

The educational value of finding the causes of what is, and then the causes of these causes, is so very much superior to the spurious reasoning which comes from explaining a record already known . . . that the arrangement of the . . . course in history in the inverse temporal order . . . deserves serious consideration.[6]

G. Stanley Hall, the premier developmental psychologist of his day, shared Thorndike's speculative interest in history teaching. Given Hall's concern with the development of character, it is not surprising that he saw in historical study a tool for helping students place events in a "temporal perspective as products of growth and development," a subject that, especially during adolescence, should be infused with lessons that "inspire to the greatest degree ideals of social service and unselfishness."[7] Not a battleground of competing interpretations, a tangle of ill-defined problems, or even a site for the development of critical thinking, Hall's history would be a unifying moral force, "a thesaurus of inspiring ethical examples to show how all got their deserts in the end."[8]

Among early educational psychologists, Chicago's Charles Hubbard Judd dealt incisively with history. Judd's chapter in the *Psychology of High-School Subjects* was a treatment impressive in scope, embracing in twenty-nine pages the nature of chronological thinking, the difficulties of causal judgment ("much more complicated" in history than in science), the dangers of dramatic reenactments, the psychological difficulties presented by historical evidence, and the motivational role of social (then called "industrial") history.[9] While drawing on the work of others, including the Committee of Seven[10] and the Committee of Five,[11] Judd's discussion contains its own flourishes of insight. In a section entitled "The Intricacy of Moral Judgments," Judd dealt with the psychological inevitability of presentism, the difficulty—perhaps even the impossibility—of understanding the past on its own terms:

The modern student is . . . guided in all of his judgments by an established mode of thought . . . peculiar to his own generation. We have certain notions . . . that are wholly different from the notions that obtained at the time that England was in controversy with her American colonies. When . . . [the student] is suddenly carried back in his historical studies to situations that differ altogether from the situations that now confront him, he is likely to carry back, without being fully aware of the fallacy of his procedure, those standards of judgment and canons of ethical thought which constitute his present inheritance.[12]

In this short comment Judd anticipated issues that would occupy researchers' attention well into the final decades of the twentieth century.

In 1917, the year the United States entered World War I, history made it into the pages of the ten-year-old *Journal of Educational Psychology*. J. Carleton Bell, managing editor of the *Journal* and professor at the Brooklyn Training School for Teachers, began his tenure with an editorial entitled "The Historic Sense." (A timely second editorial examined the relationship of psychology to military problems.) Bell argued that the study of history provided an opportunity for thinking and reflection, the opposite of what he claimed went on in much instruction. However, to teachers who would aim at these lofty goals, Bell put two questions: "What is the historic sense?" and "How can it be developed?"[13] Such questions, he continued, did not concern the history teacher alone but were ones "in which the educational psychologist is interested, and which it is incumbent upon him to attempt to answer."[14]

Bell offered clues about where to locate the "historic sense." Presented with a set of primary documents, one student produces a coherent account while another assembles "a hodgepodge of miscellaneous facts."[15] What factors and ways of thought account for this discrepancy? Similarly, some college freshmen "show great skill in the orderly arrangement of their historical data," while others "take all statements with equal emphasis . . . and become hopelessly confused in the multiplicity of details."[16] Do such findings reflect "native differences in historic ability," Bell wondered, or are they the "effects of specific courses of training"? Such questions opened up "a fascinating field for investigation" for the new field of educational psychology.[17]

Bell put his finger on questions that continue to occupy us today: What is the essence of historical understanding? What determines success on tasks that have more than one right answer? What role might instruction play in improving students' ability to think? Given this forward-looking research agenda, it is sobering to examine how it unfolded in practice. In a companion piece to his editorial, Bell and his associate David F. McCollum presented an empirical study that began by sketching out the various ways historical understanding might be assessed:[18]

1. "[T]he ability to understand present events in light of the past."[19]
2. The ability to sift through the documentary record—newspaper accounts, hearsay, partisan attacks, contemporary accounts—and construct "from this confused tangle a straightforward and probable account" of what happened. This is important, especially, because it is the goal of many "able and earnest college teachers of history."[20]

3. The ability to appreciate a historical narrative.
4. "[R]eflective and discriminating replies to 'thought questions' on a given historical situation."[21]
5. The ability to answer factual questions about historical personalities and events.

Bell and McCollum conceded that this last aspect was "the narrowest, and in the estimation of some writers, the least important type of historical ability," but it was, fatefully, the one "most readily tested."[22] In a decisive move, the authors announced that the ability to answer factual questions was "chosen for study in the present investigation."[23] While perhaps the first instance, this was not to be the last in which ease of measurement, not priority of subject matter understanding, determined the contours of a research program.

Bell and McCollum composed a test of names (e.g., John Burgoyne, Alexander Hamilton, Cyrus H. McCormick), dates (e.g., 1492, 1776, 1861), and events (e.g., the Sherman Antitrust Law, the Fugitive Slave Law, the Dred Scott decision) believed by teachers to be important facts every student should know. They gave their test to 1,500 students at the upper elementary (fifth through seventh grades), secondary, and college levels. In the upper elementary grades, students answered 16 percent of the questions correctly; in high school (after a year of U.S. history), 33 percent; and in college, after a third exposure to history, 49 percent. Taking a stand customarily reserved for country preachers, and more recently for secretaries of education and op-ed columnists, Bell and McCollum indicted the educational system and its charges: "Surely a grade of 33 in 100 on the simplest and most obvious facts of American history is not a record in which any high school can take pride."[24]

Six years later, in 1923, D. H. Eikenberry replicated these findings, though on a smaller scale.[25] He found that not one of thirty-four university seniors could remember who was president during the Mexican War (James K. Polk), and fewer than half could remember the president of the Confederacy (Jefferson Davis). Similar patterns emerged from a *New York Times* survey of historical knowledge given to 7,000 students in the 1940s, and little has changed since then, according to contemporary findings from the National Assessment of Educational Progress examination in American history.[26] Viewed in historical perspective, these recent results provide scant evidence for what some have claimed is a "gradual disintegration of cultural memory."[27] Instead, the consistency of these results testifies to a peculiar American pastime: the practice by each generation of testing its young, only to discover—and rediscover—their "shameful" ignorance.[28] But as Dale Whittington has shown, when test results from the early part of the twentieth century are compared with the most recent findings, we learn that there has been little appreciable change in students' historical knowledge over time,[29] despite the enormous expansion of high school enrollments in this century. If anything, the consistency of these results casts doubt on a presumed golden age of fact retention. Appeals to such an age are more the stuff of national lore and a wistful nostalgia for a time that never was than a reference to national history whose reality can be found in the documentary record.

J. Carleton Bell's colleague at the Brooklyn Training School, Garry C. Myers, took a different route in exploring historical knowledge. Myers was more interested in students' wrong answers than in their correct ones.[30] He asked 107 college women to name one fact about each of fifty historical figures. He found that fewer than 50 percent of the names were recalled accurately, with 40 percent "lost between the time of mastery and that of recall."[31] But this loss was not an erasure. Wrong answers, Myers found, were often statements of facts wrongly connected, the result of systematic efforts that followed a discernible pattern.[32] For example, Philip John Schuyler, one of four major generals commissioned by Congress during the Revolutionary War, was connected to wars ranging from the French and Indian War to the Civil War, but his status as general remained unchanged. Names like that of the abolitionist William Lloyd Garrison were confused with names that sounded similar, like President William Henry Harrison. And people with common last names, like Cyrus McCormick, the inventor of the reaper, were confused with others bearing a homonymous name, in this case John McCormack, the Irish crooner whose ballads were popular in the twenties. "Wrong answers deserve more careful study," urged Myers, anticipating future researchers' concern with error analysis, "and may give the teacher more and better information about his teaching than can be obtained from the traditional study of correct answers."[33]

Myers's study resists easy classification. On one hand, his recognition of the human tendency to "make some kind of response to a situation" foreshadowed the British social psychologist Sir Francis Bartlett's "effort after meaning" some fifteen years later.[34] On the other hand, he struck a chord that resonated with the associationism of the German psychologist Herman Ebbinhaus when he warned teachers to "exercise the greatest care . . . to insure correct recitations" so that the learner keeps "each element of his knowledge eternally associated with his mate."[35] But the recitation Myers had in mind was not mindless drill. Rather, children would "perceive facts in proper relation during study" using "hitching posts," or slots in memory, that the learner "needs to keep constantly in view."[36] Here Myers's appeal to cognitive hierarchies with major and minor points recalled an earlier Herbartian tradition and anticipated later notions of cognitive organizers popularized by David Ausubel and other pioneers of the cognitive revolution.[37]

Not all psychologists shared Myers's fascination with wrong answers, or Bell's with the historic sense. B. R. Buckingham, then editor of the *Journal of Educational Research* and professor of education at the University of Illinois, bristled in response to charges that tests of factual knowledge missed the most important aspects of historical knowing. "The case against memory has been vastly overstated," he fumed. "Even when we think we are appealing to a supposedly higher process, we may really be dealing only with a somewhat higher form of memory."[38] To support his claim, Buckingham administered questions from the "Van Wagenen Test of Historical Information and Judgment" to elementary and high school students and found a correlation of .4 between the factual items of this instrument and its "thought" items.[39] Rather than concluding that factual knowledge and historical reasoning went hand-in-hand, Buckingham made a bolder claim: What people called "historical reasoning" was actually nothing more than knowledge of facts! Buckingham argued his case by analyzing the "thought items" on the Van Wagenen test:

> The first [question on the Thought Scale] reads as follows: "Before the steamboats were made people used to travel on the ocean in sail boats. Steamboats were not made until a long, long time after the European people came to make their homes in America. How do you think these early European settlers came to America?" The acceptable answer is "in sail boats" and it is a fact. Therefore the question is a fact question although introduced by the words, "How do you think?"[40]

Buckingham believed that higher forms of historical understanding may be inferred from the factual component of the Van Wagenen scale "with substantial accuracy *without giving any other test*."[41] Moreover, he claimed, because of the relationship between factual tests and higher mental abilities in history, we actually "encour[age] the training of these higher abilities" when we administer tests of facts.[42]

Buckingham's shaky logic did not escape his contemporaries. The next issue of the *Journal of Educational Research* carried a short but stinging response by F. S. Camp, superintendent of schools in Stamford, Connecticut, who wryly identified himself as a "member of the [research] laity" but "not of the laity so far as teaching history is concerned."[43] Camp questioned the validity of Van Wagenen's scale, and particularly its ability to tap historical thinking. His own experience as a history teacher told him that it was possible to construct questions that measured students' ability to think deeply in history. For example: "Suppose Champlain in 1608 had chanced to befriend the Mohawks (Iroquois). What would probably have been the results of the New York campaign of the French in 1758?"[44] The answers to such questions, argued Camp, drew on factual knowledge, but the student, in formulating a response, "must examine, weigh and accept or reject facts; he must then organize them. And that requires staunch thinking."[45]

Camp's concerns, while perhaps persuasive to other history teachers, seemed to have little effect on test developers. As research efforts turned increasingly to scale development and refinement, historical knowledge, viewed as a menu of possibilities by Bell and McCollum, narrowed perilously toward a concentration on just one of their entrees—the ability to answer factual questions about historical personalities and events.[46] Advances in the field of educational measurement carried with them a certain antipathy to traditional forms of assessment in history classes, like essay writing.[47] According to one study, essays were "distasteful" not only to students but also to teachers, because the "scrutinizing, marking, and correcting of the student products is the teacher's greatest bugbear."[48] What if it could be shown that written work, in addition to being laborious, produced little benefit? Worse, what if the essay produced "as much harm as it does good?"[49] This was precisely the claim of F. R. Gorman and D. S. Morgan, whose study was conducted in three U.S. history classrooms.

These classes, all taught by the same teacher, were assigned different amounts of written homework. Class I was assigned "three units," Class II "one unit," and Class III none at all. Class III indeed did best on the factual outcome measure (181 points versus 175 for Class I), but the authors failed to account for the wide disparity in the entering achievement levels among students. Moreover, the researchers' homework assignments often looked more like directions for busy work than requests for thoughtful written responses (e.g., "List Lincoln's cabinet with the offices held by each" or "List the states which seceded in order, with the dates of secession").[50] When Gorman and Morgan concluded that "the popularity of written work with teachers may result from a confusion of busy work with valid learning procedures,"[51] one wonders where the confusion truly lay: with muddled teachers or with zealous researchers hell-bent on demonstrating the ineffectiveness of written assignments?

Advances in psychometrics fueled the movement toward objective testing, as did the spirit of Taylorism that swept American schools between the world wars.[52] But it would be wrong to see the focus on "objective" testing as a movement restricted to education. The fact-based image of historical knowledge fit cozily with prevailing views of knowledge in the discipline of history. As educational psychologists worked to produce reliable and objective history scales, university historians tried to extricate themselves from their humanistic roots so as to emerge as scientists who would, as the saying went, "cross an ocean to verify a comma."[53] This doggedly factualist approach, as Peter Novick has argued, helped distinguish professional historians from their amateur colleagues, a distinction necessary if history was to become a full-fledged member of the academic community.[54] It is no coincidence, then, that at almost the same time that L. W. Sackett was presenting his refinement of a world history scale in the pages of the *Journal of Educational Psychology*, a scale that would "nearly eliminate the subjective factor in grading history,"[55] the *American Historical Review*'s editorial policy was being formulated to exclude from its pages "matters of opinion" in favor of "matters of fact capable of determination one way or another."[56] This was an age characterized not by a breach between school and academy, but by a tightly woven nexus.

Following World War I, with the ascent of behaviorism as the dominant research paradigm of American psychologists, the concerns of a J. Carleton Bell or an F. S. Camp were all but abandoned.[57] Even in the odd study that took up history, the focus rarely veered from how to apportion facts so that they could be easily committed to memory.[58] The earlier concerns of Charles Judd with history's distinctive psychological features were overshadowed by sweeping learning theories that applied equally to all domains. Well into the 1970s, the psychologist Robert Gagné could blithely claim that learning was not unique to subject matter and that there was "no sound rational basis for such entities as 'mathematics learning,' 'science learning,' 'language learning' or 'history learning,' except as divisions of time devoted to these subjects during a school day or term."[59] Not until a decade later would this position meet serious challenges among mainstream psychologists of learning.

Ironically, some of the features of history learning that Judd identified may have contributed to its neglect by researchers. The lack of consensus about right answers in history complicated the measurement of outcomes, for if researchers deemed tests of facts trivial and term papers (often the product of historical understanding at the college level) unwieldy, they were faced with the forbidding prospect of creating wholly new measures. Other factors doubtless came into play. The rise of social studies on American soil presented new challenges to researchers because of the conceptual and epistemological differences in the disciplines brought under its umbrella. Further, in contrast to mathematics, where an active research community of subject matter and curriculum experts borrowed from and contributed to psychological theorizing, there was no such group among social studies educators. Research conducted by this latter group was usually a one way street: Psychological concepts were borrowed, but little was offered in return. These factors—and doubtless others—contributed to a period of relative neglect in research on the learning and teaching of history from the end of World War I to the advent of the cognitive revolution.

DEVELOPMENTS IN GREAT BRITAIN: PIAGET, PEEL, AND BEYOND

While American researchers focused on paired associates and running rats through mazes, psychologists in Great Britain followed a different lead. From the late 1950s to well into the 1970s, the theories of Jean Piaget provided the framework for understanding the school curriculum. In a twenty-eight-year span beginning in 1955, no fewer than two dozen theses and dissertations on historical learning from a Piagetian perspective were produced in Great Britain.[60] Although recent British work on history has ventured into different areas, it is impossible to conceive of it apart from its Piagetian roots.

Among the most ambitious research programs was that associated with E. A. Peel, a past president of the British Psychological Society and a professor of educational psychology at the University of Birmingham. For Peel, Piaget's theory was the key to understanding children's school performance, a means of classifying and systematizing the types of thinking required by different school subjects. Noting that Piaget's work had direct bearing on math and science, Peel set out to extend the theory to children's textual reasoning, particularly their comprehension of written materials in English and history. The essence of understanding in the latter subject, according to Peel, was not to be found in lists of facts but in synthetic forms of thought, like the ability to grasp "cause and effect, a capacity to follow a sustained argument and a power to evaluate."[61]

Although Peel often addressed history in his theoretical writings,[62] it was his student, Roy N. Hallam,[63] who gave historical research in the Piagetian tradition its biggest push. Hallam gave one hundred British high school students, ranging in age from eleven to nearly seventeen, three textbook passages, one on Mary Tudor, another on the Norman conquest, and the third on the civil wars in Ireland, as well as a series of questions on each. For example, after reading the passage about the Norman conquest, students were asked whether it was right for William to destroy northern England. Hallam classified students' responses according to Piagetian categories of intellectual development. Not relating the question to the information provided was scored as "pre-operational thinking"; a well-organized answer that did not go beyond the text was classified as "concrete operational"; and going beyond the text by stating hypotheses and checking them against the text was rated "formal operational."

Of Hallam's one hundred adolescents, only two answered questions consistently at the highest level, that of formal operations. Such findings, and similar results from Peel's other colleagues, led Hallam to conclude that systematic thinking appeared later in history than in math or science.[64] Hallam speculated that this is because history confronts the child with "an 'environment' which envelops the inner motives of adults living probably in another century with mores markedly different from those of the twentieth century."[65] The abstract nature of history, argued Hallam, "can perplex the most intelligent of adults."[66]

It is useful to step back from Hallam's study to see how the ways in which research is framed and executed can predetermine its results. First, students were asked questions that had little connection to what they studied in class. How they might have performed had their instruction stressed the formal aspects of historical reasoning remained an open question. Second, students may have been confused by Hallam's questions.[67] Consider, for example, the ones that accompanied the passage on Mary Tudor: "Mary Tudor thought that God wanted her to take England back to the Catholic church. (a) What would God have thought of her methods? (b) Can you think of any reasons why Mary Tudor should use such methods to make people follow her religion?"[68] What on earth were students to answer in response? For his part, Hallam was anything but tentative about the meaning of his findings: History, for children younger than fourteen, "should not be too abstract in form, nor should it contain too many variables."[69]

The desire to isolate the basic psychological processes embedded in learning history created challenges for Piagetian researchers. One problem was how to minimize the effects of students' prior knowledge, which was viewed as introducing unwanted variation to experimental results. Margaret F. Jurd tried to solve this problem by writing "historical" scenarios about three imaginary countries, Adza, Mulba, and Nocha.[70] Students were presented with a chart showing parallel events in two of these made-up countries and had to predict what would happen in the third. In Mulba, for example, "Richard became dictator" after "having led his people to victory against invaders," while in Adza, Henry became king after his father's death.[71] Students were then given a list of five events in Nocha's history, from a buildup in military spending to a decline in standard of living, and asked to order events in the correct sequence using comparative data from Adza and Mulba. Jurd interpreted students' performance in Piagetian terms. Success hinged on "identifying . . . one or more variables and the kinds of relations which might be thought to exist between them."[72] Students who identified only one variable and made no classification of it were judged "preoperational," while those who coordinated multiple variables while holding others constant were judged to be exhibiting formal operational thought.

By creating imaginary countries or restricting historical information to short textbook passages, Jurd, Hallam, and others attempted to control for students' prior knowledge. But there was something odd about decontextualizing historical events (or inventing fictional history) in a field that stresses the centrality of context.[73] Filtered through Piagetian lenses, historical reasoning came to resemble the textbook version of hypothetical-deductive reasoning in the natural sciences, complete with formalized techniques for induction and deduction and strategies for the coordination and classification of variables. The final result was a depiction of historical reasoning that was more persuasive among psychologists than among historians.[74] Reduced to sets of logical relations and tests of hypotheses, the history in such studies bore only a faint resemblance to the rich hybrid of narration, exposition, and imaginative reconstruction familiar in the discipline.

It is easy to find fault with quixotic efforts to strip away historical context to get at historical cognition. But such criticism should not obscure the fact that Peel, Hallam, Jurd, and others were the first psychologists since J. Carleton Bell to reopen the question of the "historic sense." Their efforts reminded researchers that the best indication of historical reasoning was not children's selection of a right answer, the "mere repetition of learnt facts," but the nature of children's reasoning, their ability to connect ideas, and the justifications they offered for their conclusions.[75] Although these researchers may have gone overboard in drawing conclusions based on limited data, they are to be credited with invigorating a field and launching projects whose influence is felt today.

One question that remains from Piagetian research on history was its impact on practice. In the opinion of Henry G. Macintosh, the past secretary of the British Southern Regional Examinations Board, Piagetian studies caused many history teachers "to undervalue the capacities of their own students and [helped] to ensure that their own teaching methods [made] it a self-fulfilling prophesy."[76] Similar observations came from John Fines, a history educator who claimed that a whole generation of teachers had been "cowed by Piagetian analysis."[77] While it is difficult to assess the accuracy of these claims, it is clear that Piagetian research lent support to the historian G. R. Elton's claim that serious work in history could not begin until students entered university.[78] It is also clear that these pessimistic assessments spurred on other research efforts, particularly those aimed at discovering a brighter side of students' historical capabilities.

This was precisely the challenge before the members of the Schools Council History 13–16 Project. Founded at the University of Leeds in 1973 with approximately sixty participating schools, it grew in ten years to include 20 percent of all British high schools.[79] Its original mission was a reconsideration of the nature of history and its relevance in secondary schools, but in its totality the project offered nothing less than a comprehensive model of the psychology of the subject matter.[80]

The project drew heavily on Paul Hirst's theory of academic disciplines as forms of knowledge. Hirst believed that the disciplines were more than groupings of related topics but constituted fundamentally different ways of knowing.[81] Accordingly, all knowledge forms exhibited four characteristics: (a) a body of concepts and key ideas—a common vocabulary; (b) distinctive ways of relating these concepts and ideas—a "syntax" for this vocabulary; (c) characteristic ways of establishing warrant for truth claims, such as the psychologist's appeal to the laboratory, or the historian's to the documentary record; and (d) distinctive forms of inquiry, such as the chemist's use of X-ray spectroscopy or the physicist's use of a linear accelerator.

Project founders argued that traditional history instruction constitutes a form of information, not a form of knowledge. Students might master an agreed-upon narrative, but they lacked any way of evaluating it, of deciding whether it, or any other narrative, was compelling or true. Denis Shemilt, the evaluator of the project and later its director, compared students from traditional history classes to drama students who could talk "sensibly about the separate scenes and characters of King Lear, but do not know what a play is."[82] Put differently, such students possessed copious amounts of historical information but had no idea where this information came from.

The Schools Council three-year curriculum began in the eighth grade. It took a nonchronological approach to history, beginning with a course called "What Is History?" that introduced students to the nature of historical evidence, the nature of reasoning from evidence, and problems of reconstruction from partial and mixed evidence. Other parts of the curriculum engaged students in historical research projects and thrust them into intensive inquiries on selected topics (e.g., Elizabethan England, Britain in the years 1815–1851, the American West, the rise of communist China, the Arab–Israeli conflict). Still other topics, like the history of medicine, were included in the curriculum because they exposed students to practices, beliefs, and ways of thinking radically different from their own.

An evaluation of the project conducted in the late 1970s contained three components: (a) a comparison of 500 project and 500 control students on a series of historical concept tests; (b) a matched-pairs comparison of seventy-five project and seventy-five control students on other concept tests (subjects were matched according to sex, IQ, and socioeconomic status); and (c) a matched-pairs study of seventy-eight pairs in which researchers engaged students in interviews about the nature of historical inquiry.[83] But before comparisons could be made between project students and the control group, project staff first had to invent measures and coding schemes to capture the "form of knowledge" approach to history. For example, students' responses about the nature of history from the matched-pairs interviews were coded using one of four levels spanning the range of historical conceptualization. Level I responses had a "just because" quality. Events happened because they happened, with no inner logic other than their arrangement in temporal sequence. Level II responses viewed history with "an austere, Calvinistic logic," equating historical reconstruction with slotting pieces of a puzzle into a pre-existing form.[84] At Level III, adolescents had a dawning awareness of a disjuncture between historical narratives and "the past," recognizing that the former involved selectivity and judgment and could never reflect the latter in all its complexity. At Level IV, students transcended the search for overarching historical laws and came to understand historical explanation as context-bound and context-sensitive.

The two highest levels of this typology were attained by 68 percent of project students versus 29 percent of the control group. The lowest level was occupied by 15 percent of control-group students versus 1 percent of project students. In each of the three evaluation components, project students outperformed their counterparts from traditional classrooms. For example, 50 percent of control-group students were unable to differentiate between historical and scientific knowledge, versus only 10 percent of project students. And when students were asked to compare history and mathematics, 83 percent of control students saw math as more difficult than history, versus 25 percent of project students. As one student from the control group put it, "In history you just look it up, math you work it out"; another control-group student added, "From one formula in Maths you get three or four others following, but history has no pattern."[85]

The overall picture emerging from the evaluation supported the idea that adolescents could be taught to understand history as a sophisticated form of knowledge. Yet Shemilt's evaluation study was not the story of unqualified success, for, as he noted, the difference between control students and project students could be compared "to the difference between stony, derelict ground barely able to support a few straggling weeds and a cultivated but undisciplined garden in which a few splendid blossoms struggle to show through."[86]

Even so, the portraits of adolescent reasoning offered by project students contrasted sharply with the barren images of adolescent reasoning offered by the Piagetians. This contrast was not lost on John Fines, who in his introduction to the evaluation report noted that project students "seem to be performing much more hopefully than the Piagetians first thought."[87] Yet, while Shemilt was careful to distinguish the Schools Council effort from the Piagetians, the Schools Council Project—from the nature of its measures to its levels of attainment, and even the graphic layout of its results—is impossible to conceptualize apart from that research tradition. One feels Piaget's presence at every turn, acting sometimes as touchstone, at other times as provocateur, and at yet other times as nodding observer, always at hand if not always acknowledged.

To be sure, Shemilt recognized the debt to Piaget in several places and even signaled a certain optimism about the applicability of Piagetian constructs, provided that they were first "specifically tailored" to the exigencies of history.[88] Left unacknowledged, however, was a certain similarity in research approach between the evaluation study and what some have called the Piaget-Peel-Hallam tradition,[89] a shared tendency by both approaches to thrust children into the role of mini-philosopher, with questions more germane to a discussion in metaphysics than one in history (e.g., "Does the fact that things are inevitable mean that we have no control over them?" "If an event can be altered, if it can be changed, how can it be inevitable?").[90] No doubt such questions have a bearing on historical understanding. But there is danger in equating students' responses to abstract queries with how they might respond when dealing with concrete historical materials. As the psycholinguists have taught us, it is one thing to use the pluperfect flawlessly and quite another to explain how we do it.

In its totality, the evaluation study of the History 13–16 Project yielded the most in-depth look at adolescent historical reasoning to date. Given the complexity of this portrait, one might expect similar attention to be devoted to the other half of the equation—the knowledge, understanding, and practices of the teachers who participated in the project. Here the evaluation study offered fewer insights. Like the traditional pre/post experiment, the 13–16 Evaluation Study provided some sense of where students began and provided evidence that they were different at the end. But beyond an appeal to written curricular materials, it was at a loss to explain change. What did teachers *do* in classes filled with Level I students? How did sophisticated notions of historical understanding get translated into classroom activities, explanations by teachers, or homework assignments for students? What were the key way stations along the path to higher understanding?

The History 13–16 Project provided few answers. Moreover, the question of what teachers needed to know in order to enact this curriculum was not addressed. In fact, there are clues that some project teachers may have had more in common with students functioning at Levels I and II than with those at Level IV. Responding to questionnaire items, nearly half of project teachers believed that primary sources were "necessarily more reliable than secondary sources," and 16 percent agreed with the statement that "people in the past thought and behaved in exactly the same way as people today, and that only the setting was different."[91] Shemilt's disclaimer that "teachers need to familiarize themselves with Project philosophy and objectives" surely missed the point.[82] The key question is this: How do we alter teachers' deeply held beliefs about history? *Can* we alter them?

THE COGNITIVE REVOLUTION: DEVELOPMENTS AND POSSIBILITIES

Every revolution inspires new hopes, and the "cognitive revolution" was no exception.[93] New images of school learning promised to answer questions that had puzzled researchers not only since the beginning of scientific psychology, but since humankind began asking itself what it meant to know and to learn. During the 1970s and 1980s, cognitive researchers illuminated students' thinking in an array of school subjects, from traditional ones like arithmetic, biology, physics, and geometry to newer additions to the curriculum such as computer science and economics. But amidst this efflorescence of research, history was ignored. Indeed, one of the first attempts to draw together the new work on school learning, Ellen Gagné's *The Cognitive Psychology of School Learning*, contained over 400 references—not one of which applied to history.[94]

The 1990s witnessed a dramatic change. Cognitive researchers made up for lost time by launching investigations that addressed topics from children's historical misconceptions to their reading of history textbooks, from teachers' subject matter knowledge to the assessment of expertise in history teaching. The following discussion surveys these and other developments.

Learning

One of the core insights of the cognitive approach to learning is that the learner brings to instruction a mixture of beliefs and conceptions, some true and others stubbornly false, through which new information is fil-tered. Although prior research mapped out some aspects of children's historical beliefs, particularly in the area of time and chronology, recent studies have explored their thinking on a range of topics and ideas.[95]

Gail Sinatra, Isabel Beck, and Margaret McKeown provided a sketch of the background knowledge the typical fifth grader brings to history instruction.[96] In interviews with thirty-five fifth graders prior to instruc-tion in American history and thirty-seven sixth graders following instruc-tion, students were asked questions such as "Why do we celebrate the Fourth of July?" "How did our country become a country?" and "Once there was a saying 'no taxation without representation.' What do you think that means?" Shaky understanding characterized students' responses, even after a year of instruction: 74 percent of fifth graders and 57 percent of sixth graders did not mention the war between Great Britain and the colonies in their responses, and 60 percent of all stu-dents could provide no information about the motivation of the Revo-lutionary War.

But students were hardly blank slates. Questions about the Fourth of July often elicited responses about memorials of "deaths of people who were in wars." Similarly, questions about the Declaration of Independence elicited responses ranging from the freeing of slaves to the Mayflower Compact. Like cognitive explorations in other subjects, and Myers's ear-lier work, Sinatra and her colleagues went beyond a right/wrong answer approach to explore systematic patterns in students' responses.

Bruce VanSledright and Jere Brophy also examined elementary school children's beliefs about history. They interviewed ten fourth graders about key topics in American history.[97] Although VanSledright and Brophy also found knowledge of these topics to be sparse, they found that some children were willing to construct narratives about events for which they possessed little information. One gifted story-teller, ten-year-old Helen, spun tales about Pilgrims who sailed on a boat called the *Mayflower* (adding, "That's how we got 'April showers bring May Flowers' ") and settled at Plymouth Rock, located some-where in Michigan's "upper peninsula."[98] To construct these stories, some children conflated information learned in school about different historical events, and then combined this mixture with snippets of infor-mation gleaned from cartoon shows or cultural celebrations such as Thanksgiving. VanSledright and Brophy concluded that children were able not only to construct imaginative stories about the past, but also to see patterns in these stories, overarching themes of tragedy and suspense. In this sense, young children's narrative reconstructions may be viewed as partially formed precursors of the "emplotments" used by academic historians to narrate their stories of the past.[99]

Children's fanciful elaborations can be classified within what David Perkins has called a "content frame," a set of misunderstandings about specific eras and events in American history.[100] Rosalyn Ashby and Peter Lee addressed what Perkins calls the "epistemic frame," more general and sweeping beliefs that children use to interpret the past.[101] Rather than engaging children in interviews, the strategy used in their prior work,[102] they grouped adolescents into trios and videotaped their interactions as they worked through documents about Anglo-Saxon oath-helping and the ordeal. From hundreds of hours of videotape, Ashby and Lee created a set of categories to characterize children's "historical empathy," the "intellectual achievement" of "entertain[ing] a set of beliefs and values . . . not necessarily their own."[103] Students least able to do this saw history as a "*divi* past" (from the British slang for "thick, dumb, or mentally defective"), regarding the subject with "irritated incomprehension and contempt."[104] Students occupying the middle levels of the typology began to view history as an explanatory system but made little attempt to understand the past on its own terms. Only at the highest levels did children start to recognize differences between past and present mind-sets, or historical changes in *Zeitgeist* and *mentalité*. Although Ashby and Lee viewed their typology as a way of characterizing children's thinking about the past, it may also capture aspects of adults' thinking as well. Indeed, some evidence suggests that the notion of the "timeless past," the idea that concepts from the present can be easily transported back in time, is embraced by some university students—history majors and nonmajors alike.[105]

Reading History Textbooks

Recent research efforts have also focused on students' understanding of history textbooks. The earliest work in this area applied principles of text design to the writing of textbooks.[106] Bonnie Armbruster and Tom Anderson found that typical history books failed to offer readers "considerate" treatments, or ones in which explanations allowed the reader to determine (a) the goal of an action or event, (b) the plan for attaining that goal, (c) the action that was taken in response, and (d) the outcome.[107] If a text failed to address these issues, according to Armbruster and Anderson, it failed "as a historical explanation."[108] Isabel Beck and her colleagues reached similar conclusions in a more extensive study.[109] They found that fifth-grade textbooks presumed background knowledge most children lacked. Like Armbruster and Anderson, Beck's team proposed rewriting history textbooks, using, in their words, "causal/explanatory" linkages, or linkages that connect a cause to an event and an event to a consequence.

Beck and her colleagues built on their work in text analysis to design passages that conformed to principles of cognitive text design. They conducted an experiment in which original text passages were compared with their rewritten counterparts.[110] For example, a textbook explanation about the French and Indian War that began, "In 1763 Britain and the colonies ended a 7-year war with the French and Indians," was rewritten to include material that established context and provided linkages between sentences. The new passage began, "About 250 years ago, Britain and France both claimed to own some piece of land, here, in North America."[111]

Researchers assigned 85 fourth- and fifth-grade students to original and revised text conditions and compared them according to their ability to recall ideas present in both forms. There was a statistically significant difference in recall (17 of 124 units in the original text condition versus 24 of 124 in the revised condition), providing modest support for the notion that textbooks can be revised to allow students to retain more information from them. An extension of this work showed that forty-eight fifth graders who were "provided with background knowledge" in an experimenter-led presentation were able to understand revised texts better than the originals.[112] This finding supported the notion that background knowledge helps most when readers are given well-structured texts.

The work on text design and analysis demonstrates that cognitive principles can be used to make history textbooks more "considerate." A more robust approach to improving students' understanding might teach students to deal with texts that are, by nature, inconsiderate. In a comparison of history textbooks and academic historical writing, Avon Crismore found that "metadiscourse," or indications of judgment, emphasis, and uncertainty, were used frequently in historical writing but typically edited out of textbooks.[113] For example, historians rely heavily on "hedges" to indicate indeterminacy, using such devices as modal auxiliaries ("may," "might"), certain verbs ("suggest," "appear," "seem"), and qualifiers ("possibly," "perhaps") to convey the uncertainty of historical knowledge. But Crismore found that text-books typically eliminated hedges. Such writing, she suggested, may be more "considerate," but it may also contribute to the finding that students often equate knowing history with "knowing the facts"[114] and approach their textbook with that singular goal in mind.[115] As Crismore observed:

> What happens to critical reading when attitudinal metadiscourse is delayed until adulthood and readers are not encouraged to become active participants in the reading process? . . . Young readers need to see author biases and evaluate them at an early age; textbooks and teachers need to teach them how to do this.[116]

Teaching

For the twenty-five years between 1950 and 1975, research on classroom teaching had a decidedly behaviorist cast that focused on discrete teaching acts like the frequency of classroom questions and the reinforcing qualities of teachers' responses. At the core of this approach was an assumption about the fundamental similarity among the school subjects. Variations in content were cast as "context variables" and emerged (if at all) in brief discussions about the limitations of research findings. Throughout the 1960s and 1970s, research on teaching witnessed its greatest success in the teaching of discrete skills, in which a teacher checks for understanding on a concrete outcome and then guides students in doing similar problems or exercises. But as Barak Rosenshine noted in his analysis of a history lesson on Federalist No. 10, taught by then–Secretary of Education William Bennett, research on skill teaching had virtually nothing to say about the teaching of content: "We do not even have a good name for it. . . . How does one teach this content and these ideas? The skill model does not help us much."[117]

Stanford University's Lee Shulman called the lack of research on teaching content a "missing paradigm" and went on to develop a research program to address it.[118] The Knowledge Growth in Teaching Project (1983–89) was a longitudinal study that tracked changes in teachers' knowledge from the beginning of their teacher education programs into the first and second years of full-time teaching. An examination of the knowledge growth of four history/social studies teachers was one of the first research reports (see Chapter 6 of this volume) to emerge from this project.

Work on the relationship between subject matter knowledge and teaching was extended in a series of "Wisdom of Practice" studies in which eleven accomplished teachers were observed teaching a unit on the American Revolution. Teachers also engaged in a series of interviews, ranging from an "intellectual autobiography," in which they reconstructed the high points of their high school and college education, to modified think-alouds in which they verbalized their thoughts as they read Washington's Farewell Address, Federalist No. 84 (Hamilton's argument against a bill of rights), and other primary documents. (See Chapter 8 for examples of this work.)

Gaea Leinhardt, one of the first researchers to apply cognitive principles to research on teaching, has also made major contributions to understanding the skills that teaching history demands.[119] In a case study of an experienced history teacher based on over seventy-six sessions in an Advanced Placement U.S. history class,[120] Leinhardt focused on the teacher's historical explanations, distinguishing two main types. In "blocked explanations," the teacher provided a self-contained, relatively modular explanation. In "ikat explanations," the teacher gave an abbreviated account or made a passing reference to something that was later extended and elaborated. At the beginning of the school year, the teacher provided nearly all the explanations, as students struggled with notions of multiple causation in the ratification of the Constitution or the conflicting interpretations of a Beard or a Hofstadter. As the year went on, the teacher progressively drew students into the process of formulating explanations. One measure of her success was the proportion of student talk to teacher talk, which was about 40 percent at the beginning of the year and increased almost fourfold by the thirteenth week.

This increase in student participation had an important qualitative dimension as well. Students were not simply saying more in response to the teacher's explanations; the content of their responses was characterized by an ever-increasing complexity. By January, Paul, one of the students Leinhardt analyzed, had linked the fall of a cotton-based economy to British trade policy and colonial ventures in Asia as well as to the failure of southern leaders to read public opinion in Great Britain. Students were learning not only a body of factual material but also how to use this material to craft their own interconnected historical explanations.[121]

The work on teacher knowledge represents a significant departure from the research on teaching that characterized the 1970s and early 1980s. Researchers abandoned behavioral observation schemes for intensive interviews and focused observations of a small number of teachers. Rather than brief samples of an hour or two every six months, observations in these classes tried to preserve the flow of instruction, usually over a unit but, as in Leinhardt's case, sometimes for nearly half a year. This work also ventured into new methodological territory, borrowing and modifying methods more commonly found in the anthropologist's or sociolinguist's toolbox than in the psychologist's laboratory. Rather than attempting to formulate a theory of instruction that would hold for all subjects, these investigations aimed at generating theories of the middle range, narrower and more provisional theories that applied to the teaching of a particular subject, theories that might or might not have implications for teaching physics or physical education.[122] The focus of this work was not teacher behavior isolated from teacher thought, but the deep and fundamental nexus between what teachers know and what they do.

This research offers compelling portraits of exemplary teaching. But the strength of this work—its finely etched accounts of knowledge use in action—may also be its weakness. Like museum pieces that arrest the attention and focus it on the here and now, these images tell us more about what is than about how it came to be. Was the subject matter knowledge of these teachers a consequence of their undergraduate training or a covariate of it? How did these teachers learn to socialize students into history as a way of knowing? What did their failures look like, and how did they learn from them? Since no teacher is going to become a master by taking a two-day workshop on developing historical explanations, how do we alter teachers' deep-seated epistemic beliefs about the nature of history? This last question has special meaning, for at the core of this new work on teaching is the assumption that the lessons learned from experts can be used to teach novices. But how, exactly, do we turn portraits of excellence into programs that develop it? These are just some of the unanswered questions that arise from new research on teachers' subject matter knowledge in history.

CONCLUSION

Current research on history teaching and learning is characterized by diverse investigations that reflect the vigor of cognitive approaches. In several areas, history has not been the final beneficiary of insights gleaned from research on other subjects, but the site where these insights first germinated and took root.

There are several reasons to think that the new interest in history is more than a passing fad. There is a growing recognition by educators and policymakers that questions of historical reasoning carry implications that go well beyond the curricular borders of history.[123] History offers a storehouse of complex and rich problems, not unlike those that confront us daily in the social world. Examining these problems requires an interpretive acumen that extends beyond the "locate information in the text" skills that dominate many school tasks. Understanding how students deal with such complexity, and how teachers aid them in doing so, would not only provide a knowledge base for improving school history but would also inform theories of reading comprehension, which are surprisingly mute about the processes used to form interpretations of complex written texts.[124]

Three additional developments promise to keep the spotlight on history. First, recent attention to narrative, which sees the formation of narrative as a "cognitive achievement,"[125] stands to gain much by extending its scope to the formation of historical narratives.[126] This topic is already being taken up with increasing self-awareness by professional historians, and psychologists would have much to contribute to this effort.[127] Second, new technologies such as hypermedia and computer data bases have created possibilities in history that were unimaginable a few years ago. A variety of efforts are under way that explore technology's role in enhancing historical understanding.[128] Finally, history has already been the site of new developments in student and teacher assessment and promises to continue to be a rich development site in the future.[129]

Psychologists interested in history have traditionally looked to the extensive body of historiographic writings for clues to the nature of historical thinking. This storehouse of essays and monographs, composed largely by historians and philosophers of history, looks at historical works not for what they disclose about the War of 1812, daily life in the Middle Ages, or the demise of French Indochina, but for what they say about historical knowing more generally.[130] The strategy of looking carefully at written histories and inferring from them the processes used in their composition offers many insights. The problem with using this approach to build a theory of teaching and learning is that the final products of historical thinking can be explained by appealing to wholly different intermediate processes.[131] Historiography teaches us how to recognize skilled cognition but gives us scant advice for how to achieve it.

There is a second way to understand what it means to think historically. Less developed than the historiographic tradition, this approach examines the steps and missteps that lead to the formation of historical interpretations and conclusions. This work is carried out by researchers who conduct empirical studies into how students, teachers, and historians come to understand history.[132] It asks questions about what people know and how they come to know it. In so doing, this approach wrests questions of epistemology from the clouds and turns them into objects of empirical inquiry.[133]

Such research would hark back to the beginning of the twentieth century, when the American Psychological Association and the American Philosophical Society held joint meetings because the psychologist and the philosopher were often one and the same. As a research strategy, this approach would trace its intellectual ancestry not to Edward Thorndike, who displayed little patience with questions philosophical,[134] but to Wilhelm Wundt. Contrary to his popular image as an experimentalist singularly determined to establish psychology as an empirical science,[135] the lesser known Wundt was a man whose empirical investigations informed and were informed by his writings on epistemology, logic, and ethics, a man who argued that psychology and philosophy were so interdependent that, separated from one another, both would atrophy.[136] At its heart, historical understanding is an interdisciplinary enterprise, and nothing less than a multidisciplinary approach will approximate its complexity. In this regard, present efforts suggest that the future will be richer than the past.

NOTES

This chapter originally appeared in the *Handbook of Educational Psychology*, edited by Robert Calfee and David Berliner (New York, 1996). Since its appearance there has been an explosion of new work on teaching and learning history. Edited collections of this work include Peter N. Stearns, Peter Seixas, and Sam Wineburg, *Knowing, Teaching, and Learning History: National and International Perspectives* (New York, 2000), and James F. Voss and Mario Carretero, *Learning and Reasoning in History* (Portland, Oreg., 1998). See, as well, the special issues of the *Journal of Narrative and Life History* (1994, no. 4) and *Culture & Psychology* (1994, no.

1), both of which were edited by James V. Wertsch. Updated literature reviews include a short co-written piece, Richard Paxton and Sam Wineburg, "History Teaching," in the *Routledge International Companion to Education* (London, 2000); Suzanne M. Wilson, "Review of History Teaching," in Virginia Richardson, ed., *Handbook of Research on Teaching* (New York, 2001); and James Voss's "Issues in the Learning of History," *Issues in Education: Contributions from Educational Psychology* 4, no. 2 (1998), 163–209. The review that appears here has been updated slightly and edited for a general audience.

1. I limit my focus to work in English while recognizing that important work has appeared in other languages. See, for example, J. Pozo and Mario Carretero, "El Adolescente Como Historiador" [The adolescent as historian], *Infancia y Aprendizaje* 23 (1983), 75–90; Bodo von Borries, "Geschichtslernen und Persönlichkeits-entwicklung" [The learning of history and the development of self], *Geschichts-Didaktic* 12 (1987), 1–14; V. A. Kol'tsova, "Experimental Study of Cognitive Activity in Communication (with Specific Reference to Concept Formation)," *Soviet Psychology* 17 (1978), 23–38. For an overview of trends in history teaching in Europe and the Middle East, see Bodo von Borries, ed., *Youth and History: A Comparative European Survey on Historical Consciousness and Political Attitudes Among Adolescents* (Hamburg, Germany, 1997).

2. For example, Michael Frisch, "American History and the Structure of Collective Memory: A Modest Exercise in Empirical Iconography," *Journal of American History* 75 (1989), 1130–55; M. M. Miller and Peter N. Stearns, "Applying Cognitive Learning Approaches in History Teaching: An Experiment in a World History Course," *History Teacher* 28 (1995), 183–204; Peter Seixas, "Historical Understanding Among Adolescents in a Multicultural Setting," *Curriculum Inquiry* 23 (1993), 301–27; and Peter Seixas, "When Psychologists Discuss Historical Thinking: A Historian's Perspective," *Educational Psychologist* 29 (1999), 107–9.

3. Michelene T. H. Chi, Paul J. Feltovich, and Robert Glaser, "Categorization and Representation of Physics Problems by Experts and Novices," *Cognitive Science* 5 (1981), 121–52.

4. For an example of British work that predates this tradition, see Frances Collie, "The Problem Method in the History Courses of the Elementary School," *Journal of Experimental Pedagogy and Training College Record* 1 (1911), 236–39; and R. E. Aldrich, "New History: An Historical Perspective," in Alaric K. Dickinson, Peter J. Lee, and Peter J. Rogers, eds., *Learning History* (London, 1984), 210–24.

5. Edward L. Thorndike, *Educational Psychology—Briefer Course* (New York, 1923), 345.

6. Edward L. Thorndike, *Education: A First Book* (New York, 1912), 144.

7. G. Stanley Hall, *Educational Problems*, vol. 2 (New York, 1911), 285–86.

8. Ibid., 296.

9. Charles Hubbard Judd, *Psychology of High-School Subjects* (Boston, 1915), 384.

10. Committee of Seven, American Historical Association, *The Study of History in Schools* (New York, 1899).

11. Committee of Five, American Historical Association, *The Study of History in Secondary Schools* (New York, 1911).

12. Judd, *High-School Subjects*, 379.

13. J. Carleton Bell, "The Historic Sense," *Journal of Educational Psychology* 8 (1917), 317.

14. Ibid., 317.

15. Ibid., 318.

16. Ibid.

17. Ibid.

18. J. Carleton Bell and David F. McCollum, "A Study of the Attainments of Pupils in United States History," *Journal of Educational Psychology* 8 (1917), 257–74.

19. Ibid., 257.

20. Ibid.

21. Ibid., 258.

22. Ibid.

23. Ibid.

24. Ibid., 268–69.

25. D. H. Eikenberry, "Permanence of High School Learning," *Journal of Educational Psychology* 14 (1923), 463–81.

26. Allan Nevins, "American History for Americans," *New York Times Magazine* (May 3, 1942), 6, 28–29; cf. Bernard DeVoto, "The Easy Chair," *Harper's Magazine* (June 1943), 129–32; Diane Ravitch and Chester E. Finn, Jr., *What Do Our 17-Year-Olds Know? A Report on the First National Assessment of History and Literature* (New York: 1987).

27. Chester E. Finn and Diane Ravitch, "Survey Results: U.S. 17-Year-Olds Know Shockingly Little About History and Literature," *American School Board Journal* 174 (1987), 32.

28. This characterization as "shameful" comes from Ravitch and Finn, *17-Year-Olds*, 201. See the parallels in a Canadian context, Jack Granatstein, *Who Killed Canadian History?* (Toronto, 1998). For a penetrating critique of Granatstein's failure to consider his findings in a comparative context, see Chris Lorenz, "Comparative Historiography: Problems and Perspectives," *History and Theory* 38 (1999), 25–39.

29. Dale Whittington, "What Have 17-Year-Olds Known in the Past?" *American Educational Research Journal* 28 (1991), 759–80.

30. Garry C. Myers, "Delayed Recall in History," *Journal of Educational Psychology* 8 (1917), 275–83.

31. Ibid., 277.

32. Ibid., 282.

33. Ibid.

34. Garry C. Myers, "Confusion in Recall," *Journal of Educational Psychology* 8 (1917), 174; Francis C. Bartlett, *Remembering: A Study in Experimental and Social Psychology* (New York, 1932).

35. Myers, "Confusion," 175. For an overview of Ebbinhaus's ideas, see Gordon H. Bower and Ernest R. Hilgard, *Theories of Learning*, 5th ed. (Englewood Cliffs, N.J., 1981).

36. Myers, "Confusion," 175.

37. David P. Ausubel, "The Use of Advance Organizers in the Learning and

Retention of Meaningful Verbal Material," *Journal of Educational Psychology* 51 (1960), 267–72.

38. B. R. Buckingham, "A Proposed Index in Efficacy in Teaching United States History," *Journal of Educational Research* 1 (1920), 164.

39. M. J. Van Wagenen, *Historical Information and Judgment in Pupils of Elementary Schools* (New York, 1919).

40. Buckingham, "Proposed Index," 168.

41. Ibid., 170, emphasis in original.

42. Ibid., 171.

43. F. S. Camp, "Wanted: A History Scale Maker," *Journal of Educational Research* 2 (1920), 517.

44. Ibid., 518.

45. Ibid.

46. For example, C. L. Harlan, "Educational Measurement in the Field of History," *Journal of Educational Research* 2 (1920), 849–53; C. W. Odell, "The Barr Diagnostic Tests in American History," *School and Society* 16 (1922), 501–3; and L. W. Sackett, "A Scale in United States History," *Journal of Educational Psychology* 10 (1919), 345–48.

47. See R. B. Weaver and A. E. Traxler, "Essay Examinations and Objective Tests in United States History in the Junior High School," *School Review* 39 (1931), 689–95.

48. F. R. Gorman and D. S. Morgan, "A Study of the Effect of Definite Written Exercises Upon Learning in a Course of American History," *Indiana School of Education Bulletin* 6 (1930), 80–90.

49. Ibid., 90.

50. Ibid., 81.

51. Ibid., 90.

52. Raymond Callahan, *Education and the Cult of Efficiency* (Chicago, 1962).

53. Peter Novick, *That Noble Dream: The "Objectivity Question" and the American Historical Profession* (Cambridge, England, 1988), 23.

54. Ibid.

55. Sackett, "A Scale," 348.

56. Cited in Novick, *Noble Dream*, 200.

57. Among the scattered and short-lived exceptions was the work of M. Clark, "The Construction of Exercises in the Use of Historical Evidence," in T. L. Kelly and A. C. Krey, eds., *Tests and Measurements in the Social Sciences* (New York, 1934), 302–39.

58. H. F. Arnold, "The Comparative Effectiveness of Certain Study Techniques in the Field of History," *Journal of Educational Psychology* 33 (1942), 449–57.

59. Robert M. Gagné, "The Learning Basis of Teaching Methods," in N. L. Gage, ed., *The Psychology of Teaching Methods: Seventy-fifth Yearbook of the National Society for the Study of Education* (Chicago, 1976), 30.

60. Martin B. Booth, "Skills, Concepts, and Attitudes: The Development of Adolescent Children's Historical Thinking," *History and Theory* 22 (1983), 101–17. See Booth's update on developments in Great Britain, "Cognition in History: A British Perspective," *Educational Psychologist* (1994), 61–70, as well as Peter Lee,

"History Education Research in the UK: A Schematic Commentary," paper presented at the annual meeting of the American Educational Research Association, New Orleans, 1999.

61. E. A. Peel, "Understanding School Material," *Educational Review* 24 (1972), 164.

62. For example, E. A. Peel, "Some Problems in the Psychology of History Teaching: Historical Ideas and Concepts," in W. H. Burston and D. Thompson, eds., *Studies in the Nature and Teaching of History* (London, 1967), 159–72; and E. A. Peel, "Some Problems in the Psychology of History Teaching: The Pupil's Thinking and Inference," ibid., 173–90.

63. Roy N. Hallam, "Logical Thinking in History," *Educational Review* 19 (1967), 183–202.

64. For example, D. Case and J. M. Collinson, "The Development of Formal Thinking in Verbal Comprehension," *British Journal of Educational Psychology* 32 (1962), 103–11; see the references to other studies cited in E. A. Peel, "Experimental Examination of Some of Piaget's Schemata Concerning Children's Perception and Thinking, and a Discussion of Their Educational Significance," *British Journal of Educational Psychology* 29 (1959), 89–103.

65. Hallam, "Logical Thinking," 195.

66. Ibid.

67. See Martin B. Booth, "Ages and Concepts: A Critique of the Piagetian Approach to History Teaching," in Christopher Portal, ed., *The History Curriculum for Teachers* (London, 1987), 22–38.

68. Quoted in Booth, "Skills, Concepts, and Attitudes," 104.

69. Roy N. Hallam, "Piaget and Thinking in History," in M. Ballard, ed., *New Movements in the Study and Teaching of History* (London, 1970), 168. Peter Lee has recently reminded us that Hallam's research program embraced both historical and religious thinking, a fact that should temper this critique of Hallam's work. See Peter Lee, "History Across the Water: A U.K. Perspective on History Education Research," *Issues in Education: Contributions from Educational Psychology* 4 (1998), 211–20.

70. Margaret F. Jurd, "Adolescent Thinking in History-Type Material," *Australian Journal of Education* 17 (1973), 2–17; and Margaret F. Jurd, "An Empirical Study of Operational Thinking in History-Type Material," in J. A. Keats, K. F. Collis, and G. S. Halford, eds., *Cognitive Development: Research Based on a Neo-Piagetian Approach* (New York, 1978), 315–48.

71. Jurd, "Operational Thinking," 322.

72. Ibid.

73. See James West Davidson and Mark Hamilton Lytle, *After the Fact: The Art of Historical Detection* (New York, 1982); see also the extensive discussion of context in J. H. Hexter, *The History Primer* (New York, 1971).

74. See Bernard Bailyn, "The Problems of the Working Historian: A Comment," in Sidney Hook, ed., *Philosophy and History* (New York, 1963), 93–101; and Louis O. Mink (Brian Fay, Eugene O. Golob, and Richard T. Vann, eds.), *Historical Understanding* (Ithaca, N.Y., 1987).

75. Hallam, "Logical Thinking," 198.

76. Henry G. Macintosh, "Testing Skills in History," in Portal, *History Curriculum for Teachers*, 184.

77. John Fines, "Introduction," in Denis Shemilt, ed., *Schools Council History 13–16 Project* (Edinburgh, 1980), iii. Peter Lee believes that Piaget's influence on British history teaching has been exaggerated. See his "History Across the Water," 211–20.

78. G. R. Elton, "What Sort of History Should We Teach?" in Ballard, *New Movements in the Study and Teaching of History*.

79. H. Dawson, cited in L. W. Rosenzweig and T. P. Weinland, "New Directions of the History Curriculum: A Challenge for the 1980s," *History Teacher* 19 (1986), 263–77.

80. Denis J. Shemilt, *History 13–16: Evaluation Study* (Edinburgh, 1980).

81. Paul H. Hirst, "Liberal Education and the Nature of Knowledge," in R. S. Peters, ed., *Philosophy of Education* (Oxford, 1973), 87–101. Schools Council founders were influenced as well by notions of "structure of the disciplines" as formulated in Jerome Bruner's *Process of Education* (Cambridge, Mass., 1961).

82. Denis J. Shemilt, "The Devil's Locomotive," *History and Theory* 22 (1983), 15.

83. Shemilt, *History 13–16*. A "matched-pairs" design pairs a student in the new curriculum with a student similar in background and ability who has studied the traditional curriculum. It is a common research design in psychological experimentation.

84. Shemilt, "Devil's Locomotive," 7.

85. Shemilt, *History 13–16*, 20.

86. Ibid., 14.

87. Fines, "Introduction," ii.

88. Shemilt, *History 13–16*, 50–52.

89. See Matt T. Downey and Linda S. Levstik, "Teaching and Learning History," in James P. Shaver, ed., *Handbook of Research on Social Studies* (New York, 1991), 400–410.

90. Shemilt, *History 13–16*, 14.

91. Ibid., 76.

92. Ibid.

93. Howard Gardner is generally credited with inventing the term "cognitive revolution." See his readable history of the transition from behaviorism to cognitivism in *The Mind's New Science: A History of the Cognitive Revolution* (New York, 1985).

94. Ellen D. Gagné, *The Cognitive Psychology of School Learning* (Boston, 1985).

95. Gustav Jahoda, "Children's Concepts of Time and History," *Educational Review* 15 (1963), 87–104; R. N. Smith and P. Tomlinson, "The Development of Children's Construction of Historical Duration," *Educational Research* 19 (1977), 163–70. See also Downey and Levstik, "Teaching and Learning History," 400–410.

96. Gail M. Sinatra, Isabel L. Beck, and Margaret G. McKeown, "A Longitudinal Characterization of Young Students' Knowledge of Their Country's Government," *American Educational Research Journal* 29 (1992), 633–62.

97. Bruce VanSledright and Jere Brophy, "Storytelling, Imagination, and Fanciful Elaboration in Children's Historical Reconstructions," *American Educational Research Journal* 29 (1992), 837–61.

98. Ibid., 846.

99. Hayden White, *Metahistory: The Historical Imagination in Nineteenth Century Europe* (Baltimore, Md., 1973).

100. David N. Perkins and R. Simmons, "Patterns of Misunderstanding: An Integrative Model for Science, Math, and Programming," *Review of Educational Research* 58 (1988), 303–26.

101. Rosalyn Ashby and Peter J. Lee, "Children's Concepts of Empathy and Understanding in History," in Portal, *History Curriculum for Teachers*, 62–88.

102. See Alaric K. Dickinson and Peter J. Lee, *History Teaching and Historical Understanding* (London, 1978); and Alaric K. Dickinson and Peter J. Lee, "Making Sense of History," in Dickinson, Lee, and Rogers, *Learning History*, 117–54. Peter Lee, Rosalyn Ashby, and Alaric Dickinson have launched a major study into children's historical reasoning. See Peter Lee, Alaric Dickinson, and Rosalyn Ashby, "Just Another Emperor: Understanding Action in the Past," *International Journal of Educational Research* 27 (1997), 233–44.

103. Ashby and Lee, "Children's Concepts," 63.

104. Ibid., 68.

105. David Lowenthal, "The Timeless Past: Some Anglo-American Historical Preconceptions," *Journal of American History* 75 (1989), 1263–80.

106. For example, Bonnie J. F. Meyer, *The Organization of Prose and Its Effects on Memory* (New York, 1975); and T. A. van Dijk and Walter Kintsch, *Strategies of Discourse Comprehension* (New York, 1983).

107. Bonnie B. Armbruster and Tom H. Anderson, "Structures of Explanations in History Textbooks, or So What If Governor Stanford Missed the Spike and Hit the Rail?" *Journal of Curriculum Studies* 16 (1984), 247–74.

108. Ibid., 249.

109. Isabel L. Beck, Margaret G. McKeown, and Erika W. Gromoll, "Learning from Social Studies Texts," *Cognition and Instruction* 6 (1989), 99–158.

110. Isabel L. Beck, Margaret G. McKeown, Gail M. Sinatra, and J. A. Loxterman, "Revising Social Studies Texts from a Text-Processing Perspective: Evidence of Improved Comprehensibility," *Reading Research Quarterly* 26 (1991), 251–76.

111. Ibid., 257.

112. Margaret G. McKeown, Isabel L. Beck, Gail M. Sinatra, and J. A. Loxterman, "The Contribution of Prior Knowledge and Coherent Text to Comprehension," *Reading Research Quarterly* 27 (1992), 79–93.

113. Avon Crismore, "The Rhetoric of Textbooks: Metadiscourse," *Journal of Curriculum Studies* 16 (1984), 279–96.

114. See expansions of this point in Robert F. Berkhofer, Jr., "Demystifying Historical Authority: Critical Textual Analysis in the Classroom," *Perspectives: Newsletter of the American Historical Association* 26 (February 1988), 13–16; Carl N. Degler, "Remaking American History," *Journal of American History* 67 (1980), 7–25; James L. Lorence, "The Critical Analysis of Documentary Evidence: Basic Skills in the History Classroom," *History Teaching: A Journal of Methods* 8 (1983), 77–84.

115. J. D. McNeil, "Personal Meanings Versus Test-Driven Responses to Social Studies Texts," *Reading Psychology* 10 (1989), 311–19.

116. Crismore, "Rhetoric of Textbooks," 296. Richard J. Paxton has begun a research program that examines how students respond to textbooks that better approximate authentic historical writing. See Richard J. Paxton, " 'Someone with

Like a Life Wrote It': The Effects of a Visible Author on High School History Students," *Journal of Educational Psychology* 89 (1997), 235–50; and Richard J. Paxton, "A Deafening Silence: History Textbooks and the Students Who Read Them," *Review of Educational Research* 69 (1999), 315–39.

117. Barak Rosenshine, "Unsolved Issues in Teaching Content: A Critique of a Lesson on Federalist Paper No. 10," *Teaching and Teacher Education* 2 (1986), 301–8.

118. Lee S. Shulman, "Paradigms and Research Programs in the Study of Teaching: A Contemporary Perspective," in Merlin Wittrock, ed., *Handbook of Research on Teaching*, 3rd ed. (New York, 1986), 3–36.

119. Gaea Leinhardt, "Expertise in Mathematics Teaching," *Educational Leadership* 43 (1986), 28–33; Gaea Leinhardt and James G. Greeno, "The Cognitive Skill of Teaching," *Journal of Educational Psychology* 78 (1986), 75–95.

120. Gaea Leinhardt, "Weaving Instructional Explanations in History," *British Journal of Educational Psychology* 63 (1993), 46–74.

121. Since the original publication of this review, Gaea Leinhardt has written several important analyses of skilled history teaching. See, for example, Kathleen M. Young and Gaea Leinhardt, "Writing from Primary Documents: A Way of Knowing in History," *Written Communication* 15 (1998), 25–68; and Gaea Leinhardt, "Lessons in Teaching and Learning History from Paul's Pen," in Peter N. Stearns, Peter Seixas, and Sam Wineburg, eds., *Knowing, Teaching, and Learning History: National and International Perspectives* (New York: 2000), 223–45.

122. Robert K. Merton, *Social Theory and Social Structure*, 3rd ed. (New York, 1968).

123. For example, Bradley Commission on History in Schools, *Building a History Curriculum: Guidelines for Teaching History in Schools* (Washington, D.C., 1988); California State Department of Education, *History–Social Science Framework for California Public Schools, K–12* (Sacramento, 1988); Bernard R. Gifford, *History in the Schools* (New York, 1988). For a recent example of research that examines sophisticated textual interpretation, see Joan Peskin, "Constructing Meaning When Reading Poetry: An Expert–Novice Study," *Cognition and Instruction* 16 (1998), 235–63.

124. See I. Athey and Harry Singer, "Developing the Nation's Reading Potential for a Technological Era," *Harvard Educational Review* 57 (1987), 84–93; and Walter Kintsch, "Learning from Text," *Cognition and Instruction* 3 (1986), 87–108.

125. See David R. Olson, *The World on Paper* (New York, 1994).

126. See E. B. Freeman and Linda S. Levstik, "Recreating the Past: Historical Fiction in the Social Studies Curriculum," *Elementary School Journal* 88 (1988), 329–37; and Linda S. Levstik and Christine C. Pappas, "Exploring the Development of Historical Understanding," *Journal of Research and Development in Education* 21 (1987), 1–15.

127. For example, Tom Holt, *Thinking Historically: Narrative, Imagination, and Understanding* (Princeton, 1990); and William Cronon, "A Place for Stories: Nature, History, and Narrative," *Journal of American History* 78 (1992), 1347–76.

128. For example, Jon Nichol and J. Dean, "Computers and Children's Historical Thinking and Understanding," in R. Ennals, R. Gwyn, and L. Zdravchev, eds., *Information Technology and Education: The Changing School* (West Sussex, England, 1986), 160–76; Gavriel Salomon, "Transcending the Qualitative–Quantitative Debate: The Analytic and Systemic Approaches to Educational Research," *Educa-*

tional Researcher 20 (1991), 10–18; and Katheryn T. Spoehr and Luther W. Spoehr, "Learning to Think Historically," *Educational Psychologist* 29 (1994), 71–77. For exciting developments on the relationship between technology and history see http://historymatters.gmu.edu, as well as Randy Bass and Roy Rosenzweig, "Rewiring the History and Social Studies Classroom: Needs, Frameworks, Dangers, and Proposals" (U.S. Department of Education, Washington, D.C., 1999).

129. See Martin B. Booth, "A Modern World History Course and the Thinking of Adolescent Pupils," *Educational Review* 32 (1980), 245–57. See also Eva Baker, "Learning-Based Assessments of History Understanding," *Educational Psychologist* 29, no. 2 (Spring 1994), 97–106.

130. For example, Carl Becker, *Everyman His Own Historian* (Chicago, 1935; reprint ed. 1966); Berkhofer, "Demystifying"; Marc Bloch, *The Historian's Craft* (Manchester, England, 1954); Cronon, "A Place for Stories"; Davidson and Lytle, *After the Fact;* Degler, "Remaking American History"; David Hackett Fischer, *Historians' Fallacies: Toward a Logic of Historical Thought* (New York, 1970); Louis Gottschalk, *Understanding History: A Primer of Historical Method* (Chicago, 1958); Hexter, *History Primer;* Allan Megill, "Recounting the Past: 'Description,' Explanation, and Narrative in Historiography," *American Historical Review* 94 (1989), 627–53; Novick, *Noble Dream;* W. J. Dibble, "Four Types of Inferences from Documents to Event," *History and Theory* 3 (1963), 203–21; William H. Dray, *Philosophical Analysis of History* (New York, 1966); Haskel Fain, *Between Philosophy and History: The Resurrection of Speculative Philosophy of History Within the Analytic Tradition* (Princeton, 1970); Maurice Mandelbaum, *The Problem of Historical Knowledge* (New York, 1938); Mink (Fay, Golob, and Vann, eds.), *Historical Understanding;* Jörn Rüsen, *Studies in Metahistory* (Pretoria, South Africa: Human Sciences Research Council, 1993); Quentin Skinner, ed., *The Return of Grand Theory in the Human Sciences* (Cambridge, Mass., 1985); Michael Stanford, *The Nature of Historical Knowledge* (New York, 1986).

131. See K. Anders Ericsson and Herbert A. Simon, *Protocol Analysis: Verbal Reports as Data* (Cambridge, Mass., 1984); Jill Larkin, "Teaching Problem Solving in Physics: The Psychological Laboratory and the Practical Classroom," in David T. Tuma and F. Reif, eds., *Problem Solving and Education: Issues in Teaching and Research* (Hillsdale, N.J., 1980), 111–25.

132. See note 2.

133. See Kenneth A. Strike and George J. Posner, "Epistemological Perspectives on Conceptions of Curriculum Organization and Learning," in Lee S. Shulman, ed., *Review of Research in Education* (Itasca, Ill., 1976), 10–141.

134. See Geraldine M. Joncich, *The Sane Positivist: A Biography of Edward L. Thorndike* (Middletown, Conn., 1968).

135. For example, Edwin G. Boring, *A History of Experimental Psychology* (New York, 1929).

136. M. G. Ash, "Wilhelm Wundt and Oswald Külpe on the Institutional Status of Psychology: An Academic Controversy in Historical Context," in W. G. Bringmann and R. D. Tweney, eds., *Wundt Studies* (Toronto, 1980), 396–421; Steven Toulmin and David E. Leary, "The Cult of Empiricism in Psychology, and Beyond," in David E. Leary and S. Koch, eds., *A Century of Psychology as Science* (New York, 1985), 594–617.

CHALLENGES FOR THE STUDENT

3

On the Reading of Historical Texts

Notes on the Breach Between School and Academy

n an essay about reading historical texts, William Willcox asks us to consider two accounts of the storming of the Bastille, one by a member of the *ancien régime* and the other by a Jacobin:

> No matter how honest the two men may have been, the event described by one has a quite different flavor from that described by the other. The historian can never see the event itself, in Ranke's famous phrase, *wie es eigentlich gewesen;* he can see it only through witnesses, and is as dependent on their eyes and emotions as on their pens. This is not to say that he must share their bias; quite the contrary. But he must understand it in order to allow for it.[1]

The call to "understand the bias" of a source is quite common in the reflective writings of historians. Yet as a guild, historians have been uncharacteristically tight-lipped about how they do so.[2] This is unfortunate, for the process is by no means self-evident. How exactly do historians put emotion back into the inanimate texts that they read? How do they provide voices to people who have been dead hundreds or thousands of years? And what about students of history, for whom a historical text is most often a textbook? Are they capable of engaging in this form of textual animation? Do students realize that they are as dependent on authors' hearts as on their heads?

In asking these questions I draw on my research with historians and high school students who "thought aloud" as they reviewed a series of historical documents. I begin by providing an overview of what I learned from historians, sketching in broad strokes an image of the skilled reader of history. Next, I compare this image to what emerged from an analysis of high school students' responses to these same documents. I then speculate about the source of differences between historians and students. I end by outlining some of the implications of this work for how we define the place of history in the school curriculum.

THE SKILLED READING OF HISTORY

Let me begin by explaining how my readings with historians and students were generated. I sat down with eight historians and taught them to think aloud as they read documents about the Battle of Lexington, the opening volley of the Revolutionary War. (The same procedure was followed for eight high school students, but more about them later.) The think-aloud technique asks people to verbalize their thoughts as they solve complex problems or read sophisticated texts. It departs from experimental research by focusing on the intermediate processes of cognition, not just on its outcomes. Moreover, thinking aloud differs from its discredited ancestor, introspection, in two ways: First, it asks people to report their thoughts as they are heeded in memory, not minutes or days later; and, second, it asks people to verbalize the contents of their thoughts, not the processes used to generate them.[3]

I purposely recruited historians with varied specialties and backgrounds.[4] Some were steeped in the colonial period, but others, such as a specialist in Japanese history and a medievalist, knew little more about the Revolution than what they remembered from high school. The texts I assembled were similarly varied, from eyewitness accounts and newspaper articles to materials rarely considered in historical research, such as a passage from a school textbook and a piece of historical fiction.[5] In addition to asking historians to think aloud, I asked them to rank each document in terms of its trustworthiness as a historical source.

The first text set the stage for the other seven documents they would read. This was a letter sent on April 28, 1775, by Joseph Warren, president of the Massachusetts Provincial Congress, to Benjamin Franklin, the colonists' representative in London. After the bloodshed at Lexington, Warren assembled depositions from eyewitnesses, attached a cover letter, and sent the bundle off to Franklin. In his letter, he characterized the events at Lexington as "marks of ministerial vengeance against [Massachusetts-Bay] for refusing with her sister colonies a submission to slavery."[6] Jack, a specialist in Native American history well versed in the colonial period, read this sentence and remarked:

> What I think of is a book I read by Rakove[7] talking about how one of the problems at the time was getting the colonies to hang together, and to try to get some unity. So the "refusing with her sister colonies" is kind of an appeal to the other groups.

The subtlety of this comment is easily missed. To begin, this is not a commentary on the literal text read by the historian, for there is nothing in the text about discord or disunity among the colonies. Furthermore, while it might make sense to see the letter as an "appeal," the letter was sent to Franklin for circulation among members of Parliament, so the appeal is literally directed to Great Britain. Indeed, what Jack sees here cannot be found on the page or represented in a diagram of textual propositions. What is most important to him is not what the text says, but what it does.

And what does the text do, according to Jack? First of all, it casts the confrontation at Lexington not as a minor squabble between nervous farmers and tired soldiers, but as a meeting of the broadest import—a fateful clash between representatives of the king and those of the thirteen American colonies. The phrase "refusing with her sister colonies" carries a dual purpose: It provides a frame in which to view the deaths of eight men, and it asks readers in Baltimore or Savannah (to whom this document would also be circulated) to bind their own fates to their northern cousins. In other words, this "appeal" was only partly designed to stir passions in London; it was also intended to rally the forces at home.

It is not the literal text, or even the inferred text (as that word is commonly used), that this historian comprehends, but the subtext, a text of hidden and latent meanings. Subtexts of historical documents can be divided into two distinct but related spheres: the text as a rhetorical artifact and the text as a human artifact. In the first sphere, the text as a rhetorical artifact, historians try to reconstruct authors' purposes, intentions, and goals. But the subtext goes beyond a reconstruction of the author's intentions, beyond the use of language as a linguistic technology for persuasion. In fact, many subtexts include elements that work at cross-purposes with authors' intentions, bringing to the surface convictions authors may have been unaware of or may have wished to conceal. These aspects fall into the second sphere, the text as a human artifact that frames reality and discloses information about its author's assumptions, world view, and beliefs. Such a reading leaps from the words authors use to the types of people authors are, a reading that sees texts not as ways to describe the world but as ways to construct it.

Let's return to Jack's reading of the Warren letter. What did he need to know in order to see this letter as an appeal to the other colonies? To be sure, he needed to know the secondary literature of the Revolution—in fact, he quotes a monograph by the historian Jack Rakove. But some of the eight historians I studied lacked such detailed knowledge and could not identify the Battle of Saratoga, virtual representation, the Townshend Acts, the Proclamation of 1763, and internal taxation—stock identification questions in a chapter review of a U.S. history textbook and part of a short quiz I gave to historians as part of the task.[8] Yet even among these "less knowledgeable" historians, we see the same general approach, if not the same specificity, in how they read documents. For example, Fred, the medievalist, made this comment on Warren's letter:

> It's a way to try and get people in England to see things their way; it's encouraging loyalty to the king but it's saying the government has messed up. It clearly shows that the Regular troops are guilty of the violence at Lexington. . . . It's not just a recapitulation of events, but it in fact frames events in terms of . . . the relationship of the crown to its government, and these are two different things.

Despite his lack of factual knowledge (he answered only a third of the identification questions), Fred's reading bears a strong likeness to that of his more knowledgeable colleagues. For Fred, the document goes beyond a neutral description of events and attempts to "affect people's opinions," to reassure them that, despite the bloodshed at Lexington, the colonists still pledge "allegiance to the king."[9] In this reading, the letter "frames events" in terms of the relationship of the crown to its government, with the colonists pledging loyalty to the former while indicting the policies of the latter. In other words, Warren's letter absolves the king by laying the guilt at the feet of his appointees.

In both of these readings, the literal text is only the shell of the text comprehended by historians. Texts come not to convey information, to tell stories, or even to set the record straight. Instead, they are slippery, cagey, and protean, reflecting the uncertainty and disingenuity of the real world. Texts emerge as "speech acts,"[10] social interactions set down on paper that can be understood only by reconstructing the social context in which they occurred. The comprehension of text reaches beyond words and phrases to embrace intention, motive, purpose, and plan—the same set of concepts we use to decipher human action.

THE READING OF SCHOOL TEXTS

The view of texts as speech acts may apply to the primary sources I gave historians, but what about school texts? On the surface, such texts are worlds apart from the patently polemical documents these historians reviewed. It would seem that the school text, written so that students can read and retain the information it contains,[11] falls into a different category and would be less amenable to subtextual readings. To test this, I had historians read the following excerpt from an American history textbook:

> In April 1775, General Gage, the military governor of Massachusetts, sent out a body of troops to take possession of military stores at Concord, a short distance from Boston. At Lexington, a handful of "embattled farmers," who had been tipped off by Paul Revere, barred the way. The "rebels" were ordered to disperse. They stood their ground. The English fired a volley of shots that killed eight patriots. It was not long before the swift-riding Paul Revere spread the news of this new atrocity to the neighboring colonies. The patriots of all of New England, although still a handful, were now ready to fight the English. Even in faraway North Carolina, patriots organized to resist them.[12]

When asked to rank the relative trustworthiness of the eight documents, historians ranked this excerpt dead last, even less trustworthy than an excerpt from Howard Fast's novel *April Morning*. And for good reason, since the above passage contradicts primary accounts from both British and American sides, neither of which portrays the minutemen as "standing their ground" or "barring the way." But beyond noting the factual inconsistencies of this account, historians constructed elaborate subtexts of its latent meaning. Fred's comment on this passage was fairly representative: "[The excerpt] aggrandizes the heroism and resolve of the people who begin the war on our side. They are informed, they ride fast horses, and they stand their ground."

Students' responses followed a different course. I should begin by noting that these eight students were no ordinary group. They had average SAT scores of 1227, well above the national average for college-bound seniors. Their grade point averages (GPAs) were equally distinguished, with a mean of 3.5, and with two of eight students maintaining a perfect 4.0. Moreover, these students, when compared with their peers, knew a lot of history. All had taken four years of history courses, and all scored significantly higher than a national sample on items from the history examination of the National Assessment of Educational Progress (NAEP). [13] In short, these students represented the successes of our educational system.

The responses of Derek,[14] an ambitious college-bound senior, are illuminating. Derek maintained a perfect 4.0 GPA, scored 630 (verbal) and 690 (math) on his SAT, and was enrolled in an Advanced Placement American history course when I interviewed him. As I listened to and later analyzed Derek's reading of these documents, I was struck by how well he embodies many of the features of the good reader described in the education literature. He carefully monitors his comprehension and uses reading strategies such as backtracking when meaning breaks down; he pauses and formulates summaries after each paragraph; and he tries to connect the content of what he reads to what he already knows.[15] Nonetheless, Derek rated the textbook as the most trustworthy of the eight documents he reviewed. Despite excellent reading skills and in-depth factual knowledge, Derek believed that the textbook excerpt was "just reporting the facts—'The rebels were ordered to disperse. They stood their ground.' Just concise, journalistic in a way, just saying what happened." Nor was this response atypical. Another student characterized the textbook as "straight information," a neutral account of the events at Lexington Green. For such students, the textbook, not the eyewitness accounts, emerged as the primary source.

Overall students had little problem formulating the main idea of these documents, predicting what might come next, locating information in the text, and answering literal and inferential questions about the content of the text. When analyzing the textbook, however, few students recognized that labeling the encounter at Lexington as an "atrocity" slants events and sets off associations with other "atrocities"—the Holocaust, My Lai, Kampuchea. None accounted for the quotation marks bracketing the word "rebels" or speculated about the author's intentions in putting them there. Students displayed little sensitivity to the contrast drawn between the "embattled farmers" and the troops of King George, a contrast that appeals to our tendency to side with the underdog. Unlike historians, no student commented on the progression in the description of the colonists, who go from "embattled farmers" to "rebels" and finally, shedding their quotation marks, emerge as "patriots." No student noticed how the text hedges on the firing of the first shot, yet is constructed so that a causal relationship is easily perceived between the statements "The 'rebels' . . . stood their ground" and "the English fired a volley of shots." In sum, students failed to see the text as a social instrument skillfully crafted to achieve a social end.

We should not be overly critical of students, since these aspects of text, while central to the skilled reading of history, are rarely addressed in school curricula or in the educational or psychological literature on reading comprehension.[16] For example, one article on skilled reading lays out a "Taxonomy of Comprehension Failures," cataloging the things that can go wrong during reading. The authors cite such problems as the failure to understand a word, the failure to understand a sentence, the failure to understand the relationship between sentences, and the failure to understand how the whole text fits together. But no mention is made of the failure to understand the author's intention, the failure to grasp the polemic of the text, the failure to recognize the connotations (not just the denotations) of words, the failure to situate the text in a disciplinary matrix, or the failure to do any of a host of other things that loom large when reading historical texts. Similarly, these aspects of reading are overlooked when researchers train their lens on "comprehension monitoring." Because skilled comprehension is viewed as a relatively fluid and automatic process, comprehension monitoring is often seen in light of what might be called the "medical model of reading"—something readers do when they are in trouble or bogged down.

Annemarie Palincsar and Ann Brown, for example, see skilled reading as a relatively automatic process until "a triggering event alerts [readers] to a comprehension failure." At that point, expert readers must "slow down and allot extra processing to the problem area. They must employ debugging devices or active strategies that take time and effort."[17] But with texts that have larger rhetorical and social purposes, readers may also "slow down and allot extra processing" for reasons we have yet to understand. For instance, as historical texts become rich and conceptually dense, readers may slow down not because they fail to comprehend, but because the very act of comprehension demands that they stop to *talk* with their texts. This is the point behind Roland Barthes's distinction between "readerly" (*lisible*) and "writerly" (*scriptible*) texts.[18] Readerly texts are conventional documents that convey nonproblematic, straightforward messages, like how one changes the oil of a car or how a volcano spews forth lava. Such texts conform to ordinary expectations of meaning and are often processed passively and automatically. However, writerly texts, in the words of David Harlan,

> challenge the conventions that isolate and identify meaning in the readerly text. In order to find meaning in the "writerly" text, the reader has to enter the text personally, has to participate actively in the fabrication of whatever meaning is to be carried away.[19]

How do skilled readers of history enter into the text to "participate actively in the fabrication of meaning"? How do they "write" texts while reading them? One way they do so is by simulating an interpsychic process intrapsychically. In plain English, they pretend to deliberate with others by talking to themselves.[20] Keen observers of the reading process have long noted this phenomenon. For example, in a prescient essay that anticipated later trends in reader-response theory, Walker Gibson claimed that we read texts by simulating two readers, an "actual reader" and a "mock reader."[21] The actual reader is an overall monitor of the meanings constructed during reading. But the mock reader is the reader who allows himself or herself to be taken in by rhetorical devices, to feel their effect, and to experience the associations triggered by crafted prose. When texts are straightforward and highly probative, the distance between the actual and the mock reader is minimal—indeed, there may be no distance at all. But with other texts, a chasm can form between the actual and the mock reader, and when this distance becomes too great, the actual reader intercedes and says with finality, "Enough! This text is not to be believed."

The voices of actual and mock readers were audible in the protocols of historians, but other voices could be heard as well. The reading of history is complicated by the fact that historians are rarely the intended audience for the documents they review. As eavesdroppers on conversations between others, historians must try to understand both the authors' intentions and the audiences' reactions, all the while gauging their own reactions to this exchange. Indeed, sometimes the mock reader becomes a mock writer, joining in to rewrite a document with an author long departed. The example in Table 3.1 illustrates the dynamic interplay of this process.

Alice, a specialist in seventeenth-century England who trained at the University of Wisconsin, read Joseph Warren's cover letter to Benjamin Franklin. Table 3.1 shows an excerpt from her protocol. The first three lines, a congeries of pronouns, convey the complexity of reading history: Who are all these people? The protocol begins with the historian as actual

TABLE 3.1
Excerpts from Alice's Reading of Joseph Warren's Cover Letter

TEXT	PROTOCOL
Friends and fellow subjects:	1. Again, I think I dealt with the rhetoric there,
	2. you know, we know that once you know the
	3. true story, you will sympathize with us.
hostilities are already commenced in	4. I mean here is who really started the hostilities.
the colony by the troops under the	5. It's a way of telling, you know, we are loyal
command of General Gage,	6. fellow subjects but, you know, look what's
	7. happened under this ministry.
and it being of the greatest importance	8. Again, between the lines one reads, either
that an early, true, and authentic ac-	9. you're not getting any account at all, you
count of this inhuman proceeding	10. know, the news is being withheld [unclear],
should be known to you,	11. or you're not getting a true account, or
	12. you're not getting an authentic account, and
	13. right away I'm going to tell you that it's an
	14. "inhuman proceeding." Presumably,
	15. again the rhetoric of it is that if you
	16. knew about it, and you may not know about
	17. it because you have not gotten a true, authentic
	18. account, you would see how inhuman this
	19. was, and again you would be on their
	20. [side], the presumption is that you're an ally
	21. and that we have indeed a common enemy,
	22. the common enemy being the minister who
	23. may not have given you a true and authentic
	24. account and tried to withhold this
	25. information from you or may have tried at
	26. least to put the information in such a way
	27. that you are not aware of how inhuman this
	28. proceeding was. Again, "alarming
	29. occasion," again this sense of urgency is
	30. being emphasized here.
By the clearest depositions relative to this	31. And there again, the inhabitants, so-called,
transaction, it will appear that on the night	32. you know, have done absolutely nothing in
preceding the nineteenth of April instant	33. this account to call down any kind of military
. . . the Town of Lexington . . . was alarmed,	34. action. They're just inhabitants, they're not
and a company of the inhabitants mustered	35. described as armed, they're not described as
on the occasion; that the Regular troops,	36. military, they're not described as having done
on their way to Concord, marched into the	37. anything provocative and immediately, as they
said town of Lexington, and the said company,	38. see the Regulars, they begin to disperse. In
on their approach, began to disperse.	39. other words, we are as innocent as lambs.
These, brethren, are marks of minis-	40. "Vengeance" is very strong of a word, typical
terial vengeance against this colony,	41. kind of overlay.
for refusing, with her sister colonies,	42. Note "we're not alone in this fellows" [laughter].
a submission to slavery. But . . .	43. A pregnant "but". . . you still have
	44. time to intervene, we're still loyal, but we're
	45. hard pressed. We still use the "royal
	46. sovereign," we are still fellow subjects of the King.

Note: Text in italics was part of the primary source document that Alice read aloud.

reader (line 1), acknowledging that she has already commented on a particular aspect of the text. But in line 2 she quickly assumes the role of mock writer, co-constructing the text with Warren (as indicated by the use of "we" in line 2 and "us" in line 3) to address their joint audience—not as "them," but as "you," the inhabitants of Great Britain and, later, King George himself. Lines 4–7 further highlight the flow of communication between actual and mock reader. In line 4, the mock reader begins by laying bare the subtext of the sentence "hostilities are already commenced." Monitoring the mock reader, the actual reader offers a clarifying "It's a way of telling," but then flips back to the voice of the mock reader—"we are loyal fellow subjects" (lines 5–6). In the next section (lines 8–30), we find an explicit statement by the actual reader that she is constructing a message not found in the manifest text. Here again "you" refers to the mock audience, for whom the historian (taking on the voice of Joseph Warren) provides a running subtextual commentary. In lines 31–39, the historian summarizes what she has read ("they're not described as . . ."), but adds a few interpretive markers such as "so-called" (line 31). In the final comment of this section (line 39), Alice turns from a review of the text to a summary of the subtext, again taking the voice of the mock reader: "we are as innocent as lambs."

In this excerpt, reading simulates the give and take of social exchange. First we hear Warren's voice, enunciating the real message behind his stilted prose. Next there is "you," the citizens of Great Britain or King George himself. Then there is "we," a reference to the historian as mock writer co-constructing the text with Warren. Finally, there is the "I" of the actual reader, who acts as stage director for this cast of mental characters, dictating their lines, monitoring what they say, and ultimately noting the breach between her own understanding and the claims made by the mock reader. And it is this "I" who ultimately breaks down in laughter at the disparity between her own thoughts and those of the characters she has created.

Written words fail to capture the elements of burlesque that characterize this reading. This is a ludic reading that jokes and jibes, that adopts mock-heroic and mock-tragic voices, and that ultimately degenerates into laughter when the actual and mock reader become so estranged that they barely recognize each other. Indeed, the historian's laughter in line 42 hints at this breach. The mock reader turns into an object of ridicule enunciating her lines in melodramatic parody.

Here reading moves beyond an author–reader dialogue to embrace a set of conversations—exchanges between actual and mock reader, between mock writer and mock audience, between mock reader and mock audience, and between any one of these characters and the "I" of the actual reader. Instead of a single "executive" directing a top-down process, mature readers of history may create inside their own heads an "executive board," where members clamor, shout, and wrangle over controversial points.[22] Texts are not "processed" as much as they are resurrected, and the image of reader as information processor or computing device, which often dominates current discussions of reading, seems less apt than another metaphor: the reader as necromancer.

To illustrate how readers reconstructed authors from their textual remainders,[23] let me describe another one of the sources I used, a diary entry by Ezra Stiles, president of Yale College in 1775. Stiles not only wrote about his life as a college administrator but described in great detail the unfolding events of his day. His entry about Lexington began: "Major Pitcairn [the British commander] who was a good man in a bad cause, insisted upon it to the day of his death, that the colonists fired first. . . . He expressly says he did not see who fired first; and yet believed the peasants began."[24] At this point, Mary, a specialist in Japanese history, commented:

> Ezra Stiles for all his supposed democracy comes across as very kind of classist in a way. I mean, you can tell that Pitcairn is from the same class as Stiles. Maybe not, but they both are men of integrity because of their upbringing, so he's "a good man in a bad cause." And I get that sense from some of the terms that Stiles uses—I don't know what Stiles's background is but I assume he's not aristocratic but he's educated, probably a man of the cloth if he was president of Yale in the late eighteenth century; at that point probably most of them were clergy. So he was educated even if not a noble. But Pitcairn probably was, because until World War II, I believe, most British commanders were, or its officers were, from nobility of some sort.[25]

In Mary's reading, Ezra Stiles is a "classist" (based on his haughty tone and his use of "peasants"), a cleric (based on textual cues and her background knowledge), well-educated but probably not a member of the aristocracy, and a hypocrite (based on the discrepancy between Stiles's patriotism and his reference to his compatriots as "peasants"). Elsewhere Mary talks about Stiles's motives for writing, but here her comments are not about the author's intentions but about the man himself. Similarly, when Tom, an expert on Portuguese colonization in the New World, read Stiles's entry, he deepened his voice and dangled his pencil from his mouth as if it were a pipe:

I'm thinking [voice deepens]: a nice Yale man trying to say something, you know, [voice deepens again] "Major Pitcairn was a veeeeery good man." I'm just thinking that this is the voice of reason, Ivy League high Episcopalian orthodoxy. . . . "Peasants"—it's just a great word . . . I mean here we are reading about the American Revolution. After all, it's supposed to be a bunch of yeoman farmers vigorously defending their rights and here is the president of Yale . . . whose ancestors came from England and who made enough money to send him to Yale and get him to be president of Yale. . . . This is the elite talking about the peasant.[26]

In both of these readings, texts are not lifeless strings of facts, but the keys to unlocking the character of human beings, people with likes and dislikes, biases and foibles, airs and convictions. Words have texture and shape, and it is their almost tactile quality that lets readers sculpt images of the writers who use them. These images are then interrogated, mocked, congratulated, or dismissed, depending on the context of the reading and the disposition of the reader. In such readings, authors, as well as texts, are decoded.

But the converse is also true: Just as readers decode authors, so texts decode readers. Because texts present plays of potentialities, not sets of meanings forever fixed, the think-aloud protocols I obtained may tell us more about those who read these texts than about those who wrote them.[27] In the above protocol, the word that riles the historians is "peasants," a word that calls up images of class struggle between peasants and elites. Whatever Ezra Stiles writing in 1775 may have meant, in the minds of these two historians, educated at Harvard and Stanford in the latter half of the twentieth century, Stiles's peasants become the peasants of Marx and Engels, who join with the urban proletariat to overthrow the bourgeoisie. Yet, when we look at the historical uses of "peasant" in the *Oxford English Dictionary*, we find that the word can simply mean "one who works on the land, either as small farmer or as laborer . . . one who relies for his subsistence mainly on the produce of his own labor and that of his household." So what did Ezra Stiles mean?

It is no doubt problematic to attach the connotations of "peasant" found in *Das Kapital*, written in the latter half of the nineteenth century, to Ezra Stiles's entry of 1775. In fact, one could argue that these two historians have got it wrong: Stiles was not making a distinction between rich and poor, privileged and downtrodden, peasant and elite, but simply noting a difference between urban and rural, between those who, like himself, earned their bread by administering a college and those who earned it by the sweat of their brow.

If only the problem were that simple! The *Oxford English Dictionary* enumerates other ways in which "peasant" was used before and during Stiles's lifetime. As early as 1550, the word had taken on pejorative connotations, implying ignorance, stupidity, and boorishness, modified by adjectives like "buzzardly" and placed in apposition to "coward" and "rascal." So the question remains: Did Stiles think of these men as farmers, nothing more? Or did he think of them as ignoramuses, men who shared little in common with the honorable Major Pitcairn, who was, after all, a "good man in a bad cause"?

To solve this dilemma, some historians would recommend that we shed our presentist conceptions, immerse ourselves in the language of the past, feel what past actors felt, and understand the connotations that they, not we, attach to words. Only by renouncing our own condition can we come to know the past on its own terms. Historians have sometimes gone to great lengths to do this; Robert E. Lee's biographer Douglas Freeman tried to reconstruct what Lee thought by limiting himself to what Lee knew, and then writing a biography within these boundaries of knowledge and ignorance.[28]

No doubt our understanding is enriched when we learn that "peasant" has multiple meanings, but this knowledge does not put to rest the question of what Stiles meant; it simply widens it. This is why the image of the author constructed in readers' minds remains just that—an image—which, in Carl Becker's words, is always shaped by "our present purposes, desires, prepossessions, and prejudices, all of which enter into the process of knowing. . . . The actual event contributes something to the imagined picture; but the mind that holds the imagined picture always contributes something too."[29]

AN EPISTEMOLOGY OF TEXT

When we compare how historians and students read these documents, we see dramatic differences on practically any criterion we select. By itself, this news should shock no one; after all, historians know much more history. But on closer examination, this explanation tells us precious little. We simply substitute ascription for explanation when we say that historians "did better" because they are historians. What does it mean to "know more history"? What goes on when a historian of labor in the twentieth century or a medievalist who specializes in thirteenth-century Islamic texts sits down to read about the American Revolution?

One might suppose that dramatic differences in topical knowledge separated these two groups, particularly if we define such "knowledge" as the names, dates, and concepts of the American Revolution that often appear in history tests. In point of fact, two high school students answered more of the identification questions (e.g., "What was Fort Ticonderoga?" "Who was George Grenville?" "What were the Townshend Acts?") than one of the historians, and another historian got only one more answer than most students. But knowing history is more complicated than answering such questions. That students so rarely saw subtexts in what they read, that their understanding of point of view was limited to which "side" a document was on, that they rarely compared one account with another, instead searching for the right answer and becoming flustered in the face of contradictions—all hint at a need for something more than knowing names and dates.

The differences in each group's approach can be traced, I think, to sweeping beliefs about historical inquiry, or what might be called an epistemology of text. For students, reading history was not a process of puzzling about authors' intentions or situating texts in a social world but of gathering information, with texts serving as bearers of information. How could such bright students be oblivious to the subtexts that jumped out at historians? The answer may lie in an aphorism of Tertullian, the second-century church father whose first principle of biblical exegesis was *credo ut intelligam* ("I believe in order to understand"). Before students can see subtexts, they must first believe they exist. In the absence of such beliefs, students simply overlooked or did not know how to seek out features designed to shape their perceptions or make them view events in a particular way. Students may have "processed texts," but they failed to engage with them.

Such beliefs may help to explain differences in the use of the "sourcing heuristic," the practice of reading the source of the document before reading the actual text. Historians used this heuristic nearly all of the time (98 percent), while students used it less than a third (31 percent). For most students, the text's attribution carried no special weight; it was merely the final bit of information in a string of textual propositions. To historians, a document's attribution was not the end of the document but its beginning; sources were viewed as people, not objects, as social exchanges, not sets of propositions. In this sense, the sourcing heuristic was simply the manifestation of a belief system in which texts were defined by their authors.

When texts are viewed as human creations, what is said becomes inseparable from who says it. But for some students, authors and their accounts were only loosely connected. So, when one student initially read the excerpt from Howard Fast, he knew something was wrong: "You can't really believe exactly what they're saying. It's going to be, the details are going to be off." But by the time this student reached the last document, his reservations about Fast had fallen by the wayside, as elements from this fictitious account were clearly present in his under-standing. An Americanist, on the other hand, paused when he encoun-tered the claim that the colonists were drawn up in "regular order." Remembering that an earlier document described the battle formation, he flipped back to the Fast excerpt and then burst into laughter: "Oh, that's from Fast! Forget it! I can't hold on to Fast; I can't do that. But it's funny; it stuck in my mind." Here we see the opposite case: a detail is remembered, but the historian cannot remember its source. Reunited with its author, the detail is rejected, for this historian knows that there are no free-floating details—only details tied to witnesses.

The metaphor of the courtroom may help us understand these dif-ferences. Historians worked through these documents as if they were prosecuting attorneys; they did not merely listen to testimony but actively drew it out by putting documents side by side, locating dis-crepancies, and questioning sources and delving into their conscious and unconscious motives. Students, on the other hand, were like jurors, patiently listening to testimony and questioning themselves about what they heard, but unable to question witnesses directly or subject them to cross-examination. For students, the locus of authority was in the text; for historians, it was in the questions they formulated about the text.[30]

What accounts for the fact that a group of bright high school seniors displayed such a rudimentary sense of how to read a historical text? How could they know so much history yet have so little sense of how to read it? These are not simple questions, and their answers lie beyond the scope of this chapter. But, at the very least, we can point to the types of texts students have read in their history classes. Textbooks dominate history classrooms, and, as Peter Schrag has noted, history textbooks are often written "as if their authors did not exist at all, as if they were simply the instruments of a heavenly intelligence transcribing official truths."[31] Avon Crismore has documented Schrag's claim. In a dis-course analysis of history textbooks and academic and popular histori-cal texts, she found that "metadiscourse," or indications of judgment, emphasis, and uncertainty, was used frequently in historical writing but appeared rarely in conventional textbooks. Crismore found that most textbooks abjured hedges like "may" or "might," "appears" or "perhaps," providing little indication that interpretation had anything to do with the words on the page. Such writing may contribute to students' inability to move beyond the literal: "What happens to critical reading (learning to evaluate and make judgments about truth conditions) when hedges . . . are absent? When bias is not overt (as it is not in most textbooks) are young readers being deceived?"[32]

Perhaps Crismore overstates her case. Perhaps her findings and mine are little cause for alarm; perhaps students' naive beliefs about text will simply be sloughed off when they get to college. The evidence, however, suggests otherwise. For example, James Lorence, in observations of college freshmen, found beliefs similar to those described here. Many students, he wrote, "expect a document to reveal something which they may regard as 'the truth.' . . . They persist in seeking a definitive conclusion on the reliability of the source before them."[33] Similarly, Robert Berkhofer has written about the "historical fundamentalism" he encounters frequently among undergraduates, who "treat their assigned readings and textbooks, if not their teachers, as divinely inspired."[34] At Carnegie Mellon University, researchers Christina Haas and Linda Flower had undergraduates think aloud as they read a series of polemical texts. They found that college students could easily decipher the basic meaning of texts and formulate the gist of what they read. However,

> these same students often frustrate us, as they paraphrase rather than analyze, summarize rather than criticize texts. . . . We might hypothesize that the problem students have with critical reading of difficult texts is less the representations they are constructing than those they fail to construct. Their representations of text are closely tied to content: they read for information. Our students may believe that if they understand all the words and can paraphrase the propositional content of the text they have successfully read it.[35]

Indeed, students may not be the only ones who embrace these beliefs; sometimes they share them with their teachers. In a study of knowledge growth among high school social studies teachers, Suzanne Wilson and I interviewed one teacher who told us that interpretation had little role to play in historical understanding: "History is the basic facts of what happened. What *did* happen. You don't ask how it happened. You just ask, 'What are the events?' "[36] In sum, we can locate entire epochs of history— the Middle Ages, for one—when precritical notions of historiography were embraced by adolescent and adult alike.[37] The notion that such beliefs are naturally abandoned as students enter adulthood has neither data nor history on its side.

FROM WAYS OF READING TO WAYS OF KNOWING

In our zeal to arrive at overarching models of reading, we often ignore qualities of the text that give it shape and meaning. When historical texts make the journey from the discipline to the school curriculum, we force them to check their distinctiveness at the door.[38] The historical text becomes the "school text," and soon bears a greater resemblance to other school texts—in biology, language arts, and other subjects—than to its rightful disciplinary referent.[39] So, for example, the defining feature of historical discourse—its constant reference to the documentary record through footnotes—is the very aspect that drops out when historical texts become history textbooks. No wonder many students come to see history as a closed story when we suppress the evidence of how that story was assembled.

More broadly, the epistemological distinctions that first gave rise to the labels "history," "physics," "literature," and "mathematics" become eclipsed in the school curriculum. Although we carve the school day into separate periods, hoping thereby to teach students to be multilingual in various ways of knowing, we too often end up teaching a single tongue. Although students learn different vocabularies in different classes—"mitosis" in biology, "theme" in English, "Declaratory Acts" in history, and "function" in mathematics—these lexical distinctions share a common deep structure: Knowledge is detached from experience, it is certain and comes shorn of hedge and qualification, its source is textbooks and teachers, and it can be measured with tests in which every question has a right answer.[40]

The process of disciplinary homogenization is evident even in textbooks used in teacher training. So, for example, one popular reading textbook tells prospective teachers that, when reading historical documents, "students need to be guided to reading strategies for recognizing the uses of documents and for learning how to read them."[41] But rather than delineating such strategies or describing what historians do, this book directs readers to the chapter on "Reading in Science." However, approaches to "reading in the content areas" that equate reading about the structure of DNA with reading about the structure of the American Revolution obscure the underlying assumptions that give texts meaning. Even the increased emphasis on domain-specific knowledge in the cognitive psychological literature may have unwittingly contributed to this confusion by equating knowledge with information.[42] In this view knowledge itself becomes generic, classified according to the number of facts and relationships represented in a semantic net or "if/then" conditions formalized in a production system. But domains, as Louis O. Mink reminded us, go beyond compilations of facts and concepts or executions of productions. They constitute "unique and irreducible modes of comprehending the world,"[43] sweeping ways of organizing experience and conducting inquiry into who we are. Thus, the topic of Western mountain ranges means one thing to a geologist, another to a historian, and still another to Ansel Adams. Reading is not merely a way to learn new information but becomes a way to engage in new kinds of thinking.

The image of reading comprehension presented here differs dramatically from images that often emerge from the education literature. Why? First, each image has a different starting point. Most of our portraits of the "good reader" come from schoolchildren, naive readers not yet socialized into disciplinary ways of knowing. The essence of reading comprehension becomes whatever it takes to do well on the Metropolitan Achievement Test, the Nelsen-Denny, the Gates-MacGinite, or any of a host of standardized reading measures. But these tests, all of which bear a strong family resemblance, are poor approximations of the slippery and indeterminate texts we encounter in the real world. Our definition of "reading comprehension" becomes what the reading comprehension tests measure: the ability to do well on specially designed passages written by absentee authors, each passage self-contained and decontextualized from the discipline that gives it meaning; the ability to respond correctly to multiple-choice questions that presume an unambiguous right answer; familiarity with formats that disguise the fact that texts are written by people whose beliefs ineluctably creep into their prose; skill at decoding literal as opposed to latent meaning; and the ability to process independent passages rather than create intertextual connections across multiple texts. In short, reading comprehension is defined by the texts, by the readers, and by the measures we use to study it.[44]

When we abandon the controlled vocabulary of the comprehension passage and look not at schoolchildren but at people who read for a living, we end up with a different image of comprehension.[45] It is not that one of these images is right and the other wrong; clearly, each tells us different things. But we do have a problem when there is a mismatch between the questions we ask and the image of reading we select. If we ask, "What does it mean to comprehend a historical text?" and rely exclusively on what generic reading comprehension tests tell us, we may learn a great deal about reading, but little about reading history.

If this is true, what standard should we use to judge the comprehension of historical texts? Despite widespread testing of schoolchildren's comprehension of history and social studies passages, the question of standards is seldom addressed, even in an age obsessed with standards. Robert Linn lamented this situation when he wrote that "there has been a disproportionate amount of effort devoted to the solution of problems that assume the existence of a standard in comparison to answering questions about where the standard comes from in the first place."[46] And where should our standard come from? To me, there is only one defensible answer. We must look to the discipline.

For many years it often seemed that no one in the discipline was looking back. But several developments suggest a dramatic change. The report of the Bradley Commission on History in Schools represents a considerable effort by historians, professors of education, and high school teachers to sit down and ask tough questions about the school curriculum.[47] The Organization of American Historians (OAH), reversing a trend set in 1947 when it discontinued the "Teachers' Section" of its major journal, has launched the *Magazine of History*, a publication devoted exclusively to the problems and prospects of precollegiate history. And in a presidential address to the OAH, traditionally a survey of the latest advances in historiography, the University of Maryland's Louis Harlan[48] devoted his remarks to school history and the role that historians might play in its reform—a major shift from an earlier address that sounded the death knell for disciplinary efforts to improve school history.[49]

This flurry of activity has raised penetrating questions about many topics—the intellectually vacuous "expanding horizons" curriculum in the elementary school, the quality of textbooks, the warrant for claims about what students can learn, and the impact of standardized tests on student learning. These criticisms signal a valuable start in any reform effort. But the questions we most need to answer—"What would teachers have to do differently to create history classrooms where real learning takes place? How would teachers learn to teach in these different ways?"—are rarely addressed by these reports. The Bradley Commission, mostly mute on issues of pedagogy, noted that, as with life, "variety is the spice of learning," and encouraged teachers to select from a wide range of teaching methods and techniques. But exemplary teaching is not just a function of selecting the right mixture of methods, any more than historical interpretation is just a function of selecting the right mixture of documents: Variety, as Suzanne Wilson notes, may be entertaining but it is not necessarily educative.[50] Expert teaching entails not a selection of methods, but the transformation of knowledge.[51] History teachers must take what they know and create representations of content that engender new understandings among children who often come to school with scant motivation to learn. To do this is an intellectual achievement of the highest order—no less an achievement than arriving at a sophisticated understanding of the content one wants to teach.

One exception to historians' reticence on pedagogy is Tom Holt's *Thinking Historically*, published by the College Board.[52] A thoughtful meditation on his teaching of undergraduates at the University of Chicago, Holt's work contains much of value. He describes an undergraduate history course that begins with "unlearning," an attempt to disabuse students of the impression that history is a fixed story. Instead of examinations in which students list, as Woodrow Wilson once put it, "one damn fact after another," they receive primary documents and pretend to be museum curators who must annotate these documents for an exhibit. Holt purposely juxtaposes sources with opposing viewpoints and has students construct narratives that constitute ongoing conversations with the past, not "a closed catechism or a set of questions already answered."[53]

These are all intriguing ideas. But together they point to our collective ignorance, to the fact that we know little about changing students' beliefs about history.[54] Our efforts to do so, however, will surely founder if we wait until high school to teach students to ask a short story one set of questions and their history book a different set; they must learn to ask such questions when they first encounter claims about the past. In fact, when we put our assumptions about children's capabilities to the test, we find that, under the right conditions, even third graders can grasp something of history's indeterminate nature and thereby arrive at sophisticated interpretations of the past.[55]

CONCLUSION

In the early thirties, the eminent historian Carl Becker wrote a paper entitled "Everyman His Own Historian," in which he claimed that, like it or not, we are all historians.[56] What he meant was that we are all called on to engage in historical thinking—called on to see human motive in the texts we read; called on to mine truth from the quicksand of innuendo, half-truth, and falsehood that seeks to engulf us each day; called on to brave the fact that certainty, at least in understanding the social world, remains elusive and beyond our grasp. If Becker was right, then school history possesses great potential for teaching students to think and reason in sophisticated ways. Whether we exploit this potential, however, is another story.

The view of text described here is not limited to history.[57] Language is not a garden tool for acting on inanimate objects but a medium for swaying minds and changing opinions, for rousing passions or allaying them. This is a crucial understanding for reading the newspaper, for listening to the radio, for evaluating campaign promises, or for making a decision to drink a Nutrasweet product based on research conducted by the Searle Company. If students never learn to see the difference between the "contras" and the "freedom fighters," between "Star Wars" and the "Strategic Defense Initiative," between "terrorists" and "members of the PLO," if they think of these terms as neutral appellations rather than charged symbols tapping different meaning systems, they become easy marks for snake-oil vendors of all persuasions. We need to search our memories no farther back than the Bush–Dukakis presidential campaign, when "Willie Horton," a black man convicted of raping a white woman, became a household name. It took nearly five months for the subtext of this advertisement to become an issue of public debate—a more powerful indicator of national critical thinking skills than any NAEP item yet devised.

An advertisement for a new book on teaching thinking claims that we can do so with little effort—indeed, it claims that we can "teach thinking skills across the curriculum without changing lesson plans."[58] I'm not so sure. If we want students to read historical texts differently from their driver's education manuals, if we want them to comprehend both text and subtext, I think we will have to change our lesson plans—not to mention our textbooks. If nothing else, we will have to reexamine our notions of what it means to acquire knowledge from text. The traditional view, in which knowledge goes from the page of the text to the head of the reader, is inadequate. But the metacognitive view, in which knowledge is constructed by students questioning themselves about a fixed and friendly text, is equally inadequate. We could do no better than to heed the words of Robert Scholes: "If wisdom, or some less grandiose notion such as heightened awareness, is to be the end of our endeavors, we shall have to see it not as something transmitted from the text to the student but as something developed in the student by questioning the text."[59]

NOTES

This essay originally appeared in the *American Educational Research Journal* 28 (1991). It is based on a dissertation completed at Stanford in 1990 and supervised by Lee Shulman, David Tyack, and the late Dick Snow. Previous versions of this chapter benefited from comments by Larry Cuban, Catherine Crain-Thoreson, Pam Grossman, Bob Hampel, Debby Kerdeman, David Madsen, Susan Monas, Sheila Valencia, and Suzanne Wilson. An earlier version was presented at the MacArthur "Languages of Thinking" conference at Harvard University in October 1990. I thank David Olson for inviting me and for his ongoing encouragement.

A great deal of work has come out in recent years on students' reading of documents. An overview of recent developments is the review by James F. Voss, "Issues in the Learning of History," *Issues in Education: Contributions from Educational Psychology* 4 (1998), 163–209. For a provocative view of the future of teaching with primary documents on the Web, see B. Tally, "History Goes Digital: Teaching When the Web Is in the Classroom," *D-Lib Magazine* (September 1996), online: http://www.dlib.org/dlib/september96/09tally.html.

1. William B. Willcox, "An Historian Looks at Social Change," in A. S. Eisenstadt, ed., *The Craft of American History* (New York, 1966), 25.

2. For a sampling of "how to" books in history, see Henry Steele Commager, *The Nature and Study of History* (Columbus, Ohio, 1966); Wood Gray, *Historian's Handbook: A Key to the Study and Writing of History* (Boston, 1959); Allan Nevins, *Gateway to History* (Chicago, 1962); or R. J. Shafer, *A Guide to Historical Method* (Homewood, Ill., 1969). Gray waxes mystical when he says that the reading of primary sources relies on a "sort of sixth sense that will alert [historians] to the tell-tale signs" (p. 36). Two notable exceptions to this trend are J. H. Hexter, *The History Primer* (New York, 1971), and James West Davidson and Mark Hamilton Lytle, *After the Fact: The Art of Historical Detection* (New York, 1982).

3. For a detailed discussion of the think-aloud methodology and its rationale, see K. Anders Ericsson and Herbert A. Simon, *Protocol Analysis: Verbal Reports as Data* (Cambridge, Mass., 1984). See as well the very useful book by Michael Pressley and Peter Afflerbach, *Verbal Reports of Reading: The Nature of Constructively Responsive Reading* (Hillsdale, N.J., 1995).

4. Of the eight historians I studied, six held the Ph.D. and two were doctoral candidates. Four historians considered themselves to be Americanists (and had taught American history), and four did not. In terms of doctoral training, the following institutions were represented: Wisconsin (3), Stanford (2), Berkeley (2), and Harvard (1).

5. For the full text of these documents, as well as a detailed description of the

methods and procedures followed, see Samuel S. Wineburg, "Historical Problem Solving: A Study of the Cognitive Processes Used in the Evaluation of Documentary and Pictorial Evidence," *Journal of Educational Psychology* 83 (1991), 73–87.

6. Warren's cover letter can be found in Peter S. Bennett, *What Happened on Lexington Green?* (Menlo Park, Calif., 1970), 20. Warren's skills as a propagandist are detailed in Arthur B. Tourtellot, *Lexington and Concord: The Beginning of the War of the American Revolution* (New York, 1963), 212–36.

7. Jack refers here to the monograph by Jack N. Rakove, *The Beginning of National Politics* (New York, 1976).

8. These identification questions were drawn from a leading U.S. history textbook: Lewis Paul Todd and Merle Curti, *Rise of the American Nation* (Orlando, Fla., 1982).

9. These were Fred's words in response to Warren's salutation "Friends and Fellow Subjects."

10. John Searle, "What Is a Speech Act?" in Max Black, ed., *Philosophy in America* (Ithaca, N.Y., 1965), 221–39.

11. While the goal of the text designer may be to write clear prose, the reality is often quite different. For a critique of history textbooks from the perspective of cognitive psychology, see Isabel L. Beck, Margaret G. McKeown, and Erika W. Gromoll, "Learning from Social Studies Texts," *Cognition and Instruction* 6 (1989), 99–158.

12. Samuel Steinberg, *The United States: A Story of a Free People* (Boston, 1963), 92. Reprinted in Bennett, *What Happened*, 31.

13. Diane Ravitch and Chester E. Finn, Jr., *What Do Our 17-Year-Olds Know? A Report of the First National Assessment of History and Literature* (New York, 1987), 267–69.

14. This is the student briefly described in Chapter 1.

15. Sometimes prior knowledge got in the way of Derek's understanding of historical events. I explored the downside of prior knowledge in Samuel S. Wineburg, "Probing the Depths of Students' Historical Knowledge," *Perspectives: Newsletter of the American Historical Association* 30 (1992), 20–24.

16. William S. Hall, "Reading Comprehension," *American Psychologist* 44 (1989), 157–61.

17. Annemarie Palincsar and Ann Brown, "Reciprocal Teaching of Comprehension-Fostering and Comprehension-Monitoring Activities," *Cognition and Instruction* 1 (1984), 117–75. See also Alan Collins and Edward E. Smith, "Teaching the Process of Reading Comprehension," in Douglas K. Detterman and Robert J. Sternberg, eds., *How and How Much Can Intelligence Be Increased* (Norwood, N.J., 1982), 173–85.

18. Roland Barthes, *S/Z* (New York, 1974). Also see Barthes's provocative paper on the nature of historical texts, "Historical Discourse," in Michael Lane, ed., *Introduction to Structuralism* (New York, 1970), 145–55.

19. David Harlan, "Intellectual History and the Return of Literature," *American Historical Review* 94 (1989), 597.

20. See Lev S. Vygotsky, *Mind in Society*, ed. Michael Cole, Vera John–Steiner, Sylvia Scribner, and Ellen Souberman (Cambridge, Mass., 1978).

21. Walker Gibson, "Authors, Speakers, Readers, and Mock Readers," *College English* 11 (1950), 265–69. See also Louise M. Rosenblatt, *The Reader, the Text, the Poem* (Carbondale, Ill., 1978), 131–75.

22. This point is from Alan H. Schoenfeld, who recognized a similar phenomenon in his work with expert mathematicians. See his *Mathematical Problem Solving* (Orlando, Fla., 1985), 140–41.

23. Dominick LaCapra says that historians "enter into a 'conversational' exchange with the past" and engage in "a dialogue with the dead who are reconstituted through their 'textualized' remainders." See his *History and Criticism* (Ithaca, N.Y., 1985). This quotation appears on p. 37.

24. F. B. Dexter, ed., *The Literary Diaries of Ezra Stiles* (New York, 1901).

25. This quotation has been edited slightly for readability.

26. I thank David Madsen for pointing out Tom's error: Ezra Stiles and Yale were Congregationalist, not Episcopalian.

27. For a related point made in a different context, see Margaret S. Steffensen, Chitra JoagDev, and Richard C. Anderson, "A Cross-Cultural Perspective on Reading Comprehension," *Reading Research Quarterly* 15 (1979), 10–29.

28. See the discussion of Freeman in Henry Steele Commager's *Study of History*. Commager summed up his views on the futility of Freeman's approach this way: "There are many things to be said for accepting our limitations and looking at the past through the eyes of the present, but this is the most persuasive: no matter how hard we try, that is what we do anyway" (p. 59).

29. Carl L. Becker, "What Are Historical Facts?" in Hans Meyerhoff, ed., *The Philosophy of History in Our Time* (Garden City, N.Y., 1959), 132.

30. This metaphor comes from Robin G. Collingwood, *The Idea of History* (Oxford, 1946). Collingwood (p. 249) noted, "As natural science finds its proper method when the scientist, in Bacon's metaphor, puts Nature to the question . . . so history finds its proper method when the historian puts his authorities in the witness-box, and by cross-questioning extorts from them information which in their original statements they have withheld, either because they did not wish to give it or because they did not possess it." Collingwood follows in the footsteps of Voltaire, who wrote that "when reading history, it is but the only business of a healthy mind to refute it."

31. Peter Schrag, "Voices in the Classroom: The Emasculated Voice of the Textbook," *Saturday Review* 21 (January 1967), 74. For a similar view of the history textbook, see Frances FitzGerald's *America Revised* (New York, 1980), especially pp. 149–218.

32. Avon Crismore, "The Rhetoric of Textbooks: Metadiscourse," *Journal of Curriculum Studies* 16 (1984), 295.

33. James L. Lorence, "The Critical Analysis of Documentary Evidence: Basic Skills in the History Classroom," *History Teaching* 8, no. 2 (1983), 78.

34. See Robert F. Berkhofer, Jr., "Demystifying Historical Authority: Critical Textual Analysis in the Classroom," *Perspectives: Newsletter of the American Historical Association* 26 (February 1988), 13–16.

35. Christina Haas and Linda Flower, "Rhetorical Reading Strategies and the Construction of Meaning," *College Composition and Communication* 39 (May 1988), 30–47. For an example from the world of reading legal texts, see Elizabeth Fajans and Mary R. Falk, "Against the Tyranny of Paraphrase: Talking Back to Texts," *Cornell Law Review* 78 (1993), 163–205.

36. See Chapter 6 in this volume.

37. See the chapter on "The Rationality of History," in Lionel Gossman, *Between History and Literature* (Cambridge, Mass., 1990).

38. See, for example, a column on "teaching with documents" in *Social Education* in which the authors reprinted a policy statement on the recruitment of nurses during the Civil War. The document included the following statement, "Matronly persons of experience, good conduct or superior education and serious disposition, will always have a preference. Habits of neatness, sobriety, and industry are prerequisites." In their section on teaching activities, the authors make no reference to the subtext of this document and how students could be taught to decipher it. Instead, such activities as the following are recommended: "Ask your students to discuss what qualifications are necessary for a nurse today" or "Ask students to locate evidence to support or disprove the following: The Civil War was the bloodiest war in American history." See Wynell Burroughs, Jean Mueller, and Jean Preer, "Teaching with Documents: Surgeon General's Office," *Social Education* 66 (January 1988), 66–68.

39. John Seely Brown, Alan Collins, and Paul Duguid, "Situated Cognition and the Culture of Learning," *Educational Researcher* 18 (1989), 32–42.

40. Ibid.

41. H. Alan Robinson, *Teaching Reading, Writing, and Study Strategies: The Content Areas* (Boston, 1983), 181.

42. See Gregory G. Colomb, "Cultural Literacy and the Theory of Meaning: or, What Educational Theorists Need to Know About How We Read," *New Literary History* 20 (1988), 411–50.

43. Louis O. Mink, "Modes of Comprehension and the Unity of Knowledge," in Brian Fay, Eugene O. Golob, and Richard T. Vann, eds., *Historical Understanding* (Ithaca, N.Y., 1987), 36.

44. Some of these criticisms of comprehension tests have been discussed by others. See, for example, Peter Winograd and Peter Johnston, "Considerations for Advancing the Teaching of Reading Comprehension," *Educational Psychologist* 22 (1987), 219–20. For a fresh approach to comprehension, see Rand J. Spiro, Walter P. Vispoel, John G. Schmitz, Ala Samarapungavan, and A. E. Boerger, "Knowledge Acquisition for Application: Cognitive Flexibility and Transfer in Complex Content Domains," in Bruce K. Britton and Shawn W. Glynn, eds., *Executive Control Processes in Reading* (Hillsdale, N.J., 1987), especially pp. 184–93.

45. If we looked at others who read for a living—literary critics, to name one group—we would probably arrive at still another image of comprehension.

46. Robert Linn, cited in Mary E. Curtis and Robert Glaser, "Reading Theory and the Assessment of Reading Achievement," *Journal of Educational Measurement* 20 (Summer 1983), 133–47.

47. See the Bradley Commission on History in Schools, *Building a History Curriculum: Guidelines for Teaching History in Schools* (Washington, D.C., 1988) along with its fuller statement, *Historical Literacy: The Case for History in American Education*, ed. Paul A. Gagnon (New York, 1989).

48. Louis R. Harlan, "Social Studies Reform and the Historian," *Journal of American History* 77 (1990), 801–11. Some of Harlan's proposals, such as the call for summer institutes in which teachers can "revitalize their teaching by learning of the latest and best historical scholarship" (p. 809), may themselves benefit from the lessons of the past. For a gloomy assessment of the impact of the large-scale history institutes of the 1960s, see Karen B. Wiley and Jeanne Race, *The Status of Precollege Science, Mathematics, and Social Science Education: 1955–1975*, vol. 3: *Social*

Science Education (Boulder, 1977). For an analysis of why these institutes had so little influence, see Richard H. Brown, "History as Discovery: An Interim Report on the Amherst Project," in Edwin Fenton, ed., *Teaching the New Social Studies in Secondary Schools: An Inductive Approach* (New York, 1966), 443–51.

49. James L. Sellers, "Before We Were Members—the MVHA," *Mississippi Valley Historical Review* 40 (1953), 21.

50. See Suzanne M. Wilson, "The Pedagogy of History: A Recommendation for Research," paper presented at the FIPSE/FIRST Conference, Washington, D.C., 1990.

51. Lee S. Shulman, "Knowledge and Teaching: Foundations of the New Reform," *Harvard Educational Review* 57 (1987), 1–22.

52. Tom Holt, *Thinking Historically: Narrative, Imagination, and Understanding* (New York, 1990). See also Richard J. Paxton and Sam Wineburg, "History Teaching," in Miriam Ben-Peretz, Sally Brown, and Robert Moon, eds., *Routledge International Companion to Education* (London, 2000).

53. Holt, *Thinking Historically*, 13.

54. A task force of the American Historical Association reached the same conclusion: "Concerning the cognitive abilities of students of college age that equip them to learn history, our knowledge is meager. The task force urges that research on this topic be undertaken. The findings would contribute much to the rethinking of the history major and the manner in which history courses are taught." *Perspectives: Newsletter of the American Historical Association* 30 (May/June 1990), 18.

55. See Suzanne M. Wilson, "Mastodons, Maps and Michigan: Exploring Uncharted Territory While Teaching Elementary School Social Studies," Elementary Subject Center Series, Technical Report no. 24 (ED 326470), Institute for Research on Teaching, Michigan State University (East Lansing, 1990). See also Martin Booth, "Ages and Concepts: A Critique of the Piagetian Approach to History Teaching," in Christopher Portal, ed., *The History Curriculum for Teachers* (London, 1987), 22–38. See as well my essay review "A Partial History," *Teaching and Teacher Education* 14 (1998), 233–43.

56. Carl Becker, "Everyman His Own Historian," *American Historical Review* 37 (1932), 221–36.

57. As Charles Bazerman has argued, even such straightforward texts as research notes on the molecular structure of nucleic acids communicate beliefs about the status of knowledge and the role of the knower. See his artful reading of subtexts in "What Written Knowledge Does: Three Examples of Academic Discourse," *Philosophy of the Social Sciences* 11 (1981), 361–87. See also Gay Gragson end Jack Selzer, "Fictionalizing the Readers of Scholarly Articles in Biology," *Written Communication* 7 (January 1990), 25–58.

58. Iris M. Tiedt, Jo E. Carlson, Bert D. Howard, and Kathleen S. Oda Wantanable, *Teaching Thinking Skills in K–12 Classrooms* (Needham Heights, Mass., 1989).

59. Robert Scholes, *Textual Power: Literary Theory and the Teaching of English* (New Haven, 1985), 14.

Reading Abraham Lincoln

A Case Study in Contextualized Thinking

onjure up in your mind the lanky figure of Abraham Lincoln, the sixteenth president of the United States, "Honest Abe" from Kentucky, commander in chief during the Civil War, and author of one of the most important documents in American history—the Emancipation Proclamation. Consider these words on the topic of race relations from the man often referred to as the "Great Emancipator":

> I have no purpose to introduce political and social equality between the white and black races. There is a physical difference between the two, which in my judgment will probably forever forbid their living together upon the footing of perfect equality, and inasmuch as it becomes a necessity that there must be a difference, I . . . am in favor of the race to which I belong, having the superior position. I have never said anything to the contrary.[1]

How are we to regard these words? At the very least they complicate the image of Lincoln as enlightened benefactor of African Americans. Have we been duped? Is the image of this American "patron saint" a sham? Perhaps, as Lerone Bennett claimed at the height of the Black Power movement, the image of Lincoln as "Great Emancipator" should be replaced by the image of Lincoln as "White Supremacist."[2]

An earlier version of this chapter was previously published in Mario Carretero and James F. Voss, eds., *Cognitive and Instructional Processes in History and the Social Sciences* (Hillsdale, N.J., 1994). Reprinted by permission of Lawrence Erlbaum Associates.

"Great Emancipator" or "White Supremacist"? How would we even go about answering such a question? What assumptions about the past enable us (or make it impossible for us) to understand Lincoln well enough to render judgment?

Judging past actors by present standards wrests them from their own context and subjects them to ways of thinking that we, not they, have developed. Presentism, the act of viewing the past through the lens of the present, is a psychological default state that must be overcome before one achieves mature historical understanding. The 1989 Bradley Commission promised that historical study sharpens the ability to "perceive past events and issues as they were experienced by people at the time . . . the develop[ment] of historical empathy as opposed to present mindedness."[3] When we consider the fundamental disciplinary understandings we want students to learn and, by extension, teachers to possess, the ability to think about the past on its own terms is certainly among them. If teachers of history cannot "think in time," we can have little faith in their students' ability to learn to do so.

What does such *contextualized* thinking look like, and how can we promote its development? Had my goal been for readers to think contextually at the beginning of this chapter, I could have committed no graver error than to display Lincoln's words shorn of any qualifying detail. For to think contextually means that words are not disembodied symbols transcending time and space. We cannot separate Lincoln's words at the beginning of this chapter from the occasion on which they were uttered (a debate with Stephen A. Douglas, Lincoln's rival for a fiercely contested senatorial seat), the location of this debate (Ottawa, Illinois, a hotbed of antiblack sentiment), the kinds of people who witnessed the debate (largely supportive of Douglas and suspicious of Lincoln), and the fact that both Lincoln and Douglas addressed these people not as prophets or moralists but as candidates courting votes. Nor can we ignore what Douglas said to spark Lincoln's response, or the words Lincoln uttered immediately following the passage quoted. And what about the other things Lincoln said in Havana, Illinois, a week earlier, or in Freeport, Illinois, a week later? Such considerations just begin to scratch the surface when we think about what we would need to create a historical context for the brief passage heading this chapter.

In trying to weave a context for Lincoln's words, I have focused mostly on piecing together the temporal and spatial context: the exigencies of the moment that might explain Lincoln's motivation and intention. But other forms of context—the climate of opinion, *mentalité*, or *Zeitgeist*; the biography of a complex human being and his style with words and utterances; the linguistic practices of the 1850s—must also be considered when thinking about the meaning of Lincoln's words.

How do readers use the fragments of the past that we call primary sources to weave historical contexts? How are coherent interpretations formed from documentary evidence, given its partial and elliptical nature? What kinds of knowledge are needed to produce such interpretations? What is the role of formal study in the development of contextualized thinking? And what about the *inability* to create a context? What does "noncontextualized," or anachronistic, thinking look like? What beliefs and processes give rise to and sustain anachronistic thinking? These were some of the questions that motivated this study, an enterprise we have come to think of as a form of "applied epistemology" because it neither falls into existing categories of psychological work nor qualifies as anything resembling academic history.

TYING KNOTS; OR, WHAT COGNITIVE TASKS SHARE WITH DEEP SEA FISHING

Observing contextualized thinking is more complicated than it might seem. We can try to infer it from historians' written accounts, but this approach discloses few clues about the crucial decision points that allow sophisticated reasoning to emerge. Historians edit out from their published works their hunches and faltering first steps, their miscues and fruitless pursuits down blind alleys. Yet it may be such homey and unshorn aspects of historical thought that provide the best clues about how sophisticated historical thinking emerges. If this is the case, some way has to be found to capture people in the act of contextualized thinking—in the moments of confusion before an interpretation emerges, while indecision and doubt reign and coherence remains elusive. Here is where the cognitive task comes in, an environment that allows us to study under controlled conditions phenomena that are irritatingly hard to grasp in the field.[4]

The choices before the task maker are endless, even when a set of research questions has been specified. Which time period to study, which documents to draw on, how many genres to include, and so on— the vistas of possibility are limitless. One response to this complexity is to throw up one's hands, recognize that any choice is arbitrary, and refuse to be overly concerned with decisions of topic, genre, and time period. In this case, one set of documents is as good as any other.

I hold the opposite position. Designing a task to capture historical reasoning can be likened to tying the knots of a fishing seine—the hardest work begins in dry dock. If fishermen's knots are too big for the prizes they seek, they will end up with all sorts of worthless creatures, while the real beauties slip unnoticed through the net. If the knots are too small, the nets will yield so much plankton and seaweed that the larger beasts lodged in the catch will be obscured. Tying knots, then, is not just a tedious process, but one that demands tremendous clarity of purpose. So it is with task design. In putting together this task, we sought to explore contextualized thinking by choosing a topic and period that was at once close to and remote from present concerns, for the heart of contextualized thinking is an awareness of continuity and discontinuity with the past. This consideration eliminated topics such as Anglo-Saxon ordeals, too remote from contemporary experience, and the assassination of John Kennedy, too close to our time (as well as being overexposed).[5] We chose to explore Lincoln's views about race because race is an enduring issue in American society, but one that can only be understood historically.[6] Our set of documents began with an exchange on the campaign stump, a feature of nineteenth-century American life that has much in common with modern electioneering. On the other hand, the topic under debate—the status of the slave and the justification for slavery—is an issue difficult for the modern mind to fathom.

We built a progression into our document set because historical reasoning has been referred to as *adductive*, a process of "adducing answers to specific questions so that a satisfactory 'fit' is obtained."[7] We constructed the task so that the documents we provided to readers became increasingly complex, hoping thereby to see how historical explanations that account for increasing complexity are adduced. Before selecting the final documents, we reviewed well over a thousand speeches, letters, notes, and addresses by Lincoln and his contemporaries.

PARTICIPANTS

The data for this chapter were drawn from a larger study on how different people (gifted high school students, beginning and experienced teachers, and historians with diverse specializations—see Chapter 1) think about historical texts. Here the discussion focuses on the thinking of two prospective public school teachers, drawn from a larger sample of pre-service teachers enrolled in a fifth-year teacher certification program at the University of Washington. The program requires all applicants to possess a bachelor's degree in a liberal arts discipline. Ted, a thirty-two-year-old white male, majored in history as an undergraduate and planned to find work as a history/social studies teacher upon graduation. Ellen, a thirty-four-year-old white female, was a physics major who had spent considerable time in the private sector before beginning her teacher education program. Ted's undergraduate course work was typical of the history majors in our larger sample of twelve prospective teachers. His program of study included ancient history, modern Latin American history, Afro-American history, women's history, and a seminar on the history of Iran, as well as other required survey courses. Ellen had taken two history courses as part of her college's distribution requirements. Because the number of courses taken is widely used as a proxy for subject matter knowledge, a comparison between "high-knowledge" and "low-knowledge" individuals seemed an interesting route to pursue.

PROCEDURE

Prior to engaging in a think-aloud task using the Lincoln documents, all of the teachers in our study were interviewed about their prior historical course work, particularly at the university level. We then taught them how to "think aloud"[8] and showed them a list of six rules to "keep in mind," taken from the work of David N. Perkins.[9] These rules included guidelines such as "say whatever's on your mind," "don't over-explain or justify," and "don't worry about complete sentences."[10]

My goal here is to recreate for the reader the unfolding of contextualized thinking. The presentation is sequential, following the order of the documents presented to the teachers. I invite readers to "read over the shoulders" of these two teachers, asking themselves how they would link document to document or try to weave a context for Lincoln's words. Although the full think-aloud task spans seven documents written over a 127-year period, space limitations prevent us from going beyond the fifth document here. Joining Ted and Ellen are the voices of some of the major interpreters of Lincoln and race relations in the United States: Winthrop Jordan, George Fredrickson, Don E. Fehrenbacher, Richard Weaver, Richard Hofstadter, and others.

IMAGES OF THOUGHT

The first document was by Stephen A. Douglas, Lincoln's opponent in the 1858 senatorial campaign. It begins with Douglas claiming that

Lincoln supported giving the franchise to slaves and the right to run for public office and serve on juries. In making these claims, Douglas established his own position as one "in favor of confining citizenship to white men" and opposed to Negro citizenship "in any and every form." He then went on to claim that Lincoln believed the "Negro was born his equal" and is "endowed with equality by the Almighty." Document 4.1 shows the document in the form in which it was presented to readers.

For Ted, the history major, the name Stephen A. Douglas sounded "really familiar . . . I don't remember too [many] good things about him, but nothing specific." The majority of Ted's comments during this reading were aimed at establishing textual coherence, a basic understanding of the surface meanings of the text. Only when asked what the document disclosed about Lincoln did Ted venture anything that might be called an interpretation: "Well, this makes it seem like Lincoln was much more . . . on the side of the Negro. But I think that there is probably another view to that."

Ellen, on the other hand, although also lacking detailed knowledge of Lincoln's views, was struck by the "incredibly racist language" of Douglas's speech, but noted that "it is not inflammatory" but "matter of fact, documented belief—this is obviously true, everyone knows it." When asked what the document told her about Lincoln, she said that it told her little. Instead she referred to a mental image that came to her while reading:

> When I was reading it I wasn't actively thinking of Lincoln. I was actively reading the words and thinking more of Stephen Douglas on the platform, orating and delivering this to a crowd. Who would be in the crowd listening and what the culture was at this time and why this was acceptable to say in 1858 but is now not acceptable to say.

Several things are worthy of note here. First, Ellen immediately began to build a social context for this utterance—political hustings, roaring crowds, and the speaker's awareness of the sensibilities of his listeners. But the second thing she does is more subtle—she recognizes the discrepancy between her own beliefs and those reflected in this document. By calling attention to issues of "acceptability" and recognizing that what struck her as "incredibly racist" would have been considered "matter of fact, documented belief," Ellen wove together two facets of context: issues of the social occasion and issues of *mentalité*, the sweeping modes of thought that formed the mental landscape of the day. She tried

In 1858, Abraham Lincoln ran against Stephen A. Douglas for a seat in the U.S. Senate. The two engaged in a series of seven public debates, which attracted national attention. Although Lincoln lost the election, he became widely known for his views on slavery. The following is an excerpt from Douglas's address to Lincoln in their first debate at Ottawa, Illinois, August 21, 1858.

If you desire Negro citizenship, if you desire to allow them to come into the State and settle with the White man, if you desire them to vote on an equality with yourselves, and to make them eligible to office, to serve on juries, and to judge your rights, then support Mr. Lincoln and the Black Republican party, who are in favor of the citizenship of the Negro. For one, I am opposed to Negro citizenship in any and every form. I believe this government was made . . . by White men, for the benefit of White men and their posterity forever, and I am in favor of confining citizenship to White men, men of European birth and descent, instead of conferring it upon Negroes, Indians and other inferior races.

Mr. Lincoln, following the example and lead of all the little abolition orators, who go around and lecture in the basements of schools and churches, reads from the Declaration of Independence, that all men were created equal, and then asks how can you deprive a Negro of that equality which God and the Declaration of Independence award to him. He and they maintain that Negro equality is guaranteed by the laws of God, and that it is asserted in the Declaration of Independence. . . . I do not question Mr. Lincoln's conscientious belief that the Negro was made his equal, and hence his brother, but for my own part, I do not regard the Negro as my equal, and positively deny that he is my brother. . . . [Lincoln] holds that the Negro was born his equal and yours, and that he was endowed with equality by the Almighty, and that no human law can deprive him of these rights. . . . Now, I do not believe that the Almighty ever intended the Negro to be the equal of the White man. . . . For thousands of years the Negro has been a race upon the earth, and during all that time, in all latitudes and climates, wherever he has wandered or been taken, he has been inferior to the race which he has there met. He belongs to an inferior race, and must always occupy an inferior position.

Source: Abraham Lincoln, *Speeches and Writings*, vols. 1–2 (New York, 1989), 504–5.

Note: Material in italics was added at the beginning of the document for introductory purposes and to provide bibliographic information.

Document 4.1. Speech by Stephen A. Douglas

here to understand a world in which such views were expounded, not by thugs or fringe elements, but by future senators and the voters who elected them. It is the creation of foreignness in relation to the past, not the creation of continuity, that characterizes Ellen's contextualized thinking in this instance.

Document 4.2 is one of the most famous texts from the Lincoln–Douglas debates, the *Ur*-text of the "Lincoln as White Supremacist" school. Viewed in its entirety, this document appears less easy to classify than the shortened excerpt at the beginning of this chapter. Nonetheless, it is impossible to avoid asking whether Lincoln was a racist. In fact, to pose this question—and to formulate an answer based on evidence—thrusts us into the epicenter of historical reasoning. It is worth quoting Donald Fehrenbacher in this regard:

> Anyone who sets out conscientiously to answer [whether Lincoln was a racist] will soon find himself deep in complexity and confronting some of the fundamental problems of historical investigation. In one category are various questions about the historian's relation to the past: Is his task properly one of careful reconstruction, or are there more important purposes to be served? Does his responsibility include rendering moral judgments? If so, using what standards—those of his own time or those of the period under study? Then there are all the complications encountered in any effort to read the mind of a man, especially a politician, from the surviving record of his words and actions. For instance, what he openly affirmed as a youth may have been silently discarded in maturity; what he believed on a certain subject may be less significant than the intensity of his belief; and what he said on a certain occasion may have been largely determined by the immediate historical context, including the composition of his audience.[11]

As Ted read Lincoln's reply to Douglas, he felt a certain familiarity. Initially he sensed that he had seen the document before, and by the sixth line, this feeling had grown stronger: "Yes, I *have* read this before." Lincoln's statement that "he was in favor of the race to which he belonged" strengthened Ted's view that Lincoln was not the "Great Emancipator" of textbooks, but someone who wanted "to reunite the states, not just get rid of slavery." "Yeah, see, now this makes Lincoln seem more bigoted and not so altruistic." By the end of the document, Ted's prior understanding of Lincoln was confirmed:

> Lincoln was not so much in the interest—working in the interest of the black man, for altruistic sense . . . he does say that they deserve equal treatment, in a way, but still he's not giving them equal—he's not giving them . . . equality in personhood.

For Ted, Lincoln's words stand starkly alone. They mirror Lincoln's beliefs, unfiltered by the occasion on which those beliefs were expressed or the social ends Lincoln tried to achieve in expressing them.

Ellen, in contrast, devoted over one-third of her comments (107 words out of 306 spoken) to creating a social context. Lincoln's statement of the Negro's equality in the second part of the document prompted the comment that appears in Table 4.1, where Ted's comments are presented for comparison.

What does this document disclose about Lincoln in Ellen's view? Very little, it seems. When asked how this document illuminated Lincoln's views, she affirmed her earlier reading: "I view [Lincoln] in the context of how I view a politician trying to get elected—that they'll say anything, do anything to get elected. And that you can't trust them." Ellen's reading contrasts sharply with Ted's. For Ted, Lincoln's response provided evidence of bigotry. For Ellen, on the other hand, there is no mention of

---

From Abraham Lincoln's reply to Stephen A. Douglas at Ottawa, Illinois, August 21, 1858.

I will say here . . . that I have no purpose directly or indirectly to interfere with the institution of slavery in the States where it exists. I believe I have no lawful right to do so, and I have no inclination to do so. I have no purpose to introduce political and social equality between the white and black races. There is a physical difference between the two, which in my judgment will probably forever forbid their living together upon the footing of perfect equality, and inasmuch as it becomes a necessity that there must be a difference, I, as well as Judge Douglas, am in favor of the race to which I belong, having the superior position. I have never said anything to the contrary, but I hold that notwithstanding all this, there is no reason in the world why the Negro is not entitled to all the natural rights enumerated in the Declaration of Independence, the right to life, liberty and the pursuit of happiness. I hold that he is as much entitled to these as the White man. I agree with Judge Douglas [that the Negro] is not my equal in many respects—certainly not in color, perhaps not in moral or intellectual endowment. But in the right to eat the bread . . . which his own hand earns, he is my equal and the equal of Judge Douglas, and the equal of every living man.

Source: Abraham Lincoln, *Speeches and Writings*, vols. 1–2 (New York, 1989), 512.

Document 4.2. Lincoln's reply to Douglas

TABLE 4.1
Comparison of Ellen's and Ted's Readings of Document 4.2

| Text | PROTOCOL | |
	Ted	Ellen
But in the right to eat the bread which his own hand earns, he is my equal and the equal of Judge Douglas, and the equal of every living man.		
	He seems to be giving him equal, equal rights as far as living, but, like he says, perhaps, not morally or intellectual. He's still saying that the white man is superior, but that doesn't take away the rights of the living and life.	When I read this, and think about Lincoln, I think of him in terms of a politician, a guy trying to get elected. I've kind of got this mental picture of a Roger Ailes type, you know the spin doctor who pushes his campaign director, who pushes the media director, I guess you go through Reagan's media director. Whispering in his ear, saying now this is what you got to say to this crowd. To put the right spin on this particular issue. So it, again, when I'm thinking of Lincoln, I'm viewing him as a politician, in kind of a slimy way. The kind of way I think a lot of politicians [are]. They say whatever is convenient to the crowd that's listening to them, and you never really know what they're thinking.

bigotry, no mention of what the document says about Lincoln other than the fact that, like other politicians, he spoke out of both sides of his mouth. Instead, the document points to a social context she knows well—one in which candidates say what is needed to earn votes.

Ellen's framing of Lincoln as a disingenuous politician seeking to get elected falls within a well-established interpretative tradition. Richard Hofstadter, who profiled Lincoln in his *American Political Tradition*, characterized Lincoln's words in the earlier document as appealing at once to abolitionists and "Negrophobes."[12] Remarking on a speech Lincoln gave in Chicago on July 10, 1858 ("Let us discard all this quibbling about this man and the other man, this race and that race . . . and unite as one people") and comparing it with a speech Lincoln gave in

Charleston on September 18, 1858 ("I as much as any other man am in favor of having the superior position assigned to the white race"), Hofstadter remarked that it was

> not easy to decide whether the true Lincoln is the one who spoke in Chicago or the one who spoke in Charleston. Possibly the man devoutly believed each of the utterances at the time he delivered it; possibly his mind too was a house divided against itself. In any case it is easy to see in all this the behavior of a professional politician looking for votes.[13]

Both Ellen and Hofstadter resolved apparent contradictions in Lincoln's words by appealing to the exigencies of a political campaign. Because Lincoln needed to woo voters from both camps, he needed to talk out of both sides of his mouth. But the "divided Lincoln" interpretation is not the only way to understand these documents.

Lincoln's statements in Document 4.2 thrust us into the dilemma of contextualized thinking. If we presume an essential continuity in race relations, we see inconsistencies in Lincoln's words. These inconsistencies in turn lead us to create a context to explain why, for instance, Lincoln would say different things to different people. But if we begin with the belief that clear language and pure logic are themselves historical, then we are open to different responses in the face of apparent inconsistencies. Inconsistencies become opportunities for exploring our discontinuity with the past, the inevitable consequence of trying to bridge spatial and temporal gaps across the ages.

Recall that what is at issue between Douglas and Lincoln is an implied syllogism flowing from the Declaration of Independence. If, as the Declaration stated, "all men are created equal," and if, as Douglas stated, "the Negro is not my equal," then, by Douglas's definition, the Negro is not to be considered a man. If this was the question Lincoln addressed, his views were unequivocal.

In his *Ethics of Rhetoric*, Richard Weaver demonstrated how Lincoln "argued by definition," a strategy that attacked a problem by whittling away at the side issues to reveal its unambiguous inner essence.[14] Although other statesmen examined slavery from the perspective of history, comparative politics, the Bible, or the exigencies of the moment, Lincoln's tack was to argue from first principles. His "Speech at Peoria" provides insight into this style of argument. In this case, Lincoln told his audience that he would focus on the "naked merits" of the issue of slavery. He began his speech with the question of the genus of man, precisely the issue at the heart of the exchange in Documents 4.1 and 4.2:

Equal justice to the South, it is said, requires us to consent to the extending of slavery to new countries. That is to say, inasmuch as you do not object to my taking my hog to Nebraska, therefore I must not object to your taking your slave. Now, I admit that this is perfectly logical, if there is no difference between hogs and Negroes. But while you thus require me to deny the humanity of the Negro, I wish to ask whether you of the South yourselves have ever been willing to do as much?[15]

If the slave was mere chattel, like a hog or cow, then why, asked Lincoln, was the seller of slaves treated differently from the seller of hogs?

You despise him utterly. You do not recognize him as a friend, or even as an honest man. Your children must not play with his; they may rollick freely with the little Negroes, but not with the "slave dealer's" children. If you are obliged to deal with him, you try to get through the job without so much as touching him. It is common with you to join hands with men you meet; but with the slave dealer you avoid the ceremony—instinctively shrinking from the snaky contact. If he grows rich and retires from business, you still remember him, and still keep up the ban of non-intercourse upon him and his family. Now why is this? You do not so treat the man who deals in corn, cotton, or tobacco?[16]

Lincoln hammered at his point with other examples. How, for instance, should Southerners label the 433,643 free blacks living in the United States at that time? Moreover, how did their freedom come about, at great financial sacrifice to their owners, if these same owners did not feel that the "poor Negro has some sense of natural right to himself"? It is worth quoting Weaver's summary:

Lincoln could never be dislodged from his position that there is one genus of human beings; and early in his career as lawyer he had learned that it is better to base an argument upon one incontrovertible point than to try to make an impressive case through a whole array of points. Through the years he clung tenaciously to this concept of genus, from which he could draw the proposition that what is fundamentally true of the family will be true also of the branches of the family. Therefore since the Declaration of Independence had interdicted slavery for man, slavery was interdicted for the Negro in principle.[17]

If we look carefully at Lincoln's response in Document 4.2, we see aspects that are easily overshadowed by its charged language. Notice that the only point Lincoln was willing to concede unequivocally to Douglas is a "physical difference between the two races," but from then on Lincoln equivocated. There is only *"perhaps"* a difference in moral or intellectual endowment, Lincoln said. This "perhaps" goes unnoticed by most contemporary readers, but even to raise the possibility that the two races were morally and intellectually equivalent must be viewed against the backdrop of mid-nineteenth-century racism. The

Stanford historian George Fredrickson has argued that here Lincoln followed in the footsteps of his Republican mentor, Henry Clay, who advocated gradual emancipation and early in his career declared that blacks "are rational beings, like ourselves, capable of feeling, of reflection, and of judging of what naturally belongs to them as a portion of the human race."[18]

Fredrickson's appeal to Clay interweaves aspects of the *Zeitgeist* with Lincoln's personal biography. What appears as a hairsplitting distinction between moral and legal rights was a meaningful difference in Lincoln's mind and in the minds of many of his contemporaries. Because we cannot fathom a world in which such a distinction would be viewed as "progressive," we tend to view Lincoln's statements as contradictory and inconsistent, or worse—as hypocritical and self-serving.

For Ted, Lincoln's words cast light on Lincoln's soul, and the image perceived was that of a bigot. For Ellen, Lincoln's words disclosed more about the social situation than the naked truth about the man in that situation. What Weaver, Fredrickson, and others suggest is that the "naked truth" is more veiled than we think.

The third document was drawn from a different time in Lincoln's life and exemplifies a different genre of documentary evidence. Unlike the public response to Douglas, Document 4.3 was a private letter to Mary Speed of Kentucky, the wife of Joshua Speed, a close friend. In this letter, Lincoln described a journey on a Mississippi riverboat on which a group of slaves were literally being sold down the river.

Several aspects of this document make it provocative. First, historians typically consider the genre of a document when making judgments of probity, and, in the absence of other information, they tend to regard personal correspondence as more probative than public pronouncements.[19] Second, the substance of this document presents, at first glance, a perplexing contrast. Faced with the scene of slaves chained to each other in close quarters, Lincoln felt compelled to remark, not on human misery, but on human happiness.

The first point at which an interpretation seemed to form in Ted's mind (see Table 4.2) was when Lincoln described the slave who had an "over-fondness for his wife." When Ted was asked if his image of Lincoln had changed or stayed the same, he replied:

> Well, I'm still kind of not sure. It's probably [a document] that I would have to read again, and really, I'd like to know more about this. Where was he really going with this idea? What was his total summation, rather than "God

Abraham Lincoln, writing to Mary Speed, a personal friend, September 27, 1841.

By the way, a fine example was presented on board the boat for contemplating the effect of condition upon human happiness. A gentleman had purchased twelve Negroes in different parts of Kentucky and was taking them to a farm in the South. They were chained six and six together. A small iron clevis was around the left wrist of each so that the Negroes were strung together precisely like so many fish upon a trot-line. In this condition they were being separated forever from the scenes of their childhood, their friends, their fathers and mothers, and brothers and sisters, and many of them, from their wives and children, and going into perpetual slavery . . . yet amid all these distressing circumstances . . . they were the most cheerful and apparently happy creatures on board. One, whose offense for which he had been sold was an over-fondness for his wife, played the fiddle almost continually; and the others danced, sung, cracked jokes, and played various games with cards from day to day. How true it is that "God renders the worst of human conditions tolerable . . ."

Source: Abraham Lincoln, *Speeches and Writings*, vols. 1–2 (New York, 1989), 74.

Document 4.3. Letter to Mary Speed

renders the worst of human conditions tolerable"? He seems to be saying that it is kind of unfortunate that people, that [they] could make the best of worst conditions. . . . So it gives him a sense of being caring. Which I do believe that he was. Yet, on the other hand, like I said, that the little, seeing Blacks as just happy-go-lucky people, that kind of image. I don't know. It's offensive to me. So, I don't like to read it, I guess.

Several aspects of this comment deserve note. First, Ted was sufficiently self-aware to know that the document leaves him uncertain, and that to understand it better he should probably read it again. Second, there is an elaboration of Ted's earlier image of Lincoln as bigot, though the comment about Lincoln "being caring" hints at some vestige of the "patron saint" view of the sixteenth president. Finally, Ted displayed an awareness of his emotional reactions to the text, reactions to images that he perceived as deeply bigoted.

Ellen's reading was remarkably similar (see Table 4.3). The letter generated perplexity: How can Lincoln be so callous as to mistake human misery for cheerfulness? But is Lincoln really as callous as his

TABLE 4.2
Ted's Interpretation of Document 4.3

TEXT	PROTOCOL
One, who offense for which he had been sold was an over-fondness for his wife, played the fiddle almost continually;	
	I was having trouble with that sentence—*whose offense for which he had been sold*—okay, so that's why he was sold.
was an over-fondness for his wife, played the fiddle almost continually	
	So he looks like the happy jovial little boy.
and the others danced, sung, and cracked jokes, and played various games with cards from day to day.	
	They were just playing up to the image that they were happy little people in their form of life. . . . He seems to be saying that they're—they're good people, but they're portraying that stereotypical image of the little happy "negro" no matter what the conditions are. They "enjoy" their circumstances.

words suggest? What missing pieces of context might lead us to view the Speed letter differently?

Was Lincoln blind to the suffering of people wrenched from their homes and families? What better evidence could there be for a gross insensitivity to the pain of slaves than these words to Mary Speed? George Fredrickson had in mind how Lincoln's words in the Speed letter would strike the modern ear when he wrote:

> Such philosophizing was hardly indicative of antislavery zeal, and it can easily be condemned as a manifestation of complacency, insensitivity, or lack of imagination. But it was nevertheless based on the assumption, increasingly rare in the 1840s, that blacks responded to conditions in a way that could be understood in terms of a common humanity and not as the result of peculiar racial characteristics.[20]

It is difficult to imagine a world in which the human status of slaves was in question, but that is precisely the world into which Abraham Lincoln was born. Trying to reconstruct a world we cannot completely know

TABLE 4.3
Ted's and Ellen's Interpretations of the Speed Letter

READER	TEXTUAL PROMPT	PROTOCOL
Ted	*. . . and the others danced, sung, cracked jokes, and played various games with cards from day to day.*	They were just playing up the image that they were all happy little people in their forms of life.
Ellen	*. . . and all the others danced, sung, cracked jokes, and played various games with cards from day to day. How true it is that "God renders the worst of human conditions tolerable . . ."*	It's kind of a depressing—I'm really depressed when I read this. That there were people that were being sold into slavery, being separated, and somehow, that the people in power could justify this by saying, "Look how happy they are. Look how beautiful they are. They don't mind." They're just—kind of like this is their lot in life. This is what they were brought into existence to be. When I think about Lincoln, I mean, well, at least he is clearly cognizant . . . that they are being separated. But how can he feel that they're happy? Doesn't—I mean those two conditions aren't—can't code this together. That you'd be separated from your family, your home, and your brothers and sisters and children and yet be happy and cheerful. How does he know they were cheerful?

may be the difference between a contextualized and an anachronistic reading of the past.

Ted had relatively little to say about Document 4.4, the last of three documents by Lincoln presented to him.[21] He noted that he was broadly familiar with plans for colonies of freed slaves and that reading this document did little to influence his views about Lincoln one way or the other. Ellen, on the other hand, used it to flesh out her image of Lincoln. She began with its temporal aspects, noting that the address was delivered in the middle of the Civil War. As she read it, a different image of Lincoln formed in her mind:

> [Lincoln] is conscientiously trying to deal with a problem that is something that apparently made sense in that time frame. And I get the feeling that he is wrestling with something that doesn't really have a good solution. This is the best you can have for now. So I kind of see him as problem-solver . . . not the slimy politician trying to give [unclear]. [He is a] CEO or some type of

decision-maker trying to deal with a problem or acute problem. He was real one-dimensional in the first article [Doc. 4.2], kind of a slimy politician. Then he has another side with the letter to Mary Speed, kind of human. And now this is again another, it's beginning to fill out, but now I see him more as the chief executive and trying to deal with problems, trying to balance a war, thinking ahead, what are we going to do after the war and sort of coming up with—and this is prior to the Emancipation Proclamation. Is this prior to the Emancipation Proclamation? Yes, this is prior. So, I mean he may have had this idea in mind, so he's thinking forward, and how are we going to deal with this huge number of slaves? Maybe colonizing is certainly a viable option in 1862. It kind of reminds me of what the British did with Australia. Ship all the undesirables down to Australia.

Ellen provided a richly intertextual reading here. She made reference to two of the three previous documents, and her understanding of Document 4.4 was formed with these earlier documents as backdrop. What emerged in her mind was an image of a multifaceted human being, a "slimy politician" in one instance, a caring person in another, and in this document a CEO engaged in strategic planning. There seems to be a

---

Colonization of freed blacks was an idea proposed early in the nineteenth century. Many whites who opposed slavery actively advocated colonization, maintaining that true freedom and equality could be realized only by relocating the black population. Abraham Lincoln had long favored the idea, and, in 1862, a sum of money was appropriated by Congress to aid in a colonization program. The following is from Lincoln's "Address on Colonization," delivered to a group of free black men at the White House on August 14, 1862.

Why . . . should the people of your race be colonized, and where? If we deal with those who are not free at the beginning, and whose intellects are clouded by slavery, we have very poor materials to start with. If intelligent colored men . . . would move in this matter, much might be accomplished. It is exceedingly important that we have men at the beginning capable of thinking as White men, and not those who have been systematically oppressed. . . . The place I am thinking about having for a colony is in Central America. . . . The country is a very excellent one for any people, and with great natural resources and advantages, and especially because of the similarity of climate with your native land—thus being suited to your physical condition.

Source: Abraham Lincoln, *Speeches and Writings*, vols. 1–2 (New York, 1989), 368.

Document 4.4. Address on Colonization

recognition that such a plan, although outlandish today, made more sense in the latter half of the nineteenth century. The analogy to Australia represented a search for parallels that would further contextualize Lincoln's plan. To understand Lincoln, Ellen combined elements of the *Zeitgeist* with a chronology of the Civil War, and in so doing began to form the basis for a biographical context of Lincoln's life.

John Bell Robinson begins his address (Document 4.5) by advancing a religious argument for slavery: "God himself has made them for usefulness as slaves and requires us to employ them as such and if we betray our trust and throw them off on their own resources, we reconvert them into barbarians." These are powerful words that strike us as absurd, but we should recognize that a religious justification for slavery goes back to the inception of English contact with Africa.[22] Reading John Bell Robinson, Ted bristled at ideas foreign to his own views on race. When Robinson linked slavery to the divine mission, he blurted: "My mind is going, *Argh!* I can't describe it in words." When Robinson stated that if Negro slaves were sent back to Africa, they would fall back into "heathenism and barbarism in less than fifty years," Ted composed himself and responded: "Is that what he thinks they were—*barbarians*—I mean it's putting down their own natural life style and culture as they were, which I don't think should be done." And when he was asked if reading Robinson's words shed any light on Lincoln's views, with which he had been reacquainted in the previous three documents, Ted responded: "No, because it's, I don't see Lincoln being addressed in this or, rereading his name who wrote it, that name doesn't sound familiar and I can't connect it to Lincoln at all."

How should we construe Ted's reading? On one level, of course, Ted is right. John Bell Robinson is "putting down the natural life style" of the Africans he knew, and his words smack of intolerance and disrespect for people unlike himself. But on another level, Ted's comments provide a glimpse into a view of the past shared by many college students, a view David Lowenthal characterized as a "timeless past," in which the constructs we use to make sense of our present ("racism," "bigotry," "tolerance," "multicultural understandings") stand as static categories unchanged across time and space.[23] In such a past, John Bell Robinson should have thought differently. But to be fair to Mr. Robinson, he also should not have been born into a world that, as Winthrop Jordan and George Fredrickson remind us, exalted the white European male as the standard by which humanity was to be judged.

From Pictures of Slavery and Anti-Slavery: Advantages of Negro Slavery and the Benefits of Negro Freedom Morally, Socially, and Politically Considered *by John Bell Robinson, a White pro-slavery spokesperson, Pennsylvania, 1863, p. 42.*

God himself has made them for usefulness as slaves, and requires us to employ them as such, and if we betray our trust, and throw them off on their own resources, we reconvert them into barbarians. Our Heavenly Father has made us to *rule*, and the Negroes to serve, and if we . . . set aside his holy arrangements for the good of mankind and his own glory, and tamper with his laws, we shall be overthrown and eternally degraded, and perhaps made subjects of some other civilized nation. . . . Colonization in their native land of all the Negroes would be so nearly impracticable, that it will never be done, and no other spot on this green earth will do for them. It would be the height of cruelty and barbarism to send them anywhere else. If they could all be colonized on the coast of Africa, they would fall back into heathenism and barbarism in less than fifty years.

Document 4.5. Benefits of Slavery

We also see what contextualized thinking does *not* look like when Ted tells us that Robinson teaches him nothing about Lincoln. Ted is right in saying that Robinson does not mention Lincoln. But on another level, Ted is wrong, for Robinson tells us a great deal about the mental landscape that prevailed in Lincoln's day. Robinson is a marker at one end of that landscape, just as William Lloyd Garrison (see Document 4.6) is a marker at the other end. In a universe of ideas of different textures, what is the texture of Lincoln's ideas? Where can he be located on the spectrum of ideas?

This question provided a stumbling block for Ellen as well. Robinson's document elicited from Ellen no spontaneous comments about Lincoln. She was consumed by Robinson's charged words, drawing comparisons with Adolf Hitler's "Final Solution." Robinson's statement that repatriated slaves would "fall back into heathenism and barbarism" sparked this response:

I mean I can't believe that anybody thinks this. I can't believe! I mean this is awful. It really doesn't impact how I think about Lincoln. I'm really focused on this guy. I'm just outraged! The thing that is really strange is that, again, I can picture him speaking in some type of lecture hall, and again this being delivered and it not being—this is pretty inflammatory stuff, but I mean it probably wasn't all that inflammatory back in 1863. [It] kind of emphasizes

> *From an editorial by William Lloyd Garrison appearing in the* Genius of Universal Emancipation, *February 12, 1830. Garrison (1805–79) was a leading white abolitionist and worked for a short time as the assistant editor of the* Genius *before beginning his own antislavery periodical in 1831.*
>
> I deny the postulate, that God has made . . . one portion of the human race superior to another. No matter how many breeds are amalgamated—no matter how many shades of color intervene between tribes or nations—give them the same chances to improve, and a fair start at the same time, and the result will be equally brilliant, equally productive, equally grand.

Document 4.6. Statement on Abolition

how one section of the population viewed slaves as subhumans and we're doing this for their own good and if we didn't bring them into our servitude that they would be heathens and they'd be lost.

Ideally Ellen would have recognized that Robinson's religious justification for slavery is precisely the kind of statement Lincoln eschewed. Indeed, when Lincoln did refer to God in the context of slavery, it was to comment on the common bond under God shared by people of different races (Document 4.3). In this sense, Robinson and Lincoln could not have been further apart.

CONCLUSION

These two teachers differed dramatically in their approach to the documents. For Ted, the history major, Lincoln's views corresponded directly to the words in these documents; Ellen, the physics major, was wary of pursuing the "real" Lincoln through these documents, trying instead to understand the different Lincolns who responded to different circumstances. Further distinguishing Ellen's reading from Ted's were her many intertextual connections across documents. We view these cross-references as attempts to create a context within the confines of this task by reconstructing the climate of opinion in which Lincoln dwelled. At the end of the task, when Ellen encountered Lerone Bennett's claim that Lincoln was a "tragically flawed figure who shared the racial prejudice of most of his white contemporaries," she was able to use what she had learned in this task to add texture to this statement.[24] Agreeing in part with Bennett's assertion, Ellen added this qualifier: "Lincoln clearly wasn't on the same wavelength as . . . Robinson." Moreover, she contextualized Bennett's article itself: "1968, let's see, that was a year, this is just prior to the Bobby Kennedy and Martin Luther King assassinations."

Throughout the task, Ellen gauged Lincoln's views without losing sight of her own. She was able to disapprove without being astonished. She could reject and still understand. When reading Stephan Douglas, she called attention to the "incredibly racist language," but noted that "it's not inflammatory. It's matter of fact, documented belief—this is obviously true, everyone knows it. It's what they would call conventional wisdom, common knowledge." Ellen here achieved a fundamental historical understanding. The past is not mere prologue to the present but is discontinuous with it. The distance she created between her own views and those of the people she read about allowed her to view history, in Louis O. Mink's words, as a "standing invitation to discover and enter into modes of seeing quite different from our own."[25] What Ellen understood is analogous. What white society saw in 1850, what allowed this society to propagate the institution of slavery on American soil, is not what we see today.

The two teachers here present the puzzle of an inverse relationship, or so it would seem, between academic training in history and the disposition to think contextually. This pattern, however, is not entirely anomalous; our early findings, although based on a very small sample (twelve teachers), showed no clear-cut relationship between undergraduate major and the ability to create a historical context.

This finding, tentative and provisional, is not entirely new to researchers concerned with teachers' subject matter knowledge.[26] The undergraduate major proceeds on the assumption that students have mastered fundamental disciplinary conceptions prior to coming to the university. It is precisely these fundamental conceptions that are at the center of teaching that discipline to the young. But, as is often the case, the notions presumed to exist in the minds of college freshmen, sophomores, juniors, and seniors are rarely checked, tested, or assessed. In many cases, the foundation assumed by university instructors is a figment of their imaginations.

When history majors come to M.A. programs in teaching, we presume that they know their history. The job of teacher education is to teach prospective teachers about teaching. But what happens when

assessments such as these, assessments that allow us to examine fundamental disciplinary assumptions, undermine our confidence in students'
fundamental knowledge? The job of teacher education becomes doubly
complicated when, in the midst of teaching people how to teach, we
realize that we first must teach them how to know.

I end this chapter with the "so what" question, for one hears a great
deal nowadays about "authentic assessments" that tap students' ability
to "think like historians." These pronouncements are often greeted
with enthusiastic nods, often by people who never ask a prior—and, in
my eyes, more basic—question: Why should we care if students, or
teachers for that matter, are able to think like historians?

Historical thinking of the type described here, and in particular the
disposition to think about the past by recognizing the inadequacy of
one's own conceptual apparatus, is essential in teaching people how to
understand others different from themselves. If we never recognize that
our individual experience is limited, what hope is there of understanding people whose logic defies our own, whose choices and beliefs appear
inscrutable when judged against our own standards?

Many questions remain: We do not know how, exactly, people learn
to think contextually. We do not know where they learn it when they
do. We do not even know the role of formal study in its development.
We are convinced, however, of one thing: The ability to think contextually is not, in David Hackett Fischer's words, some "pristine goal of
scholarly perfection":[27]

> If we continue to make the . . . error of conceptualizing the problems of a
> nuclear world in prenuclear terms, there will not be a postnuclear world. If
> we persist in the error of applying yesterday's programs to today's problems,
> we may suddenly run short of tomorrow's possibilities. If we continue to
> pursue the ideological objectives of the nineteenth century in the middle of
> the twentieth, the prospects of a twenty-first are increasingly dim.[28]

Reason, as Fischer reminds us, is a pathetically frail weapon in the face
of the problems that threaten to rend our society and our world. It is,
however, the only weapon we possess.

NOTES

This chapter was prepared for a conference on "Reasoning in History and the
Social Sciences" at Autonoma University of Madrid in October 1992. It first
appeared in print, with Janice Fournier as second author, in a book based on the

conference: Mario Carretero and James F. Voss, eds., *Cognitive and Instructional Processes in History and the Social Sciences* (Hillsdale, N.J., 1994); an overview appeared in *History News* 48 (1993). Using the same documents and procedure, I studied how historians read these documents (see Chapter 1). A full description of that study appeared in *Cognitive Science* 22 (1998), 319–46.

1. Abraham Lincoln, *Speeches and Writings*, vols. 1–2 (New York, 1989), 512.

2. Lerone Bennett, Jr., "Was Abe Lincoln a White Supremacist?" *Ebony* 23 (February 1968), 35–42.

3. Bradley Commission on History in Schools, *Building a History Curriculum: Guidelines for Teaching History in Schools* (Washington, D.C., 1988), 9.

4. This is not the place to offer a defense of cognitive task environments, which critics have assailed for distorting the way thinking goes on in its "natural habitat." We are currently in the midst of a pendulum swing in understanding cognition, privileging anthropological approaches over the more traditional experimental conditions of the psychological laboratory. I am deeply sympathetic to the critiques; see, for example, Michael Cole and Barbara Means, eds., *Comparative Studies of How People Think: An Introduction* (Cambridge, Mass., 1981). However, rather than thinking strategically about how to combine multiple methods, each of which bears its own liabilities, we have debased ourselves with either/or contests over which method is best. The past offers a powerful antidote to this malady of thought. See Kurt Lewin, "Defining the 'Field' at a Given Time," *Psychology Review* 50, no. 3 (1943).

5. See Alaric K. Dickinson and Peter J. Lee, "Making Sense of History," in Alaric K. Dickinson, Peter J. Lee, and Peter J. Rogers, eds., *Learning History* (London, 1984), 117–53. The pioneering work of Lee, Dickinson, and their colleague Denis Shemilt invigorated a field that had grown moribund and brittle. The questions they framed in the eighties continue to guide researchers across the globe. I cannot envision my own program of research apart from the influence of the British work on learning history.

6. See the work of Ronald Takaki, "Reflections from a Different Mirror," *Teaching Tolerance* 3 (1994), 11–15; Winthrop D. Jordan, *White Over Black: American Attitudes Toward the Negro, 1550–1812* (New York, 1968); George Fredrickson, "A Man but Not a Brother: Abraham Lincoln and Racial Equality," *Journal of Southern History* 41 (1975), 39–58.

7. David Hackett Fischer, *Historians' Fallacies: Toward a Logic of Historical Thought* (New York, 1970).

8. See Chapter 3 in this volume.

9. David N. Perkins, *The Mind's Best Work* (Cambridge, Mass., 1981).

10. Previous work with these documents showed that people with little content knowledge quickly became confused about the sequence of events in Lincoln's life. To lessen this possibility and to help orient participants to the task, we developed a timeline of major events in Lincoln's life, from his election to the Illinois legislature to his assassination. People were given this timeline and told to refer to it at any time. Documents were presented one by one, each printed on a separate page, with the source of the document appearing at the top of the page in bold italics. Once participants finished commenting on each text, they were asked to report retrospectively on "anything

else you remember yourself thinking as you read this document." If participants did not explicitly address Lincoln's views in their comments (and had not done so explicitly during the reading), they were asked, "What light does this document shed on Lincoln's views about race?"

11. Donald E. Fehrenbacher, "Only His Stepchildren: Lincoln and the Negro," *Civil War History* 20 (1974), 293–310.

12. Richard Hofstadter, *The American Political Tradition and the Men Who Made It* (New York, 1948).

13. Ibid., 116.

14. Richard M. Weaver, *The Ethics of Rhetoric* (Chicago, 1953).

15. Lincoln, *Speeches*, 325–26.

16. Ibid., 326.

17. Weaver, *Ethics*, 95.

18. Fredrickson, "Not a Brother," 42.

19. See Chapter 3 in this volume for examples of historians weighing the genre of documentary evidence. See also Louis Gottschalk, *Understanding History: A Primer of Historical Method* (Chicago, 1958).

20. Fredrickson, "Not a Brother," 44.

21. This document was accompanied by a lengthy preamble because pilot work had shown that few readers, even those with course work in this period, were familiar with Lincoln's plans to establish colonies of freed slaves in Central America.

22. See Jordan, *White Over Black*.

23. David Lowenthal, *The Past Is a Foreign Country* (Cambridge, England, 1985); David Lowenthal, "The Timeless Past: Some Anglo-American Historical Preconceptions," *Journal of American History* 75 (1989), 1263–80. For an update on Lowenthal's positions, see his *Possessed by the Past: The Heritage Crusade and the Spoils of History* (New York, 1996).

24. Bennett, "Was Abe Lincoln," 42.

25. Louis O. Mink (Brian Fay, Eugene O. Golob, and Richard T. Vann, eds.), *Historical Understanding* (Ithaca, N.Y., 1987), 103.

26. See the National Center for Research on Teacher Learning, *Findings on Learning to Teach* (East Lansing, Mich., 1992).

27. Fischer, *Historians' Fallacies*, 215.

28. Ibid.

5

Picturing the Past

lear your mind and try to conjure up images of two historical figures, a Pilgrim and a Western Settler. Does your Pilgrim wear a tall black hat with a buckle? Or a small lace cap?
Is your Settler herding cattle in bandanna and chaps? Or
tending chickens on the prairie in a sunbonnet? Why do
these particular images come to mind? And why do some of
these images come to mind more easily than others?

This brief exercise serves to introduce our topic: the role of
cultural assumptions in the learning of history. Often these
assumptions run so deep and are so taken for granted that we
do not even recognize them. In the learning and teaching of
history, assumptions play a key role. They signal what is
important in history, pushing to the forefront an easily recognized canon. Without much thought, we typically organize
history chronologically, according to eras defined by specific
political, diplomatic, and military events: the Constitutional
Convention, Reconstruction, the New Deal, the Carter presidency. At the same time, we designate other topics as "special," as additions or supplements to the main story, often
addressed in textbook sidebars but rarely in end-of-chapter
tests. Often our implicit assumptions shape our ideas about
what is central in history and what is peripheral, what to look
for and what to overlook. Our assumptions allow us not to
miss a beat when reading about "Pilgrims and their wives."

Consider how history textbooks normally treat the topic
of trade in colonial New England. The standard U.S. history

113

textbook routinely highlights the "triangular trade," the network through which the American colonies, the West Indies, and Great Britain exchanged slaves, sugar cane, and rum. One widely used text-book, *The Americans* by Winthrop Jordan and his colleagues,[1] devotes nearly three pages to the topic, introducing it with a boldfaced sub-heading, "The North Develops Commerce and Cities—Molasses and Rumbullion." These two terms, "molasses" and "rumbullion," appear later in the chapter review section and also as end-of-the-chapter vocab-ulary words. Jordan's emphasis in the telling of history is on the eco-nomic life of nation-states, which in this case means the trade and commercial activities that men engaged in.

Women appear in Jordan's colonial economy in the section headed "Family Farms," where we learn that women "performed an unending round of tasks," cooking in metal pots, baking in hollow compartments in the chimney, spinning rough cloth, and sewing it into clothes for husband and child. "They washed clothes and bedding in wooden tubs with soap they made themselves," write Jordan and his colleagues, while "men did most of the heavy outdoor work."[2]

Jordan's list of tasks, like so many other conventional histories, con-fines a woman's existence to her role as servant to husband and home.[3] This account would lead students to believe that women rarely partici-pated in the economic exchange of goods and services in colonial and post-Revolutionary New England. Imagine, however, that our assump-tions about historical importance were different. Imagine that instead of commercial enterprise, our focus was the ordinary accounts of daily life. In this version of history, we might learn about the interdependent partnership of women and men engaged in the economic support of their families and communities. Added to the production of rum would be information about what Jean Roland Martin calls "reproductive functions"—a category that includes the major life-cycle activities that marked human existence as much in 1790 as in 2001: conception and birth, rearing children, managing families and households, caring for the sick, tending to the dying and dead.[4]

Laurel Thatcher Ulrich's Pulitzer Prize–winning biography, *A Mid-wife's Tale*, provides a glimpse of what such a history might look like.[5] Ulrich begins her story with the life of Martha Ballard, a midwife who lived in Hallowell, Maine, and kept a diary during the years 1785–1812. We learn from Ulrich's reconstruction that Martha Ballard did much more than deliver babies. In the course of less than one month, between August 3 and August 24, 1787, she

> performed four deliveries, answered one obstetrical false alarm, made sixteen medical calls, prepared three bodies for burial, dispensed pills to one neighbor, harvested and prepared herbs for another, and doctored her own husband's sore throat. In twentieth-century terms she was simultaneously a midwife, nurse, physician, mortician, pharmacist, and attentive wife. Furthermore, in the very act of recording her work, she became a keeper of vital records, a chronicler of the medical history of her town.[6]

Martha's story and others like it have traditionally not been told—neither in our present textbooks nor in the diaries and accounts of her contemporaries. Henry Sewall was Martha's neighbor in Hallowell, and his diary covers roughly the same period as hers. But Sewall's diary more closely parallels Winthrop Jordan's chronicle than Martha Ballard's entries. From Martha's diary, not Henry's, we learn that Martha traveled on eight occasions to the bedside of Henry's own wife, Tabitha, before she finally delivered. We rely on Martha, not Henry, to tell us of the complications that attended Tabitha's delivery and the fees Martha charged for her services. And, finally, only Martha's diary records how Tabitha Sewall participated actively in the economy of women by making and selling bonnets. Martha Ballard details many economic exchanges, often between and among women, of clothing, health care, food, and medicine—exchanges that never appear in Henry Sewall's account books or in Winthrop Jordan's description of colonial and early American economic life. Using traditional assumptions about historical significance, we could easily imagine a textbook sidebar on Martha Ballard. But if we were to employ different assumptions about historical significance, we could just as easily see a sidebar on rum.

Of course, not all historical preconceptions hinge on gender. But the recognition of how gender frames our understanding of history allows us to question previous reports of "sex differences" in historical achievement. From J. Carleton Bell's and D. P. McCollum's 1917 study of Texas schoolchildren ("boys were markedly superior to the girls in almost every class")[7] to Diane Ravitch and Chester Finn's 1987 report on the first National Assessment of Educational Progress in History and Literature,[8] boys are reported to be superior to girls in historical knowledge. This finding is reported matter-of-factly, without considering the possibility that such differences reflect a curriculum that pays little attention to the lives of women.

Assumptions about historical importance loom large whenever we write history or school curricula, and the writers of each have traditionally been men. The philosopher Nel Noddings[9] asks why students are more likely to know about Generals Pershing and Patton than about Emily Green Balch, the winner of the Nobel Peace Prize in 1946. According to Noddings, Balch's name "does not even appear in a major encyclopedia published in the fifties," whereas lengthy entries are devoted to the two generals.[10] She asks: Are those who wage war more worthy of comment than those who wage peace?

Although in recent years the history/social studies curriculum has become an area of increased scholarly attention, the issue of gender and students' historical understanding has received attention in only a few studies.[11] In schools, however, there have been several attempts to integrate more women's and social history into existing curricula.[12] Indeed, textbook adoption criteria in California and other major states require that social studies texts reflect an equal balance of male and female contributions.[13] Have any of these efforts changed children's images of the past? This is what we set out to explore.

METHOD

Our question was straightforward: How do boys and girls picture the past? In what ways do children project themselves into historical roles when those roles are gender-neutral? We selected three kinds of historical figures, each from a different century in American history—Pilgrims, Western Settlers, and Hippies—and constructed a short questionnaire.

Since this was an exploratory study, we did not set out with a list of formal hypotheses, in part because we could find no other work that looked explicitly at how schoolchildren depicted figures from the American past. But we were not without ideas about what we might find. Decades of research on children's drawing suggested that we could expect a "gendercentric" bias; that is, boys would tend to draw male figures, and girls female ones. Over forty years of clinical psychological research has shown that when children are provided with the nonspecific prompt to "draw a whole person," they overwhelmingly draw images that reflect their own gender.[14] Further, when children are asked to draw both male and female figures they typically draw the figure of their own sex first and provide more detail to that drawing.[15] Elizabeth Koppitz, one of the leading researchers on children's drawings, sees the charge to "draw a person" as an invitation for the child to draw a picture of the person the child knows best. "The person a child knows best is himself; his picture of a person becomes therefore a portrait of his inner self."[16]

In our questionnaire we did not ask children to draw a generic "person" but to draw figures typically portrayed as male in the media and the culture at large. Would students see our prompts as invitations to depict *themselves* in the roles of Pilgrims, Settlers, or Hippies (in which case we would see equal numbers of male and female drawings), or would our questionnaire elicit a set of cultural icons typically male in form?

Each of the questionnaires dealt with only one of these figures, and each had two parts. Part 1 asked children to "think of a Pilgrim" ("Western Settler," "Hippie") and to draw their depiction "in the box below." Part 2 asked children to first read and then illustrate a short, textbook-like passage about their historical figure. We tried to design passages that were gender-neutral in form and content; our sentences used plural pronouns and were about activities in which both men and women engaged (see Appendix).[17] One of our intentions in designing part 2 was to engage students' ideas about school history. We wondered whether the textbook prose would invoke a "school history framework" that would lead to more traditional depictions of historical figures, or whether the gender neutrality of the passage would lead students to draw both male and female figures. In contrast to part 1, the prompt in part 2 asked students to illustrate the passage by drawing multiple figures: "Pilgrims farming the land," "Western Settlers in a wagon," or "Hippies at a protest." Each child, then, had two opportunities to depict the past: at the beginning of the questionnaire and following a short, textbook-like passage at the end.

SAMPLE

We administered the questionnaires to fifth- and eighth-grade students. Seventy-three fifth graders were drawn from a suburban elementary school (K–6) located in a white, middle-class community in the Puget Sound area of Washington state. We administered the questionnaire to twenty-seven boys and forty-six girls in three fifth-grade classrooms. Our second site was a middle school in a similar white, middle-class district in the same area. In this school we gave the questionnaire to fifty-one boys and thirty-seven girls from four eighth-grade classrooms. In both schools we sampled all classrooms at each grade level. We administered the questionnaire in early October, before students had much exposure to the history/social studies curriculum for their grade level. Although we did not interview teachers about the material they had covered to this point, we do not believe that they had raised the issue of sex roles in history, nor was it a topic explicitly raised by the textbooks used in their classrooms.

PROCEDURE

We introduced ourselves to the children and explained that we were interested in how "kids like you think about the past." We assured them that our questionnaire was "not a drawing contest" and that each response was important to us. We also explained that not everyone would get the same form. We distributed the three versions of the questionnaire so that about one-third of the students in each class received the form for Pilgrims, Western Settlers, or Hippies, and students sitting next to each other did not receive the same form. The questionnaire took about twenty-five to thirty minutes to complete.

ANALYSIS

Before analyzing the data, we removed the name and sex from each questionnaire so that coding would be done without knowing whether the artist was a boy or girl. We then used thirty randomly selected questionnaires to create a coding scheme for determining the sex of the figures drawn by students. In abbreviated form, the coding scheme used the following guidelines: Male Pilgrims wore pants and/or a hat with an obvious brim or crown, female Pilgrims wore a dress or skirt, bonnet, and/or had long hair; male Settlers were distinguished by pants, broad-brimmed hat, boots, or spurs; female Settlers were again distinguished by a dress or skirt, bonnet, and long hair; male Hippies had facial hair, hair that stood on end rather than hanging, short hair, or no hair, and wore a belt and/or boots; female Hippies were distinguished by a dress or skirt, flowers in hair or on clothing, earrings, and/or feminine facial features, such as bow-shaped lips or exaggerated eyelashes. Figures that could not be distinguished by these features were coded as "ambiguous." Some drawings in part 1 were coded as "multiple figures" despite the questionnaire's directions to draw a single figure. In part 2, where students were instructed to draw multiple figures, drawings were coded as (a) all male, (b) all female, (c) ambiguous, or (d) including both sexes.[18]

RESULTS

Our first impression was of the vividness of students' imaginations and the variety in their drawings. Figure 5.1 shows some of the exemplary depictions of each historical figure. We separated the data by sex of student, grade level, and historical prompt. Boys' responses showed remarkable consistency; there were no significant differences for grade level or prompt. The data shown in Table 5.1 are collapsed across grade levels; they indicate that boys responded similarly to each of the three prompts in part 1. Overall, sixty-four of the seventy-six boys who completed this task drew male Pilgrims, male Settlers, or male Hippies; in

Figure 5.1. Exemplary drawings of Pilgrims, Settlers, and Hippies (two of each): A, Male and female Pilgrims; B, Female Pilgrim; C, Male Settler; D, Male Settler; E, Male Hippie; F, Female Hippie

TABLE 5.1
Sex of Figures Drawn by Boys (N = 76) in Part 1 (Single Figure)

Sex	PROMPT			
	Pilgrim	Settler	Hippie	Totals
Male	22 (92)	21 (81)	21 (81)	64 (84)
Female	0 (0)	0 (0)	1 (4)	1 (1)
Ambiguous	0 (0)	2 (8)	4 (15)	6 (8)
Multiple figures	2 (9)	3 (12)	0 (0)	5 (7)
Total	24 (100)	26 (100)	26 (100)	76 (100)

Note: Numbers in parentheses are percentages. Percentages may not total to 100 because of rounding.

other words, 84 percent of the boys in our sample depicted male figures. The one instance in which a boy drew a female figure came in response to the Hippie prompt. The remaining eleven boys (14 percent) drew either "ambiguous" figures, most often in response to the Hippie prompt (six figures, or 8 percent of the total), or pictures of multiple figures (five, or 7 percent).

Girls' responses were less straightforward. Although no significant effects were found for grade level, girls in both fifth and eighth grades responded differently from the boys to the three prompts (Table 5.2). In general, girls drew approximately equal numbers of female and male figures. Of the eighty girls who completed part 1, twenty-eight (35 percent) drew pictures of female Pilgrims, Settlers, or Hippies, while twenty-six (33 percent) drew their male counterparts. This pattern, however, was not consistent across the prompts. Girls drew female Pil-

TABLE 5.2
Sex of Figures Drawn by Girls (N = 80) in Part 1 (Single Figure)

Sex	PROMPT			
	Pilgrim	Settler	Hippie	Totals
Male	8 (28)	15 (65)	3 (11)	26 (33)
Female	13 (45)	3 (13)	12 (43)	28 (35)
Ambiguous	0 (0)	0 (0)	11 (39)	11 (14)
Multiple figures	8 (28)	5 (22)	2 (7)	15 (19)
Total	29 (100)	23 (100)	28 (100)	80 (100)

Note: Numbers in parentheses are percentages. Percentages may not total to 100 because of rounding.

grims and Hippies more often than female Western Settlers (see Table 5.2); responding to the Settler prompt, almost two-thirds of the girls drew single male figures (fifteen of twenty-three, or 65 percent), suggesting that these girls brought a different schema to bear when "picturing" each of these historical figures.[19]

We discovered another difference between boys' and girls' drawings. Twenty students disregarded the directions in part 1 to draw a single figure and drew multiple figures instead. As shown by the totals of multiple figures in Tables 5.1 and 5.2, girls were three times as likely to make this "mistake" as boys. If "Pilgrim," "Settler," or "Hippie" did not call to mind a picture of a single historical figure, what images did these words elicit? To answer this question, we analyzed the drawings of the five boys (7 percent) and fifteen girls (19 percent) who drew multiple figures (Table 5.3).

TABLE 5.3
Description of Multifigured Drawings in Response to Single-Figure Prompt, Part 1

SEX/GRADE OF ARTIST	PROMPT	DESCRIPTION OF PICTURE
Boy, grade 8	Pilgrim	Pilgrim man in foreground, stick-figure men in background
Boy, grade 8	Pilgrim	Stick figures of Pilgrim men, dancing in a ring
Boy, grade 8	Settler	Settler man and monster figure
Boy, grade 8	Settler	"Civil War," two men shooting at each other
Boy, grade 5	Settler	"Settler Kills Indian"
Girl, grade 5	Pilgrim	Pilgrim mother with baby
Girl, grade 5	Pilgrim	Pilgrim couple, man and woman
Girl, grade 5	Pilgrim	Woman Pilgrim in foreground, man in background on ship
Girl, grade 5	Settler	Settler couple, man and woman
Girl, grade 5	Settler	Family: mother, daughter, and son
Girl, grade 5	Settler	Male and female "cowboys"
Girl, grade 5	Settler	Settler with his daughter
Girl, grade 5	Hippie	Five Hippies, male and female
Girl, grade 5	Hippie	Male and female Hippies
Girl, grade 8	Pilgrim	Pilgrim family at Thanksgiving
Girl, grade 8	Pilgrim	Pilgrim couple and Indians at Thanksgiving
Girl, grade 8	Pilgrim	Pilgrim couple, man and woman
Girl, grade 8	Pilgrim	Pilgrim man, Indian woman
Girl, grade 8	Pilgrim	Pilgrim man, Indian woman
Girl, grade 8	Settler	Settler man, and other men in background driving wagon

Note: Quotation marks indicate the actual title given to the drawing by the student.

Thirteen of fifteen multiple-figure drawings by girls (87 percent) depicted men and women together, and twelve of the fifteen (80 percent) depicted images of couples or families (see Figure 5.2). For these twelve girls, a "Pilgrim," "Settler," or "Hippie" was represented not by a single figure, but by a family or social unit.

The "family image" was not the picture elicited from boys. Boys who drew multiple figures in part 1 were no more likely to envision a past inhabited by women than were the boys who drew single figures. All five of the boys who drew multiple figures drew men (Table 5.3), and in three of five cases the images contained violent overtones (see Figure 5.3). In other words, when boys drew multiple figures, their pictures more often showed men engaged in combat than in cooperation.[20]

Would a task that instructed students to draw *multiple* figures lead to a greater number of mixed-sex pictures of Pilgrims, Settlers, and Hippies? This question was addressed by examining the responses in part 2 of the questionnaire. We wondered how the students' responses in this section, in which they were asked to illustrate a gender-neutral passage about Pilgrims, Settlers, or Hippies, would compare with their responses in part 1, the depiction of a single figure.

Again, a majority of boys (57 percent, or thirty-four of the sixty boys who completed part 2) responded by drawing male figures (Table 5.4). Although this number is less than the 91 percent who drew male figures in part 1 (recall that boys' drawings of multiple figures showed only men), none of the boys' drawings in part 2 depicted women alone. In addition, the category showing the greatest increase was not "both male and female" but "ambiguous." Although the number of boys who included women in their drawings rose from one in part 1 (the single female Hippie) to seven in part 2, the number of ambiguous figures increased fourfold. Reasons for this rise, we speculated, might include one or both of the following: the constraints of the task left students with little time or motivation to complete a detailed drawing (there were many stick-figure drawings in part 2); or the scene students were asked to illustrate (Pilgrims farming, Settlers in a wagon, or Hippies at a protest) was not suited to close-up detail.

The data from girls, however, provided little support for either explanation. While sixteen fewer boys completed part 2 than part 1, only seven fewer girls failed to complete their illustrations of textbook passages, suggesting that the time allotted to complete the questionnaire was adequate. In addition, as Table 5.5 shows, the percentage of

Figure 5.2. Examples of girls' multifigured drawings in response to single-figure prompt, part 1: *A*, Multiple figures—woman and child; *B*, Multiple figures—male and female; *C*, Multiple figures—male and female

TITLE: Settler kills Indian

TITLE: Civil WAR

TITLE: Bigest feet in the west

Figure 5.3. Examples of boys' multifigured drawings in response to single-figure prompt, part 1: *A,* Multiple figures—male; *B,* Multiple figures—male; *C,* Multiple figures—male

TABLE 5.4
Sex of Figures Drawn by Boys (N = 60) in Part 2
("Textbook" Illustration)

Sex	PROMPT			
	Pilgrim	Settler	Hippie	Totals
Male	12 (67)	12 (67)	10 (42)	34 (57)
Female	0 (0)	0 (0)	0 (0)	0 (0)
Ambiguous	5 (28)	6 (33)	8 (33)	19 (32)
Both sexes	1 (6)	0 (0)	6 (25)	7 (12)
Total	18 (100)	18 (100)	24 (100)	60 (100)

Note: Numbers in parentheses are percentages. Percentages may not total to 100 because of rounding.

girls' responses coded as "ambiguous" did not increase significantly from part 1 to part 2; even in these "far-away" scenes, girls included sufficient detail to distinguish male from female figures. (Are girls simply more conscientious students and more detail-oriented? If this is the case, then why did 19 percent of the girls disregard the directions in part 1?)[21]

Additional differences emerged in girls' and boys' responses to part 2. Although the textbook passage elicited from girls a 10 percent increase in the number of drawings that included male and female figures, it also elicited a nearly equal increase (9.5 percent) in the number of drawings containing male figures alone. As with part 1, however, the girls responded differently to each of the three prompts. After reading the textbook passage, girls drew a male Pilgrim or Pilgrims more than twice as

TABLE 5.5
Sex of Figures Drawn By Girls (N = 73) in Part 2
("Textbook" Illustration)

Sex	PROMPT			
	Pilgrim	Settler	Hippie	Totals
Male	13 (59)	14 (58)	4 (15)	31 (42)
Female	3 (14)	3 (13)	1 (4)	7 (10)
Ambiguous	1 (5)	2 (8)	11 (41)	14 (19)
Both sexes	5 (23)	5 (21)	11 (41)	21 (29)
Total	22 (100)	24 (100)	27 (100)	73 (100)

Note: Numbers in parentheses are percentages. Percentages may not total to 100 because of rounding.

often as before (59 percent versus 28 percent), while the pattern of Settler drawings across parts 1 and 2 remained largely unchanged (Table 5.6).

This finding speaks not only to the differential responses to the three historical prompts but also to the effect that reading a textbook-like passage may have on girls' conceptions of history. Is there something about textbook-like prose, even when the form and content are gender-neutral, that makes girls imagine that the past was populated mostly by men? And why, we wondered, were girls' initial pictures of the past so greatly altered by reading a textbook passage on Pilgrims (or Hippies), yet minimally affected by a passage on Western Settlers?

These response patterns led us to reexamine our questionnaire for sex bias. Although each of the prompts in part 1 asked students simply to "draw a Pilgrim (Western Settler, Hippie)," the prompts in part 2 asked students to draw a picture of either "Pilgrims farming the land," "Settlers riding in a covered wagon," or "Hippies at a protest." In effect, these prompts might be construed as asking different questions: "Who is a Pilgrim?" in part 1 versus "Who is a *farming* Pilgrim?" in part 2; "Who is a Western Settler?" versus "Who rides in a Settler wagon?"; and "Who is a Hippie?" versus "Who participates in protests?" In girls' minds, it would seem, both men and women can be Pilgrims, but Pilgrim farmers are men. (We note the historical inaccuracy here, for, with the exception of large-scale agriculture, farming in colonial times was often done by women.) Girls also pictured most Settlers as men, along with a few Settler families, and these are the same people who ride in wagons. (However, it seems that women never drove the wagon.) In boys' responses (Table 5.7), the answers to these questions were largely the same, except

TABLE 5.6
Sex of Figures Drawn by Girls in Parts 1 and 2 (Percentage)

| Sex | PROMPT | | | | | |
| | Pilgrim | | Settler | | Hippie | |
	Part 1	Part 2	Part 1	Part 2	Part 1	Part 2
Male	28	59	65	58	11	15
Female	45	14	13	13	43	4
Ambiguous	0	5	0	8	39	41
Multiple figures, both sexes	28	23	22	21	7	41

Notes: Percentages may not total to 100 because of rounding.

TABLE 5.7
Sex of Figures Drawn by Boys in Parts 1 and 2 (Percentage)

| | PROMPT | | | | | |
| | Pilgrim | | Settler | | Hippie | |
Sex	Part 1	Part 2	Part 1	Part 2	Part 1	Part 2
Male	92	67	81	67	81	42
Female	0	0	0	0	4	0
Ambiguous	0	28	8	33	15	33
Multiple figures, both sexes	8	6	12	0	0	25

Note: Percentages may not total to 100 because of rounding.

in response to the Hippie prompt. For both the boys and the girls, men and women (and many ambiguous figures) participated in protests.

Of the three prompts, the Hippie prompt elicited the greatest variation. For both boys and girls, as shown in Tables 5.6 and 5.7, the pattern of Hippie drawings was different from the patterns of Pilgrim or Settler drawings. Responses to the Hippie prompt also came closest to what we would expect if children possessed a psychological propensity to picture someone of their own sex when drawing a historical figure (similar to their responses in the generic Draw-a-Person Test). Most boys drew male Hippies and most girls drew female Hippies in response to part 1. Additionally, when illustrating the textbook passage in part 2, boys and girls more frequently included both men and women in their drawings of Hippies than in their drawings of Pilgrims or Settlers. Although still not the majority, a sharp increase is seen in the percentage of pictures including both male and female figures in the Hippie column. (The large number of ambiguous figures overall can be seen as reflecting the androgynous nature of the "Hippie" prompt.)

One possible explanation of this finding is suggested by the variety we noted in the Hippie drawings, depictions that ranged from Vietnam War protesters and Woodstock attendees to grunge rock enthusiasts and shopping mall loiterers. These images suggest that, for some students, Hippies are not historical figures but people who inhabit the present. This finding also reflects the scant coverage accorded to Hippies in history texts intended for elementary and middle-school students. Ironically, the mixed-sex images of Hippies that emerged from these drawings are historically the most accurate, while the male-biased images of

Pilgrims and Western Settlers—the genuine "historical figures" to these students—are not.

DISCUSSION

This study was not an in-depth investigation of children's conceptions of history, and the form of the questionnaire we administered sheds only partial light on how children construed the task we set for them. However, given our purpose—to understand *something* about the historical images in children's minds—the questionnaires served a useful function. They acted as a kind of mirror for students' quick reactions to three historical prompts, perhaps even their mindless reactions, in the sense in which Ellen Langer uses the term—a response that requires little thinking.[22] The drawings revealed something of students' ordinary historical conceptions, as yet untouched by special units on "Great Pilgrim Women" or "Cowgirls of the Frontier."

Most striking about the 289 pictures we evaluated are the different response patterns for girls and boys. We had a hunch that we might find a same-sex bias, particularly in the single-figure drawings of part 1; girls, we thought, would more often draw female figures, and boys more male. We also believed that the gender-neutral passages in part 2 would lead students to conjure up images of both men and women. Our predictions turned out to be fairly accurate for girls, whose drawings overall depicted a past populated by men, women, and children. But even for girls, the largest percentage of drawings depicted male figures alone. Of the 153 drawings produced by girls in parts 1 and 2 combined, fifty-eight (or 38 percent) were of men alone; drawings of women alone numbered only thirty-five (23 percent) of the total. The remaining drawings depicted men and women together (thirty-four, or 22 percent) or ambiguous figures (twenty-five, or 16 percent).

We are concerned about girls' tendency, particularly when illustrating textbook-like passages, to depict a past inhabited by fewer women than men.[23] But we are equally concerned about boys' tendency to depict a past inhabited almost exclusively by men. Women are virtually invisible in these boys' pictures, whether they show Pilgrims, Settlers, or Hippies. Of the 136 drawings produced by boys, only eight (6 percent) contained female figures; seven of these (5 percent) depicted men and women together, and only one (less than 1 percent) depicted a woman alone. In contrast, boys drew male figures exclusively in 103 drawings (76 percent); the remaining twenty-five drawings (18 percent) were coded as ambiguous. If these patterns suggest that girls view the past with less than 20–20 vision, then boys are blind in one eye.

Is it only the past that boys see this way? What about the present? Perhaps the results of this investigation speak to a more generalized tendency among boys to draw males—irrespective of time period—unless explicitly prompted to do otherwise. Such a view, however, is unsupported by the work of Sandra Weber and Claudia Mitchell,[24] who examined over 600 drawings by schoolchildren, student teachers, and experienced teachers in response to the prompt "Draw a teacher." Nearly every one of these drawings, by male and female students alike, was of a woman. In response to critics who claimed that such findings were artifacts of the research prompt, Weber and Mitchell added new prompts such as "Draw your favorite teacher," "Draw an ideal teacher," or "Draw a class at work." Insofar as the depiction of the teacher was concerned, the results were consistent: "The typical teacher portrayed in the drawings . . . was a white woman pointing or expounding, standing in front of a blackboard or desk."[25] Just as the image of the present-day teacher is gender-coded, so are the historical images of Pilgrims and Settlers. Our findings, together with those of Weber and Mitchell, suggest that any psychological tendency to draw a picture of oneself is overridden by culturally coded prompts that tap into gender stereotypes. This would seem to hold true whether stereotypes are drawn from the past or from the present.

How might we bring balance to both girls' and boys' depictions of the past? One suggestion has been to increase the salience of women's contributions to history. We might, for example, celebrate Women's History Month and line classrooms with posters of famous American women— Lucretia Mott, Harriet Tubman, Susan B. Anthony, Elizabeth Cady Stanton, and Betty Friedan. We remain skeptical. The fact is that pictures of these five women *did* line the walls of one classroom we surveyed, and the patterns there were no different from those in the other classrooms.

Lining the classroom walls with pictures of prominent women can be a well-meaning attempt to balance a male-dominated history curriculum. Such posters have a counterpart in history and social studies textbooks, which in recent years have made enormous strides in integrating the contributions of important American women.[26] But it is problematic to conclude that textbooks now present a balanced view of the past because women occupy more space. As Barbara Light and her colleagues observed in their textbook analysis, short biographies and excerpts on women "commonly appear boxed off outside the main prose, reinforcing their consideration as asides or afterthoughts."[27] Likewise, the historian Linda Kerber suggests that women make it into the history survey course only "insofar as they help men do what men wish to do, whether it be settling the frontier or keeping the factories running; for shock value, as witches or prostitutes or women air service pilots in World War II; [or] in the politics of woman suffrage, which is understood to have ended in 1919."[28]

Gerda Lerner characterizes such changes as "contributory history," or the story of how women contributed to enterprises men already deemed important.[29] Contributory history is a tempting and cost-effective strategy for textbook editors because they have only to add new material to the existing narrative. Alongside the traditional picture of Ethan Allen and the Marquis de Lafayette, they add Deborah Sampson, who "disguised as a man . . . served well in the Continental army."[30] When the section on western settlement and exploration is revised, editors replace the traditional illustration of Lewis and Clark peering westward with one that places Sacajawea, their woman scout, between them. Next to Martin Luther King, they paste Rosa Parks.

Contributory history preserves the assumptions common to traditional textbooks. History remains the story of political and economic progress acted out on a public stage. It details the plight of great people and important deeds. But contributory history leaves unchallenged the terms "progress," "great," and "important," and the reasons why some spheres of human experience matter more than others. Contributory history rests on the notion that there is a single history instead of multiple "histories," many of which go untold because their content is viewed as insignificant or unimportant. Contributory history sends us to forage through the documentary record in search of a woman rum trader but never thinks to challenge why we narrate the story of rum.

Our focus on suggested changes in school curriculum might give the impression that we think historical images originate in the classroom. We believe they do—in part. But we also recognize that these images are influenced by many sources, not just those found in school.[31] Hollywood shapes our images of Western Settlers almost certainly more than the work of historians of the West;[32] our images of Pilgrims are rendered more by Thanksgiving lore than by the intellectual histories of Perry Miller. Our questionnaire asked children to conjure up images that they encounter not only in school, but in the media, in popular culture, in church, and at home. Given the depth of these images, hanging a classroom poster or rewriting an illustration's caption seems a weak response indeed.

What happens when deep cultural assumptions are confronted head-on? Mary K. T. Tetreault accepted this challenge and designed a course on women's history for eleventh graders.[33] She found that many students had trouble reconciling the sources they read with the "real history" they had learned in previous grades. Confronted by texts that contradicted their preconceptions, these students complained that women's history was "opinioney" and subjective. The course "called into question what [students] thought was true. It created cognitive dissonance for them. . . . It confused them about what's the right way and it went against what they had always seen and heard about the proper roles and spheres of society."[34]

When we ask students to consider why one group's story is told and another's is left out, we pose for them a new set of cognitive, epistemological and emotional challenges. Decisions of inclusion and exclusion, students believe, have already been made by the textbooks. But how do textbooks decide what is important, which stories to narrate and which to silence? Traditionally, our attempts to get students to ask these questions take the form of providing them with alternative accounts, competing narratives, or even textbooks in which a narrative is presented and then commented upon by historians who represent different perspectives. Each of these activities can be a useful gesture toward getting students to see that the past comprises many stories and that different individuals have chosen to form these stories into narratives that look different, sound different, and feel different in their underlying tropes. But even these activities leave students distant from the "real action," the intellectual work of deciding how to weigh competing emphases. In reading others' work, students learn about the choices others have made, but they remain epistemological outsiders, blind to the hard choices that characterize the formation of narrative.

It is not enough to expose students to alternative visions of the past, already digested and interpreted by others. The only way we can come to understand the past's multiplicity is by the direct experience of having to tell it, of having to sort through the welter of the past's conflicting visions and produce a story written by our own hand. We have in mind here a vision of history classrooms where students learn the subject by rewriting it. Students come to develop a sensitivity to multiple stories because they have wrestled with them, not as arbiters of others' accounts but as authors of their own. This vision of history instruction

transforms a school subject from a fixed story, with questions of significance and importance sewn up, to an array of stories that invites students to consider the fullness of human experience. By questioning the
past, students illuminate their present. What activities—past and present—are worthy of attention? Whose stories and what issues are
included or left out? Who gets to decide?

Indeed, we ourselves faced these questions in selecting the three historical prompts for our questionnaire. Pilgrims and Settlers typically
receive abundant coverage in American history textbooks, while Hippies often go unmentioned. Consider, for example, the treatment of the
Pilgrims in Todd and Curti's *Rise of the American Nation*, one of the
best-selling American history textbooks.[35] From this book we learn
what the Pilgrims believed; what ordinary families ate; the kinds of
lamps they used to illuminate their houses (from "Betty Lamps" to rush-
lights); the clothing they wore; and the beliefs about authority, the
world to come, and the place of work in everyday existence that framed
the Pilgrims' conceptual universe. Indeed, for most schoolchildren the
study of Pilgrims is one of the few occasions when they learn the social
history of an era—the mores, values, habits, and world views of ordinary
people from a different time period.

In the same book that tells us so much about Pilgrims, the group of
people known as Hippies are nowhere to be found. Despite an entire
chapter on the events of the 1960s (Unit 13, "Into a New Era"), we
learn about the youth movement of that decade only in the context of
antiwar demonstrations that "disrupted the president's speeches at
public ceremonies."[36] What remains hidden from children is the
notion that these "disruptions" were nested within larger shifts in attitudes toward authority that wrought profound changes in practically
every sphere of social life, from flouting drug laws to rebellion against
conventional sexual ethics (overturning a "Puritan" notion of "living in
sin" and introducing the public embrace of "free love"); from an exploration of Eastern religious philosophies to a looser definition of appropriate dress and hair style; from attitudes about the environment
guided more by Native American beliefs than Judeo-Christian ones to
new ideas about our "daily bread"—whether in its vegetarian, organic,
or macrobiotic form. Indeed, we could make the case that Hippies
changed the fabric of American social life in ways no less profound than
the folkways of the Pilgrims. To learn about these changes, however,
today's students would have to search the monographic literature of
historians like Todd Gitlin, Staughton Lynd, Barbara Epstein, and

Maurice Isserman.[37] The histories closest at hand—students' textbooks—leave only blank spaces.

This study raises as many questions as it addresses. A follow-up study
would have us return to these same classrooms, drawings in hand, and
ask students to discuss what they drew and why. In this way we might
be able to identify the specific assumptions present in students' reasoning. It would also be illuminating to ask teachers to engage in a parallel
drawing task, for the relationship between teacher attitudes and student
understanding is far from evident. Questionnaire studies necessarily
sacrifice detail in favor of a broad sampling scheme. Further research—
research that focuses on the meanings individual students impute to
these drawings—would add texture and clarity to the questions we have
begun to ask.

CONCLUSION

We have used a relatively simple research task to raise questions about
what the typical history curriculum is and what it could be. But pictures,
even those drawn by schoolchildren, provide a window to perceptions
that sometimes dodge verbal explanation. We believe this is what
Picasso meant when he wrote that art is a lie that tells the truth about
reality. If there is any point to our work, it is this: In girls' minds, women
in history are blurry figures; in boys' minds, they are virtually invisible.
On historical grounds, this finding constitutes a serious misrepresenta-
tion. On social grounds, it perpetuates alarming and dysfunctional attitudes. On educational grounds, it poses, we hope, a challenge.

APPENDIX: TEXTBOOK-LIKE PASSAGES
USED IN THE QUESTIONNAIRE, PART 2

Pilgrims

When the Pilgrims came to Plymouth they suffered from cold weather, lack of food,
and sickness. They also had a hard time growing crops to eat. The Indians taught
the Pilgrims how to fertilize the soil by planting a fish in the ground with corn seeds.
They also taught the Pilgrims to watch their fields for a few nights to make sure that
wolves and other wild animals did not dig up the fish.

   Please draw a picture of the Pilgrims farming the land: [a box follows].

Western Settlers

In 1844 James K. Polk was elected president. He promised to expand the territory
of the United States from the Atlantic Ocean to the Pacific Ocean. Many people

packed up their belongings and moved west in covered wagons. These Western Settlers faced many difficulties in their journey. They feared wild animals, rough terrain, and harsh weather. There was little shade and often these settlers did not have much food.

Please draw a picture of Settlers riding in a covered wagon: [a box follows].

Hippies

In the 1960s, the United States entered a war in a country called Vietnam. Some Americans supported the war but others felt it was senseless and wrong. They protested against the war at universities and in front of the White House. These protesters were often called Hippies. They carried signs against the war and banners with the peace symbol on it. Many of these hippies wore scruffy clothes and headbands.

Please draw a picture of the Hippies at a protest: [a box follows].

NOTES

This essay, which was originally co-authored with Janice E. Fournier, appeared in the *American Journal of Education* 105 (1997), © 1997 by The University of Chicago. All rights reserved. I thank Janice for agreeing to let me update it for this volume. Thanks also go to readers who commented on earlier drafts: N. L. Gage, Miriam Hirschstein, Peter Seixas, and Suzanne Wilson. Phil Jackson, editor of the *American Journal of Education*, also helped us to sharpen our thinking. Finally a word of thanks goes to these aspiring artists and their teachers, without whom this study could not have been completed.

1. Winthrop D. Jordan, Miriam Greenblatt, and John S. Bowes, *The Americans: The History of a People and a Nation* (Evanston, Ill., 1985).

2. Ibid., 69.

3. See the exhaustive analysis of gender roles in history textbooks by Mary K. T. Tetreault in "Integrating Women's History: The Case of United States History High School Textbooks," *History Teacher* 19 (1986), 210–61.

4. Jean Roland Martin, *Reclaiming a Conversation: The Ideal of the Educated Woman* (New Haven, 1985).

5. Laurel Thatcher Ulrich, *A Midwife's Tale: The Life of Martha Ballard, Based on Her Diary, 1785–1812* (New York, 1990).

6. Ibid., 40.

7. J. Carleton Bell and David McCollum, "A Study of the Attainments of Pupils in United States History," *Journal of Educational Psychology* 8 (1917), 257–74. See similar comments by the father of modern achievement testing, Edward L. Thorndike, *Educational Psychology—Briefer Course* (New York, 1923), 274.

8. Diane Ravitch and Chester Finn, Jr., *What Do Our 17-Year-Olds Know? A Report on the First National Assessment of History and Literature* (New York, 1987).

9. Nel Noddings, "Social Studies and Feminism," *Theory and Research in Social Education* 20 (1992), 230–41.

10. Ibid., 231.

11. See, for example, Donna Alvermann and Michelle Commeyras, "Inviting Multiple Perspectives: Creating Opportunities for Student Talk About Gender Inequalities in Text," *Journal of Reading* 37 (1994), 38–42; Terrie Epstein, "Sometimes a Shining Moment: High School Students' Creations of the Arts in Historical Context," paper presented at the annual meeting of the American Educational Research Association, Atlanta, April 1993; Marcy Gabella, "The Art(s) of Historical Sense: An Inquiry Into Form and Understanding," *Journal of Curriculum Studies* 27 (1995), 139–63.

12. See B. Light, P. Stanton, and P. Bourne, "Sex Equity Content in History Textbooks," *History and Social Studies Teacher* 25 (1989), 18–20; Tetreault, "Integrating Women's History," 210–61.

13. "Do Textbooks Shortchange Girls?" *Social Studies Review* (1992), 3–5.

14. See, for example, Karen Machover, *Personality Projection in the Drawing of the Human Figure* (Springfield, Ill. 1949); Elizabeth Koppitz, *Psychological Evaluation of Human Figure Drawings by Middle School Pupils* (New York, 1968); M. Richey, "Qualitative Superiority of the 'Self' Figure in Children's Drawings," *Journal of Clinical Psychology* 21 (1965), 59–61.

15. Richey, "Superiority of the 'Self' Figure," 59–61.

16. Koppitz, *Human Figure Drawings*, 5.

17. In composing textbook passages, we tried to stick to the style of existing elementary school textbooks. We looked to these books for guidance: T. Helmus, V. Arnsdorf, E. Toppin, and N. Pounds, *The World and Its People: The United States and Its Neighbors* (Morristown, N.J., 1982); S. Klein, *Scholastic Social Studies: Our Country's History* (New York, 1981); J. Ralph Randolph and James W. Pohl, *People of America: They Came from Many Lands* (Austin, Tex., 1973).

18. We tested the interrater reliability of our coding scheme using approximately 20 percent of the questionnaires, which yielded a high reliability, Cohen's *Kappa* = .91, p < .001.

19. A chi-square analysis showed that the differences in these data by historical prompt were statistically significant, χ^2 (6, N = 80) = 40.1, p < .001.

20. These findings are similar to those of K. K. McNiff, "Sex Differences in Children's Art" (Ph.D. diss., Boston University, 1981).

21. To further check our analysis, we analyzed students' responses to parts 1 and 2 of the questionnaire using a repeated-measures analysis of variance, examining boys' and girls' responses to both parts. (This entailed recording students' drawings using a binary female/nonfemale coding system in which ambiguous drawings—typically stick figures—were coded as "nonfemale.") This ANOVA yielded a significant main effect for sex, F(1,130) = 12.71, p < .0005, and a significant sex × questionnaire part (part 1 versus part 2) interaction, F(1,130) = 4.95, p < .05, further showing that the difference in prompts from part 1 to part 2 had relatively little effect on boys and more so on girls.

22. Ellen Langer, *Mindfulness* (Reading, Mass., 1989).

23. See similar findings in a British context by Fiona Terry, "Women's History and Children's Perceptions of Gender," *Teaching History* 17 (1988), 20–24.

24. Sandra Weber and Claudia Mitchell, *That's Funny, You Don't Look Like a Teacher* (London, 1995).

25. Ibid., 28.

26. Tetreault, "Integrating Women's History."

27. Light, Stanton, and Bourne, "Sex Equity Content," 19.

28. Linda K. Kerber, " 'Opinionative Assurance': The Challenge of Women's History," *Magazine of History* 2 (1989), 30–34 (quotation from p. 31).

29. Gerda Lerner, "Placing Women in History: Definitions and Challenges," *Feminist Studies* 3 (1975), 5–14.

30. This quotation is from one of the market leaders in U.S. history textbooks (Harcourt Brace & Jovanovich), Lewis Paul Todd and Merle Curti, *Rise of the American Nation* (Orlando, Fla., 1982), 131.

31. See, for example, the work of Michael Frisch, "American History and the Structure of Collective Memory: A Modest Exercise in Empirical Iconography," *Journal of American History* 75 (1989), 1130–55; David Lowenthal, *The Past Is a Foreign Country* (Cambridge, England, 1985); George Lipsitz, *Time Passages: Collective Memory and American Popular Culture* (Minneapolis, 1993); David Thelan, "Memory and American History," *Journal of American History* 75 (1989), 1117–29; Vivian Sobchack, *The Persistence of History: Cinema, Television, and the Modern Event* (New York, 1996). See, as well, the series of articles assembled by James Wertsch in the *Journal of Narrative and Life History* 4, no. 4 (1994), as well as those assembled by Robert Farr in a special issue of *Culture and Psychology* 4, no. 3 (September 1998), "One Hundred Years of Collective and Social Representations."

32. See the boldly original work of Peter Seixas, who contrasted adolescents' responses to *The Searchers* and *Dances with Wolves*. Peter Seixas, "Popular Film and Young People's Understanding of the History of Native American–White Relations," *History Teacher* 26 (1993), 351–69.

33. Mary K. T. Tetreault, "It's So Opinioney," *Journal of Education* 168 (1986), 78–95.

34. Ibid., 81–82.

35. Todd and Curti, *Rise of the American Nation*.

36. Ibid., 762.

37. Todd Gitlin, *The Sixties: Years of Hope, Days of Rage* (New York, 1981); Staughton Lynd, *Intellectual Origins of American Radicalism* (New York, 1968); Barbara Epstein, *Political Protest and Cultural Revolution: Nonviolent Direct Action in the 1970s and 1980s* (Berkeley, 1993); Maurice Isserman, *If I Had a Hammer: Death of the Old Left and the Birth of the New Left* (New York, 1987).

CHALLENGES FOR
THE TEACHER

6

Peering at History Through Different Lenses

The Role of Disciplinary Perspectives in Teaching History

With Suzanne M. Wilson

Four novice teachers sit down to collaborate on planning a unit on the Great Depression. We join them in the middle of their discussion:

Jane: We really have to convey to the kids that the Depression wasn't just 1929 and the stock market crash. It had a profound impact on the lives of all Americans. Let's have them read parts of *The Grapes of Wrath*, maybe even look at some of Lange's photographs of migrant workers.

Cathy: Reading Steinbeck is great! If they don't understand the impact of the land—you know, the dust storms and the droughts—they'll miss the main point.

Bill: The main point? Now wait just a second. The economic and political issues of the thirties were just as important, if not more so, than the Dust Bowl. The stock market crash, buying on margin, FDR's economic reforms—how can you even think about teaching the Depression without emphasizing capitalism?

Fred: Sorry, folks, but you're all missing the point. How does this stuff relate to the lives of the kids? What difference does the Depression make if the kids can't see how it affected their lives? Relevance—that's the key!

Cathy, Bill, Jane, and Fred[1] are four new teachers who graduated from the same teacher education program, from which they received a master's degree in education and secondary school teaching certificates in social studies. Today, all teach social studies at different high schools in the San Francisco Bay area. Although it is unlikely that they will ever teach together on the same faculty, it is not inconceivable that they will participate in planning conversations with their colleagues similar to the one above.

This fictionalized conversation highlights the fact that these teachers think differently—very differently—about teaching history. Given their academic backgrounds, this comes as no surprise. Cathy holds a B.A. in anthropology with an emphasis in archeology. Fred majored in international relations and political science. Bill has a B.A. in American Studies. Of the four, only Jane holds a bachelor's degree in American history.

Their backgrounds are not atypical. As a group, social studies teachers are recruited from the many disciplines that make up the humanities and social sciences. In addition to teaching standard courses in American and European history, social studies teachers are called on to teach anything from anthropology and economics to sex education and family living. Once they receive their teaching credentials, these teachers may be asked to teach any course in the social studies curriculum. But what happens, exactly, when an anthropology major sets out to teach American history? Or a European history major begins teaching sociology? How prepared are our four novices to teach the assortment of courses housed under the rubric of social studies?

Suzanne Wilson and I interviewed and observed a half-dozen novice social studies teachers, among them the four who serve as the illustrative examples for this chapter. As we watched these people learn to teach, it became apparent to us early on that their disciplinary backgrounds wielded a strong—and often decisive—influence on their instructional decision making.[2] Our discussion here focuses on the influence of disciplinary perspectives on the teaching of American history. Two factors guided our selection of American history. First, it is the mainstay of many social studies departments, and in most states its teaching is mandated by law. Second, three of our four teachers taught classes in American history during their internships or first year on the job. Only Cathy, the anthropology major, had yet to teach a history course, and even for her the prospect of doing so was not far off.

Several issues arise when one reflects on how budding anthropologists, historians, and political scientists, fresh from their undergraduate and teacher training, think about history. We will explore those issues here, and also discuss some of the differences in teaching styles we observed while watching our four novices in their respective classrooms. Finally, we discuss some of the implications of our observations for teacher education and research on teaching.

CONCEPTIONS OF HISTORY

We have organized our discussion of the differences in the conceptions of history held by Cathy, Fred, Jane, and Bill along some of the dimensions that figure prominently in the teaching of history. These dimensions include the role of factual knowledge, the place of interpretation, the significance of chronology and continuity, and the meaning of causation. We discuss each of these dimensions in turn.

The Role of Fact

For Fred, the political scientist, history and fact were synonymous:

> I think knowing history is knowing . . . the facts, all the dates. Knowing all the terms, knowing when the conference in Vienna was held or what were the terms of the agreement in World War II.

Fred admitted being "no fan of history": He preferred international relations and political science because he saw these disciplines as more "general" and "thematic" than history. In Fred's mind history dealt only with the particular: "If I were in history, I would know a lot more specifics."

Bill, an American Studies major, spoke of facts as the basis of history. He drew an analogy to a "building," a "historical edifice" built on a foundation of factual information. The building's frame, however, consisted of alternative interpretations of those specifics, "alternative ways of looking" at facts. Bill was also quick to note that many facts were missing from traditional history, and he distinguished between textbook history (or what he called "elitist history") and the history of common people. Aware that much of historical writing has focused on the story of great white men, Bill was careful to acknowledge that history is also about the lives and experiences of other cultural, religious, social, and ethnic groups.

For Fred, history is fact; for Bill, history is greater than fact. Although their beliefs about history differed, Fred and Bill were of like mind when it came to facts: They were bad. Both teachers tried to dispense with facts quickly in their classrooms, shifting the spotlight from the specifics and highlighting the interpretation of those specifics. At one point, Bill explained what some teachers did when they taught about the legislation creating the National Recovery Administration (NRA) and the Agricultural Adjustment Administration (AAA), the "alphabet soup" of the New Deal:

> I have this conception that the reason why kids hate U.S. history is because teachers make them learn stuff like facts. They give them a test and they give them ten sets of letters and say, "Explain what the letters stand for and the importance of each." I think kids just go, "Blah! None of this is important!" And they are right because the facts aren't important!

Jane, our only history major, treated facts more kindly. For her, facts formed the narrative of history, the story of the past:

> History is not a stagnant set of lists of facts, the great unpopular characterization. History is an unfolding of events and people and motivation and twists and turns. It has a great deal of texture, and it *lives*.

For Jane, history forms a rich "tapestry" of classic questions and themes, great men and women, geography and natural disasters. Moreover, history is bound up with context: "As a historian, I'm trained to think of things historically as contextual. . . . I see things, I look back in the past, I see what the roots are." Facts, to Jane, are part of history, woven together by themes and questions, and, most important, embedded in a context that lends meaning and perspective.

Interpretation and Evidence

Our teachers also differed in their understanding of interpretation and the role of evidence in formulating interpretations. For Cathy, the anthropology major, interpretation and evidence were fused; understanding and interpreting the past involved, above all, a search for archeological evidence. This entailed the excavation, dating, and piecing together of artifacts:

> I like finding the objects that have been buried. . . . I like dealing with the hidden side of people. If you study someone nowadays, you have to interact with them. Sure, they have artifacts, but you are focusing on what these people are doing now, how they are interacting now. You are more involved in the present day. . . . I like what happened before.

What "happened before" is not to be found in a book. Rather, for Cathy, the past can be unearthed, touched, held in her hand. When

Cathy taught her ninth graders about interpretation, she tried to get them to stick close to the evidence, for she believed that hypotheses were most productive when they focused on things that could be known with certainty. Theories and interpretations that strayed far from the available physical evidence baffled her.

Cathy's notion of interpretation stands in stark contrast to Jane's. For Jane, interpretation went far beyond the sum of the available evidence. Interpretation was bound up with historiography, the processes and modes of inquiry of historians: "The making of history, the task of being a historian, involves very clear thinking about argument and logic, about evidence, about how to split hairs sensibly." She described historiography as analysis and synthesis:

> History is analytical in the sense that you go and break things down. It's synthetic when you engage in the process of writing history. You take things apart and then you put them back together. You try to look for connections. You look for specifics, gather evidence, make general hypotheses. You go through all those steps in a sort of scientific spirit.

Interpretation for Jane revolved around the "classic questions in history," questions that wove factual information into a complex and rich story. History was narrative and interpretation. It represented the products of the past as well as the processes of the historians engaged in reconstructing it.

Fred also recognized the importance of interpretation in social science, but for him interpretation was the purview of political scientists, not historians:

> I think history is the basic facts of what happened. What *did* happen. You don't ask how it happened. You just ask, "What are the events?" History is great as background material. Political science is different because it may need history but it takes history much further. It takes history and sees what kinds of causes were behind the event, not just the facts.

Interpretation in political science often focuses on questions of politics and economics; hence, Fred's interpretive repertoire was limited to interpretations concerning these dimensions of history. Bill, too, knew a lot about political and economic interpretations, and when he spoke about interpretation his explanations were sprinkled with terms like "the Left" and "the Right." However, he placed interpretation within the realm of the historian and acknowledged that other interpretations, divergent from his own, were possible. For example, he recognized the importance of social questions and readily admitted that he knew little about them. Because Bill recognized his blind spots, he used his preparation time to learn more about alternative interpretations, especially ones that incorporated aspects of social history.

Chronology and Continuity

These four teachers also differed in the emphasis they placed on chronology and continuity. For Cathy, history *was* chronology. When asked how she would present her ninth-grade world studies curriculum from a historical perspective, she remarked, "The historian would start with that country when it was just a little kid and how it has grown. It would be a *time thing*." Lacking knowledge of historical context, Cathy was often unable to see beyond the parade of dates and events in her textbook to catch a glimpse of the story of history, of individuals acting and shaping the course of their affairs. When teaching about China, for instance, she felt like a slave driver mercilessly pushing her students through twenty pages in the textbook on the Chinese dynasties: "The kids, you know, fight their way through it, so I have to approach it carefully, I have to set up some sort of balance doing something interesting before—some of them think that [history] is the driest part of the chapter." Viewing history, largely, as an endless string of events, often discrete and bearing little on contemporary society, Cathy could see in it little continuity or change.

Bill and Jane had richer conceptions of chronology. For these teachers, chronology and continuity were interwoven. Chronology was more than discrete dates—dates were held together by trends and themes, patterns and perspectives. While Bill and Jane could recount the story of a historical period, making reference to important people, dates, and events, chronology was not the only factor that structured their explanations. Rather, each teacher possessed a rich set of explanatory themes and concepts on which they drew to make sense of the past. For Bill, themes were largely political and economic. When talking about the connections between the New Deal and other periods in American history, for example, he spoke of the development of laissez-faire capitalism and the slow transition from an agrarian to an industrial economy. He drew connections to Lyndon Johnson's Great Society in the 1960s and the Reagan administration. Jane, whose interests lay more in the social and artistic aspects of the past, focused on cultural trends. When asked to explain what she knew of the Depression era, Jane turned first to a set of slides, each depicting a piece of artwork, a painting, or a photograph. Using these slides, she tracked changes in the national mind-set, showing how art mirrors political and social trends such as the changing role of women or the continued oppression of minorities. She spoke of chronology thus:

> I see history as a story unfolding that is important in your acquisition of a sense of yourself and your place in time, your place in history. A sense of chronology unfolding without any terrifically measured gait. But a wonderful sort of framework for seeing yourself in the universe and seeing things in the past.

Note that Jane does not equate chronology with time (it does not have the "measured gait" of years that underlies Cathy's simpler conception of chronology). Chronology, for both Jane and Bill, underlies continuity—the way in which the present connects to the past and moves, in Jane's words, "forward into the future."

CAUSATION

"For the historian there is no difference between discovering what happened and discovering why it happened," Robin Collingwood once remarked.[3] The question of cause lies at the heart of historical inquiry, and it figured prominently in the classrooms of our four teachers, but the question of cause took on drastically different meanings depending on who was behind the lectern. For instance, with Cathy at the helm, cause was not something to be endlessly pondered over in some kind of pageant of conflicting interpretations. Cause could be determined authoritatively by probing the interrelationships among the land, the climate, and human development. In the following overview of a unit she taught on Japan, Cathy sounds like an environmental determinist, awarding geography the leading role in shaping human affairs:

> We started out with geography, looked at the geography of Japan, where it was located, what the climate was. What the geology of the region was like and from that we went on, how does [geology and geography] influence the people who live there. Well, there is a problem with not enough land, a lot of people on a small island, how does that affect the way they lead their life? It affects their livelihood; they don't have enough natural resources, so what do they do about it? They go and trade with other countries. How much do they trade? Well, they're one of the nations leading in trade with the U.S., for example. Why's that? Because of the climate and geography.

Cathy's understanding of human affairs bears the stamp of her undergraduate training in physical anthropology and archeology. Her

favorite classes all dealt with the land: field courses in which she exca-
vated, plotted, and dated artifacts; museum courses in which she
learned how to display objects that had been unearthed; and courses in
ecological anthropology that focused her attention on the place of
Homo sapiens in a complex ecosystem. Cathy's understanding of social
life was also influenced by the type of training she *didn't* have: She had
no courses in economics or political science and but a single course,
Ancient Egypt, in history. Because she received little training in the
"fuzzier" social sciences, Cathy's notions of causation in the social
sphere were not marked by the strings of qualifications that characterize the explanations of, say, the interpretive historian. Teaching about
Japan, Cathy lacked the historical knowledge of Japanese culture and
history that might have tempered her "not enough natural resources,
therefore . . ." account of Japanese modernization. Largely unfamiliar
with issues of historical context, Cathy offered explanations of change
studded with generic ideas lifted from anthropology and applied
directly to specific countries. When she thought of history, she
thought only of chronology, or, as she put it, a "time thing." History
as story, as a narrative of human agents who acted on motives and passions and so influenced the course of human events, was not part of
Cathy's intellectual or instructional repertoire.

Jane's and Bill's conceptions of causation differed radically from
Cathy's. When asked to discuss the causes of the Depression, Bill
responded, "Well, of course, there is never just one cause," and went on
to list the myriad events that contributed to the financial panic of 1929.
Like Bill, Jane believed that the period was too complicated to be
accounted for by a single event like the stock market crash, or even by
a string of independent events: "History is not a linear progression. A
great white man making decisions bang, bang, bang. There are all kinds
of quirks and a rich narrative that can emerge." Causation to Jane and
Bill was a "messy" issue. Single events occur for many reasons, and these
reasons are not all discovered by digging up earth. Some causal explanations rely on theories of human motivation and psychology; others
draw on sociological and economic theories; still others make use of
wooly constructs like the "American mind-set." For Bill and Jane, cause
extended far beyond famines and droughts. Causation became a problem to be pondered, studied, argued, and advocated, but never to be
known with certainty.

HISTORY ENACTED

History carried different meanings and functioned in different ways in the classrooms of our four teachers. In Cathy's social studies classroom, history was most frequently distinguished by its absence. The countries she presented to her ninth graders seemed to exist in a temporal vacuum, decontextualized in relation to the past and responding lockstep to a generic set of geographical and geological imperatives. The generic, when applied to a specific case, is bound to be only partly correct—and in places will almost certainly be *incorrect*. Cathy's lack of contextual knowledge often prevented her from detecting inaccuracies, as was the case with a unit she taught on China.

At the beginning of the unit, Cathy asked her students to generate a list of the problems that a country would face as a result of overpopulation. Soon the blackboard was covered with a list ranging from a lack of food to a shortage of housing. When one student suggested that overpopulation would impair domestic transportation, another student raised her hand and asked why. Cathy turned to her students and asked rhetorically, "Will the government spend money on roads if people are dying from starvation?" Unencumbered by knowledge of China's pursuit of nuclear weapons development amid abject poverty, and unaware, say, of the $200 million anniversary celebration of the Marxist coup in Ethiopia, held while a famine of ghastly proportions enveloped that country, Cathy could portray governments as institutions that always acted in the best interests of their citizens.

Although history was not absent from Fred's U.S. history class, its richness and complexity were uncelebrated. Each period of Fred's class started with a lively discussion of the day's headlines. Almost reluctantly, he stopped this conversation after 20 minutes to begin the day's main activities. During class, his comments were peppered with concepts drawn from political science. Political and economic interpretations were showcased, factual information deemphasized, and social and cultural dimensions of history rarely mentioned. During a two-week unit on the Industrial Revolution, Fred dwelled on changes in the American economic system, especially the transition from cottage industries to factories. Not surprisingly, he also discussed the Robber Barons and their financial empires—"monopoly," "trusts," and "laissez-faire" were frequently heard. The social changes that paralleled the financial and industrial shifts went unmentioned.

In Fred's hands, the Industrial Revolution became representative of all revolutions, political and economic, and Fred drew sweeping comparisons across centuries by linking the American and French revolutions to the Civil War and to contemporary upheavals in Central America. Lacking knowledge of the contextual factors that make these events more different than similar, Fred presented *all* revolutions as close cousins. Possessing neither a wide knowledge of history nor an appreciation for context, Fred, like Cathy, was mostly blind to the inaccuracies he presented.

On the surface, Bill's U.S. history class looked much like Fred's. Not only did his classes begin with a discussion of current events, but his lectures also contained numerous references to political and economic history. On closer inspection, though, major differences emerged. During a unit on the Depression and the New Deal, Bill delivered a series of mini-lectures, as most history teachers do. However, the lectures were supplemented with alternative activities. During one period, students worked in small groups on an activity entitled "You Are the President." Presented with a series of problems, among them unemployment, bank failures, malnutrition, and farm foreclosures, students generated solutions and possible courses of action. Bill used this activity to foreshadow a lecture on the problems Franklin Roosevelt faced and the legislation proposed to deal with those problems. On another day, Bill used pictures taken by Farm Security Administration photographers to spark a discussion on the plight of the farmers. In another class, he xeroxed portions of *The Grapes of Wrath* and had students read them aloud. By presenting his students with social and cultural perspectives, Bill sought to balance his own strengths in political and economic history.

Jane used similar instructional strategies in her classroom, but rather than start each class with a discussion of current events, she grabbed her students' attention by turning off the lights and projecting a series of slides. She introduced a unit on the Roaring Twenties with slides of flappers, musicians, mansions like Gatsby's, California gold diggers, Model T's, and Dust Bowl farmers. She played a jazz tape and gave a short lecture on the cultural origins of jazz.

Jazz, she explained, melded blues and ragtime, and to convey this, she had her students listen to selections of each. To cap the lesson, Jane replayed the jazz tape and asked her students to identify points where they could hear either of the two earlier musical traditions. The following day, she used this musical metaphor to frame her explanation of the 1920s—the "Jazz Age." At one extreme, she explained, were the "flappers and their fellas," buying on credit and dancing the Charleston. At the other were oppressed blacks, impoverished farmers, and exploited immigrants. After this two-day introduction, Jane presented a unit that included lectures on buying on margin, readings from *The Great Gatsby* and *The Grapes of Wrath*, and a presentation of slides of the Dust Bowl. Students learned about social, cultural, political, and economic issues. They read primary and secondary source materials, studied photographs, analyzed graphs, and engaged in debate. After structuring the unit with the jazz metaphor, Jane filled individual periods with references to people, places, events. Through pictures, music, art, and dance, she breathed life into the facts of history. In her classroom the past was a drama enacted rather than a script learned by rote. Facts were not just told but sung, witnessed, and experienced.

THE INFLUENCE OF DISCIPLINARY PERSPECTIVES

The contrasts we have drawn among these four teachers suggest some ways in which their undergraduate training influenced the process and content of their instruction. For them, learning to teach involved developing a philosophy that embraced their goals for instruction as well as their strategies of instruction, but this meant learning about subject matter as well as about pedagogy. Cathy knew anthropology, but she had to teach ninth-grade "social studies," an amalgam, as her textbook put it, of "seven distinct social sciences."[4] Fred knew political science but had to teach American history, Asian history, and introductory algebra. Jane's undergraduate specialty was the early 1900s, but she was expected to teach a survey course in U.S. history, from the landing of the *Mayflower* to the landing on the moon.

No one who prepares to become a social studies teacher can know all of the subjects he or she may be called on to teach. No single undergraduate major corresponds to the demands of the typical social studies curriculum. So it is not surprising that we found Cathy and Fred at a disadvantage when they began to teach history. Bill and Jane had to scramble too as they prepared to teach units on periods of American history that they had never studied; Bill knew little about Jacksonian democracy, and Jane almost panicked when she had to lecture on the economics of the Depression. All of our teachers had as much to learn about content as about the teaching of it.

How our teachers' undergraduate training influenced their teaching is especially interesting. The curriculum they were given and the courses they subsequently taught were shaped by what they did and did not know. Fred's U.S. history course became the study of political science—he not only emphasized politics and economics but organized the entire course around those themes. Unaware of the broad structures of history, he borrowed a framework from political science to organize and sequence the new information in American history that he read about and then later taught.[5] In much the same way, Cathy used her knowledge of the structures of anthropology and archeology to make sense of the social sciences she was simultaneously learning and teaching. In using those structures, both Cathy and Fred tended to overgeneralize, as in Fred's claim that all revolutions are the same and Cathy's belief that governments act in their citizens' best interests. Generalizing across periods and events, both teachers committed a sin against which historians constantly rail: the failure to consider context.

In a sense, Fred's knowledge of political science and Cathy's knowledge of anthropology and archeology dominated their curricular choices, but in another important sense, it was their *lack* of knowledge that was most decisive in their instruction. Not knowing that history is as much interpretation as fact, they did not know enough to seek out alternative interpretations. Unaware of Beard and Bailyn, Morgan and Miller, Cathy and Fred believed that they had learned history once they had accumulated the names, dates, and events they read about in textbooks. Just as their disciplinary knowledge limited the ways in which they taught history to their students, so their *lack* of knowledge about history limited their ability to learn and understand new subject matter. The cognizance of ignorance is an important first stage in learning. In some ways, Fred and Cathy had not yet reached this stage.

Bill and Jane, on the other hand, were steeped in historical knowledge. Although these novices often had to learn new subject matter by the seat of their pants, their broader and more accurate conceptions of the discipline of history aided them in their search for new information. Each possessed an elaborate organizing scheme[6]—Bill's being primarily political and economic, Jane's social and cultural. These frameworks served each teacher equally well. With every new unit, they had a great deal to learn, but they placed this new information in frameworks they had acquired through their undergraduate training in history. Aware of the importance of interpretation and multiple causation, they were also able to seek out competing explanations for historical events and incorporate these views in their teaching. For instance, Bill knew a great deal about the political interpretations of Roosevelt's economic programs but little about minority issues related to the New Deal. His knowledge of multiple perspectives, however, made him aware of the need to search out such information. Fred and Cathy, lacking that sensitivity, spent their planning time reading textbooks and teachers' guides, becoming mired in factual information, and struggling to find ways—using the disciplinary lenses most familiar to them—to make sense of the facts.

Our teachers' disciplinary perspectives also influenced their goals for instruction. Jane loved history and appreciated its complexity and continuity. She fervently believed that students needed to be exposed to the past and could learn much from its legacy. As a historian, she wanted students to love and appreciate history. Bill, equally appreciative of history's richness, studied history primarily from a political perspective and thought that students should be aware of the ways in which the past has influenced our present political system. For him, knowledge of history meant politically empowering students. Bill's goals reflected his concern for politics; he spent less time talking about the legacy of history and more time emphasizing common political and economic themes. Fred took his passion for the present to an extreme. Dedicated to creating educated, committed citizens, he thought history important only insofar as it served this goal. If he could not see a relationship between a past event and his students' lives, he glossed over it as quickly as possible. His concern for developing conscientious citizens was laudable, but, ironically, his lack of historical knowledge prevented him from recognizing and then forging the connections between past and present that he so valued.

Cathy entered teaching as an anthropologist, and initially her goals for instruction were wedded to her discipline. However, in her first year of full-time teaching, she was assigned a ninth-grade social studies class and handed curricular materials that placed heavy emphasis on seven social sciences, not just anthropology. Given her lack of familiarity with many regions, the textbook emerged as the central tool in her instruction. Two months into the school year she remarked:

> I really do depend [on the textbook] at times. I mean, I need something like this, I mean, it keeps me focused on what direction I should be moving in. It's very detailed. . . . I would have to go to college for four years to understand completely the history of the Middle East, and here we're just

supposed to give them an overall feeling for the Middle East . . . I'm
following the book pretty closely right now because I'm not sure what the
book has to offer and so I'm taking the Middle East and going through it
chapter by chapter.

Presented with curricular materials that gave equal time to other disciplinary perspectives, Cathy was forced to rethink her understanding of the
social world. Her textbook claimed that to understand human development, seven areas of knowledge must be considered: geography, history,
political science, psychology, anthropology, sociology, and economics.
The influence on Cathy's thinking was evident. Three months into the
school year, she already viewed the book's seven-part organization as
"natural" and thought that it was "common sense" to study every culture
from these seven vantage points. An even greater transformation occurred
in Cathy's goals for her ninth graders. Influenced by her textbook's disciplinary ecumenicalism, a woman who during her student teaching wanted
to turn her students into "mini-anthropologists" now wanted to turn them
into "mini–social scientists" who "can look at the culture through all seven
aspects and tell me one or two of the important key concepts of each."

TEACHING THE WAYS OF KNOWING

These four stories have implications for both teacher training and
research on teaching in general. Cathy, Fred, Bill, and Jane know and
believe very different things about the disciplines that represent the
social sciences. Here we have used history as an illustrative example. Yet
these four individuals will be expected to teach several of these disciplines throughout their careers as social studies teachers. Their travails
suggest that knowing the structures of the disciplines they teach is critical to teaching. Had Fred and Cathy known more about history as a
discipline, they might have found it easier to learn about history and
been less likely to misrepresent that discipline to their students.

Learning about disciplines is not simply a matter of acquiring new
knowledge; it entails examining previously held beliefs. Cathy and Fred
were exposed to a great deal of historical information as social studies
teachers, but their naive and, at times, distorted conceptions of history
acted as powerful sieves through which new information was filtered.
Fred's view of history as fact was so entrenched that, when exposed to
a series of alternative interpretations of Roosevelt in a history textbook,
he assumed that they were written by a political scientist whom some

enlightened textbook writer had decided to cite. Such beliefs run deep, and uprooting them may require not the equivalent of a garden hoe, but a bulldozer.

The results reported here also have implications for research on teacher knowledge. Our teachers' "knowledge" of the subject matter was as much a product of their beliefs as an accumulation of facts and interpretations. After a year of teaching American history, Fred had learned vast amounts of historical information. He took and passed with flying colors the National Teachers Examination in history. Does this mean that Fred *knows* history?

History extends beyond knowledge of the past. It can neither be held in one's hand nor put on a shelf in a library. While the raw material of history is the past, history goes well beyond that past. Jacques Barzun explains:

> A sense of history does not reside in any set of bound books. It is something in someone's head; and that something, though born of natural curiosity, has to be cultivated in a certain way, by reading genuine history. Let me say once again what recognized, acknowledged historians have always understood to be genuine: it is a narrative that sets forth a chain of motive, action, result. The sequence in time—chronology—must be clear. Dates are important solely for this purpose of orientation in the stream of motives, actions, results. The chain need not be long . . . but it must be thick, for the motives and actions, being those of many individuals, are always tangled, and the results cannot be understood unless a full view of that preceding tangle is given.[7]

We believe that all of our new teachers were bright, articulate, caring individuals who worked hard at learning their craft. Still, not all of them possessed a robust sense of history. By choosing to use history as the focus of our discussion, we have made Cathy and Fred look less than competent, but had we chosen anthropology, our accounts of Cathy's teaching would have sparkled. Likewise, Fred would have shone had our focus been political science.

Social studies teachers have to know many things, and it is unreasonable to expect that young teachers will know enough about history *and* anthropology *and* sociology *and* economics to represent them accurately and teach them effectively. Learning is not merely an encounter with new information, for new information is often no match for deeply held beliefs. Indeed, each of our teachers is an enthusiastic learner. When one is unfamiliar with the ways of knowing in disciplines other than one's own, new information becomes a slave to the old, and fundamental beliefs go unaltered. Teaching the ways of knowing encompasses more than a methods course, and, clearly, teacher educators cannot do it alone. Creating in prospective teachers an awareness of different ways of knowing is, however, within our sights. It is a worthy goal.

NOTES

The fieldwork for this chapter was conducted in 1985–87 under the Knowledge Growth in Teaching Project, for which Lee S. Shulman was principal investigator, and funded by the Spencer Foundation. This project was a three-year study investigating the development of subject matter knowledge in new high school teachers. Both Cathy and Fred were informants in this project, beginning with their entry into their teacher education programs and continuing through their first year of full-time teaching. Each was interviewed approximately fourteen times throughout the project, and both were observed several times in their respective classrooms.

This chapter was originally co-written with Suzanne Wilson and appeared with her as first author in *Teachers College Record* 89 (1988), 525–39. It has been slightly edited and updated for this volume. Research on history and social studies teaching has expanded considerably since this paper originally appeared; see Suzanne Wilson's chapter on "History Teaching" and Peter Seixas's chapter on "Social Studies Teaching" in Virginia Richardson, ed., *Handbook of Research on Teaching*, 4th ed. (New York, 2001). See, as well, the very useful overview, geared primarily to teachers at the secondary level, by Chris Husbands: *What Is History Teaching? Language, Ideas, and Meaning in Learning About the Past* (Buckingham, England, 1996).

1. The names used here are pseudonyms. Block quotations and words within quotation marks are excerpts from transcribed interview and field notes.

2. Sigrun Gudmundsdottir, Neil B. Carey, and Suzanne M. Wilson, "Role of Prior Subject Knowledge in Learning to Teach Social Studies," Knowledge Growth in a Profession Project Technical Report No. CC-05 (Stanford: Stanford University, School of Education, 1985).

3. Robin G. Collingwood, *The Idea of History* (Oxford, 1946), 177.

4. *Exploring World Cultures* (New York, 1984).

5. We use "structure" in the sense suggested by Joseph J. Schwab, "Education and the Structure of the Disciplines," in Ian Westbury and Neil J. Wilkof, eds., *Science, Curriculum, and Liberal Education* (Chicago, 1978).

6. Richard C. Anderson, "The Notion of Schemata and the Educational Enterprise," in Richard C. Anderson, Rand S. Spiro, and William E. Montange, eds., *Schooling and the Acquisition of Knowledge* (Hillsdale, N.J., 1979), 415–31.

7. Jacques Barzun, "Walter Prescott Webb and the Fate of History," in Dennis Rinehart and Stephen E. Maizlish, eds., *Essays on Walter Prescott Webb and the Teaching of History* (College Station, Texas, 1985). For an extended discussion of the issues raised by this quotation, see Richard J. Evans, *In Defence of History* (London, 1997).

1

Models of Wisdom in the Teaching of History

With Suzanne M. Wilson

Grim portrayals of history classrooms abound. In *What Do Our 17-Year-Olds Know?*, an analysis of the findings of the 1987 National Assessment of Educational Progress, Diane Ravitch and Chester Finn describe the typical history classroom as one in which students

> listen to the teacher explain the day's lesson, use the textbook, and take tests. Occasionally they watch a movie. Sometimes they memorize information or read stories about events and people. They seldom work with other students, use original documents, write term papers, or discuss the significance of what they are studying.[1]

These findings are not the exception; sadly, they are the rule. Similar conclusions emerged from an examination of social studies instruction in Indiana in the mid-sixties,[2] and more recent research has shown few deviations.[3]

In light of this consistency, we may have reached a point of diminishing returns in studying the "typical" or "representative" classroom. We have a fairly good sense of what occurs in such classes. Instead, in our work with the Teacher Assessment Project,[4] my colleagues and I have conscientiously avoided the ordinary to focus on the extraordinary, moving from the study of the probable to a close examination of the possible.

155

To do this, we have undertaken a series of "Wisdom of Practice" studies with eleven experienced high school history teachers. (A similar set of studies was conducted with eleven math teachers.) Our work was guided by the belief that much knowledge about good teaching never finds its way into the professional literature, remaining instead in the minds of good teachers. Through a series of in-depth interviews and observations, we attempted to cull, capture, and describe what these eleven peer-nominated expert practitioners know, think, and do. What follows is an account of two of these teachers and how they think about the history they teach.

THE INVISIBLE TEACHER

It is Monday morning in Elizabeth Jensen's[5] first-period American history class. Her students, a collage of white, black, Asian, and Hispanic faces, enter her classroom and arrange their desks into three groups. On the left sits a group of "rebels"; on the right, "loyalists"; and in the front, "judges." Off to the side, with a spiral notebook in her lap and pencil in hand, sits Jensen, a short woman in her late thirties with a booming voice. Today her voice is silent as her eleventh graders begin a debate on the legitimacy of British taxation in the American colonies. Written on the blackboard is this statement: *Resolved—The British government possesses the legitimate authority to tax the American colonies.*

The first speaker for the rebels, a girl with blond curls and one dangling earring, takes a paper from her notebook and begins:

[The British say they keep] troops here for our own protection. On face value, this seems reasonable enough, but there is really no substance to their claims. First of all, who do they think they are protecting us from? The French? Quoting from our friend Mr. Bailey,[6] "By the settlement in Paris in 1763, French power was thrown completely off the continent of North America." . . . In fact, the only threat to our order is the Indians, but we have a decent militia of our own. . . . So why are they putting troops here? The only possible reason is to keep us in line. With more and more troops coming over, soon every freedom we hold dear will be stripped away.[7]

Another rebel, exuding self-confidence, rises to speak:

Aside from the moral and practical issues involved, there is another important fact to point out. The American colonies *already* tax themselves. . . . The colonies are clearly willing to pay taxes if they can be assured that the cause is just. This point was clearly demonstrated by the Virginia Legislature on May 30, 1765.[8] We were also willing to pay our share of the expenses necessary to keep peace in America. However, because we already have heavy taxes, our ability is limited. We will pay only if the method of raising taxes is decided by ourselves.

A tall African American student with a fade haircut rises from his chair and moves to the center of the loyalist contingent. He begins the loyalists' response:

Let's look at why we're being taxed—the main reason is probably because England has a debt of £140,000,000. . . . Did you know that over one-half of their debt was caused by defending us in the French and Indian War? . . . Taxation without representation isn't fair. Indeed, it's tyranny. Yet *virtual representation*[9] makes this whining of yours an untruth. Every British citizen, whether he had a right to vote or not, is represented in Parliament. Why does this representation not extend to America? . . . If it reaches over 300 miles to Manchester and Birmingham, why can it not reach 3,000 miles to America? Are they not alike British subjects and Englishmen?

A rebel rises to question the loyalists on this point.

Rebel: What benefits do *we* get out of paying taxes to the crown?
Loyalist: We benefit from the protection—
Rebel: Is that the only benefit you claim—protection?
Loyalist: You're being a bit selfish in thinking it's all right to take what is given and not [pay] taxes that are levied. How can you justify not having to pay taxes to England?
Rebel: We're not saying we shouldn't have to pay taxes. We're saying that we shouldn't have to pay taxes without being represented in Parliament— paying taxes and not having a say in what's going . . .

Before she has a chance to finish her sentence, a chorus of loyalists shout "cream, cream, cream," the term they use to signal that an alleged factual or conceptual error has been made by the other side. The loyalists now have a brief moment to state their case before the judges:

Loyalist: We *are* represented in Parliament—by *virtual representation.* We are British citizens and are represented in Parliament. We had the opportunity to . . . be *actually* represented in Britain but you [pointing accusingly at the rebels] did not want to. . . . Many citizens in Britain have virtual representation, that's all they have so it's the sa—
Rebel: No! They have *virtual* and *actual* representation.
Loyalist: No! In the larger cities, they have only virtual, so you are exactly the same as many of the British citizens in England.

For a moment, the room is a cacophony of charges and countercharges. "It's the same as in Birmingham," shouts a loyalist.[10] A rebel snorts disparagingly, "Virtual representation is bull." Thirty-two students seem to be talking at once, while the presiding judge, a thin black student with horn-rimmed glasses, bangs his gavel. But his classmates—warring loyalists and rebels—ignore him. Jensen, still in the corner, still with spiral notebook in her lap, issues her sole command of the day. "Hold still!" she thunders. Order is restored instantly, and the judges uphold the loyalists' "cream."

After opening statements by both sides followed by a day and a half of cross-examination, the debate concludes on the third day with closing statements by rebels and loyalists. The final speaker for the loyalists, with shoulder-length hair and faded denim jacket, stands to address his classmates:

> Does our country's government have the right to tax us? Of course. When the question is phrased in this manner, arguments to the contrary seem moronic. Yet our rash compatriots have taken to the idea that we should be exempt of this responsibility. . . . They are not given representation, they say, so why should they pay taxes? Simultaneously, they refused representation in Parliament . . . What do they want? A representative force that equals over half of Parliament? Of course they will be outvoted if they try to do away with colonial taxation, as would any British district that attempted such a maneuver. It's preposterous to assume that they should get a humongous representative vote, so they say that the taxes themselves are a fraud. They need no protection, seeing that Britain has taken care of France and Spain. They are quite secure in the fact that neither these nor any other countries will attack after the sound beating they received. But once ties are severed, America once again becomes a free-for-all. . . . It should be painfully clear that paying taxes will produce much less strife for all of us than if we were to commence hostilities with Britain. So I put forth a resounding plea: Please be rational. Does our country have a right to tax us? Yes.

While we did not administer pre- and posttests to her students, we view statements such as this one as powerful evidence of the type of learning that goes on in Jensen's class. Note the care this student has taken in the construction of this statement, the pains he took to imitate the language of the eighteenth century. Because he committed what linguists call a "mistake in register" (calling the rebels' request for representation *humongous*), we can see how successful he has otherwise been. He gracefully uses such phrases as "commence hostilities" and "it's preposterous to assume" to capture the spirit of an age in which the style of a message was deemed as important as its meaning. Sixteen-year-olds do not normally "put forth a resounding plea." Under Jensen's guidance, this student has immersed himself in the primary documents of the eighteenth century and has learned that language itself has a rich history.

MAKING THE TEACHER VISIBLE

While the judges wade through three days of testimony, nervousness pervades the room. Students, eager to learn the final verdict, whisper about points they might have made that would have surely swayed the judges to their side. Even though the formal debate is over, students continue to discuss eighteenth-century conceptions of parliamentary representation. Meanwhile, the judges work to reduce myriad points and counterpoints to a single decision.

For three days, Elizabeth Jensen was an invisible presence in this classroom, nestled in the corner, scribbling notes on her pad. Sometimes, unable to contain her delight, she flashed a smile at a student who had made a particularly incisive point about "salutary neglect" or the "imperatives of natural rights." But the only words she uttered (with the exception of "Hold still!") were directed to the judges to remind them every so often to sound their gavels and maintain order. During these classes, Jensen did little that would conventionally be called "teaching": She did not lecture; she did not write on the board; she did not distribute a worksheet, quiz, or test.

One might think, initially, that it is Jensen's students who allow her to sit back and, in her words, "play God." Perhaps with such seemingly motivated adolescents, any teacher would sparkle. There is no denying that Jensen's students are motivated. As self-selected honors students, they chose this class knowing that it required extra work. But Jensen's students, nearly a third of them from minority groups, are not dramatically different in background from other students in this and other large urban high schools. The comprehensive high school they attend even has the same look and feel as other urban schools—the usual cracked paint, exposed pipes, and scattered graffiti marking the stalls in the restrooms.

The impression that Jensen played only a small role in this event is a testament to her artistry. For just as we don't see the choreographers of a Broadway musical standing on stage directing a troupe of dancers, so we don't see the hand of Elizabeth Jensen as her students shape ideas and craft arguments in a debate on the legitimacy of taxation. Choreographers work tirelessly with their dancers, preparing them for the moment when they will take center stage, alone. Similarly, Jensen has learned over the years how to prepare students to be loyalists, rebels, and judges.

For example, she knows that it is not easy for adolescents to transcend the narrow realm of their experience and embrace the issues, emotions, and motivations of people whose world was vastly different from their own. What allows students to do so, in part, is knowing that the success of the activity is up to them; they know that their teacher will not step in to save them if they flounder. Sometimes this means that Jensen has to restrain herself and let a wild goose chase go on longer than it should. But she knows that she can't have it both ways. "If I enter with anything more than regulations to prevent it from becoming a shouting match . . . or [from] losing the structure," she explains, "then they are going to look to me for *all* of it."

But it is much more than a keen understanding of adolescents that allows Jensen to act as choreographer, arranging learning experiences that engage students in the search for cause and motive. Above all else, Jensen's debate rests on a *vision* of what it means to teach history, a vision that provides structure for classroom activities and infuses them with meaning.

For Jensen, history is held together by overarching ideas and themes, which lend coherence and provide a way of understanding the rich texture of human experience. And so Jensen's school year begins not with a list of explorers in a unit on the "Age of Discovery," but with a conference on "Human Nature." Students read excerpts from the writings of philosophers (e.g., Hume, Locke, Plato, and Aristotle), heads of state and revolutionaries (e.g., Jefferson, Mahatma Gandhi, and Mao Zedong), and tyrants (e.g., Adolf Hitler and Benito Mussolini). They then present these views to their classmates. Students learn that theories of human nature undergird the choices people make and that some theories depict humans as enlightened beings, just a step below angels, while others cast them as sinister wretches, just a step above beasts. When it comes time to ratify the U.S. Constitution some months later, these now-familiar figures—Plato, Aristotle, Hume, Locke, Emma Goldman, Vladimir Lenin—are reconvened to be courted by impassioned groups of Federalists and Anti-Federalists.

All of these activities exemplify the larger lesson Jensen wants to impart: The making of history is a dynamic process. What happened in the past wasn't fated or meant to be. It occurred because human actors shaped their destinies by the choices they made, just as people today shape their futures by the choices *they* make.

SETTING THE WHEELS IN MOTION

Jensen's understanding of history is fundamental to the way she captures her students' minds. For her, American history is more than particular dates, persons, or legislative acts. History centers on such themes as authority, freedom, and representation—themes that bind past to present and provide a framework for organizing the mass of information in the eleventh-grade curriculum. This framework guides her curricular decisions, allowing her to foreshadow ideas months before her students confront them. For example, when she introduces eighteenth-century views of human nature at the beginning of the year, she knows that these same issues will resurface in discussions of the Constitution, the Bill of Rights, and federalism. And long before students begin to prepare for those debates, Jensen has already laid the groundwork by introducing students to ideas that set them thinking about the nature of authority.

She does this in several ways. Two weeks before the debate between loyalists and rebels, she assigns selections from the "Student Handbook on Authority," a mimeographed booklet that corresponds to the main units of her American history course, a kind of "nontextbook" textbook. Students read a short story, "A Flogging at Sea," in which a ship's captain beats a sailor. Next they read "Two People Who Make Choices," a short article that compares Josiah Quincy, a lawyer who defended British soldiers accused of murder in the Boston Massacre, to Rosa Parks, a black woman who bucked public opinion more than a century and a half later by refusing to move to the back of a bus in Montgomery, Alabama. As students read these selections, Jensen makes the implicit explicit, bringing underlying issues to the surface. In doing so, she helps prepare students for the debate to come.

The four class sessions just prior to the debate are "research days," during which students work in small groups, studying the documents, books, and articles that Jensen has gathered to help them formulate their arguments. Groups of loyalists, rebels, and judges bustle about, shuffling books back and forth and mapping out their respective strategies. Jensen roams from group to group, acting as coach, troubleshooter, and monitor, making sure that the topic of conversation is the Revolution and not the weekend dance. "The guy who's sitting there talking to his buddy. . . I'll ask him, 'Where's your stuff?' " she explained during one observation. " 'I'm doing it tonight,' he'll say, and I'll say, 'Well, *start it now!* "

Making sure that students stay on task is only one part of Jensen's job. She is a walking encyclopedia, card catalogue, and archive, issuing suggestions and hints at a dizzying pace. "Look at the Declaration of the Virginia Legislature on page 42," she tells one group. "Did you read what Bailey says about the Proclamation of 1763?" she asks another. "Make sure you look at the chart for the real value in terms of a day's work of the different stamps in the Stamp Act," she reminds a third. Her rich knowledge of the American Revolution translates into sources and materials to give to her students. Never, though, does she deliver this information ready-made. She always conveys it in the form of a hint ("See what Bailey says about the British East India Company . . .") or a question ("How does Hacker differ from Jameson on this?").[11]

The questions that crop up in the small groups range from how long it took in 1770 to sail from Boston to London (about five weeks) to whether the opening statements had to be memorized (they did not). But every so often a student asks a question that cannot be answered in a sentence. For instance, at the judges' table, where seven students were studying selections on jurisprudence, a boy told Jensen that he feared he might be swayed, not by the persuasiveness of his peers' arguments, but by his loyalty to them as friends. Jensen stopped for a moment and thought. Judges, she gently explained, have never existed in a social vacuum. They have always had to rein in their emotions, striving to separate their prejudices from the merits of each case. As she spoke, the students looked at her, nodding their heads. Detecting the spark of recognition, she moved on.

THE VERDICT

The judges' verdict at the conclusion of the debate was both a beginning and an end. The verdict ended the debate but began the process by which students make sense of what they have learned. Jensen's pad, her running commentary on students' confusions and insights, became the basis for a debriefing session the following day. Revisiting the issues of the debate, Jensen clarified lingering misunderstandings and prepared students for the final assignment of the unit: a term paper on the legitimacy of British taxation in which students were to shape, summarize, and place their own unique signatures on the material they had learned.

Elizabeth Jensen's classroom is an anomaly. The textbook does not drive instruction; teacher talk does not drown out student talk; there are no worksheets. Students engage in a powerful intellectual process in which they embrace beliefs not their own and argue them with zest. By re-creating history, rather than just reading about it, students learn that Tories were not the villains depicted in textbooks, but ordinary people who saw their world differently from their rebel neighbors. Sometimes one could even see this learning taking place—quizzical looks turning into smiles of recognition. At the end of the debate, one girl stared at the ceiling, dazed. Slowly, she began to nod her head. "You know," she muttered to no one in particular, "we could've all been like Canada." The realization that, had the loyalists prevailed, Queen Elizabeth would appear on *our* stamps, as well as those of our northern neighbors, does not come easily to adolescents growing up in an era when America, not Britain, is the dominant world power.

The judges' final decision stunned the class. The loyalists were declared the victors; the American colonies did not sever their ties with England but reaffirmed them. As students waited for the bell to end the period, the closing speaker for the loyalists could not believe the judges' verdict. Perplexed, he asked his teacher, "Why is it that, like, in the seventh grade all you hear about is that all of these colonists all of a sudden were revolting and the British were running in mass terror? How come we're never told about this stuff?" Nodding her head as he spoke, Jensen said, "I'd like to know that, too."

THE VISIBLE TEACHER

In a high school located about 20 minutes from Jensen's, we enter another history class. The school looks much the same—similar graffiti, the same shabby exterior, a similar mixture of faces. John Price, a teacher in his early forties, paces between the chalkboard, his students, and the center of a horseshoe formation of desks. He is in the middle of a discussion of the Intolerable Acts.

Price:	In fact, these laws are called, by Mr. Jordan,[12] what?
Jim:	Intolerable Acts.
Price:	Intolerable Acts! Intolerable! We can't stand them! If you were to read an English history book, would they call these laws the *Intolerable Acts?*

Students: No!
Price: No! I don't know what they would call them, but they might call them
          something like "The Laws Essential to Establishing Law and Order
          in Boston." You see? Because they see it differently. They see tea
          being lost. They see private property being destroyed, and, in fact,
          what we are going to do today is look at the results of the Intolerable
          Acts. The British *do* send soldiers. Sam Adams is *cheering* all this! He's
          loving it! Now the British are doing *exactly* what he wanted. We have
          already had the Boston Massacre. Things calmed down; now they are
          heating up again, thanks to mistakes made by the British. And all we
          need now is an incident to set this whole thing off once again. Now,
          there was another *triggering event,*[13] and I am going to have you read
          about what actually set it off. And the way that we are going to do this
          is that we are going to read two newspaper accounts that were writ-
          ten back in 1775. So let me pass them out to you. Take one and pass
          them along. Pass them as quickly as you can; they're all the same. . . .
          This is a newspaper account describing what happened in Lexington
          on the nineteenth of April 1775. And because the language is old to
          our ears, 200 years old, I'm going to read with you the first paragraph
          to get you started on these. Listen to the sound of the language. "Last
          Wednesday, the nineteenth of April," says the reporter, "the troops
          of his Britannic majesty"—who is that?
Cindy: The king.
Price: The king. So what troops are we talking about?
Students: British troops.
Price: British troops. "Commenced hostilities upon the people of this
          province . . . upon the people of Massachusetts attended with cir-
          cumstances of cruelty, not less brutal than our venerable ancestors
          received from the vilest savages of the wilderness." . . . What did the
          British troops do?
Isabel: They treated them as badly as the Indians had treated them.
Price: Treated their ancestors on the frontier. . . . "The particulars," that is,
          the details, "relative to this interesting event, by which we are
          involved in all the horrors of a civil war, we have tried, endeavored to
          collect as well as the present confused state of affairs will admit."
          That's quite a mouthful but in essence what he is saying is: "All hell
          has broken loose in Lexington. It's like a civil war." What's a civil war?
Susie: A war inside one place.
Price: All right. Brothers fighting brothers. . . . Now, as you read this, I would
          like you to look first, before you start the article now, at the front
          board. And before we begin this, I want to make sure that you under-
          stand the difference between a *fact* and an *opinion.* It is a very impor-
          tant skill for you to develop when you are reading something and
          trying to decide whether it's the truth or not. So I'd like anyone in here
          to say any kind of statement of fact that comes to mind. Well, if you
          want you can make it the American Revolution, the colonies. What
          facts do we know about the American colonies? Give me any fact.

The exchange between Price and his students takes less than five minutes. He dominates the conversation, uttering more than 750 words, compared with the 26 words that a subset of his students contributes. Indeed, he has said more in these minutes than Jensen did during the entire three days of the debate in her class. A casual observer peering into Price's classroom might claim to have seen what other researchers have observed—teacher-dominated, whole-group instruction, with activities centered on the teacher's questions and explanations.

But something makes this classroom different. The air is electric. Students lean forward in their seats, ask thoughtful and stimulating questions, and stay in the room to continue discussions after the bell has rung. Price is pure energy—laughing, pacing, bantering with students, gesturing excitedly. No ordinary teacher, John Price is a master performer who has seized the collective imagination of thirty-five adolescents and has led them on an expedition into the past.

After this brief introductory discussion, Price directs students to read the first newspaper account. While they read, they are to look for evidence to answer a set of questions on the board. Students work quietly, independently or with a partner, while Price walks around the room answering questions. After ten minutes, the class resumes as Jenny asks, "Who wrote this?"

Price: Well, who does it look like wrote this?
Jenny: A colonist.
Price: Looks like it's an American newspaper, doesn't it? Because it looks like wherever you read here, the British are the bad, evil *savages*. . . . And the Americans, how are they described?
Jenny: Sweet.
Price: Anything else?
Jenny: Courageous.
Price: *Heroic.* They're *courageous*, standing fast. . . . See how carefully this is written to create a mood? And so, how would you respond then to the third question here? How could this news story influence the Revolution? Who was going to read it?
Mark: It could make them all hyped up.
Price: It was going to hype people up. It's adding gasoline to the fire. It's making it worse. Can you imagine that this guy was maybe a friend of someone or himself was a member of the Sons of Liberty? Trying to sway those people who are sitting on the fence and don't want to get involved.

The conversation lasts a while longer until Price directs students to the second part of the assignment, which involves reading another newspaper account and responding to a similar set of questions. The second account comes from the *London Gazette*, and, after another close reading of the text, Price discusses with his students how the author's point of view influenced this second, vastly different characterization of the Battle of Lexington.

EXAMINING THE VISIBLE TEACHER

Teaching has sometimes been compared to acting, and John Price is an actor *par excellence*—simultaneously sensitive to his audience and a master at using his body to communicate. He is keenly aware of his audience, asking them questions he knows they can answer, relating the day's lesson to what they already know, pushing them to look for evidence to support their claims.

But if Price is an actor, he is one who writes and delivers his own lines. He has no formal script, and he neither plans meticulously nor uses the textbook as a guide. Rather, he carries with him a notebook filled with bits of information collected over his seventeen years in the classroom: the number of British soldiers killed at Lexington and Concord, what Mao Zedong most admired about George Washington, notes about Tom Paine's father (a corset maker).

When the bell rings, Price is on stage—responding to student questions, interjecting anecdotes from his notebook, and using analogies and examples to illustrate his points. Just as Jensen laid the groundwork for the ratification of the Constitution by first introducing her students to eighteenth-century views of human nature, so Price introduces organizing frameworks and concepts early in the school year, thus enabling his students to cull the information presented to them and sort the wheat from the chaff. To talk about the Intolerable Acts, he had to introduce the Townshend Acts, as well as the Gaspé incident, Sam Adams, and the Committees of Correspondence. He also introduced an adaptation of Crane Brinton's model of revolution.[14] Says Price:

> I want students to see it so they'll remember it. . . . I want them to approach it from the standpoint of certain elements of revolution that are necessarily present in all revolutions. So that when they come across revolutions in the future, they'll have some signposts to look for . . . so that all the time we're studying the Revolution, they are listing these complaints, and it's a term that I began with Bacon's Rebellion—*grievances*—they know what that word means. The second thing they look for is the presence of leaders, so that when I start talking about Sam Adams or they're reading about John Hancock or the others, the Sons of Liberty and so forth, that's another signpost.

Price's students were no more surprised by his question about the differences between fact and opinion than they were about his use of the term "triggering event." Since the beginning of the semester, Price has pushed students to look for values, opinions, interpretations—starting with those of the textbook authors: "We always start with values. We start with the . . . notion . . . that they have values that influence what they say and do." This emphasis is based on Price's conception of history. "What Mr. Jordan has here in this [textbook]," he says, "that's not history. A collection of human experiences [is] too complicated for there to be one pat explanation as to what happened. . . . And that's what makes history so exciting."

While Price wants his students to appreciate and recognize the interpretive nature of history, he is not interested in making them "little historians." He acknowledges that his school expects him to teach his students a certain amount of factual information, information he values because it provides students with a sense of rootedness. But Price is well aware that in a survey course he cannot do justice to both the content of history and the processes historians use to reconstruct it: "I'm seeking a balance. . . . My mission is to really get [students] excited about some of the characters along the way . . . [and] for them to realize that there is a real excitement in how this information was discovered. . . . Those are the two things I constantly have in mind."

Like Jensen, Price is known as a "hard teacher," one who pushes students more than they have been pushed before. Unlike Jensen's class, Price's is not an honors section; instead, it consists of students who have opted to enroll in his class because of his reputation as a fine teacher. Students know that they are expected to work hard and that U.S. history is serious business.

But in this class "pushing" does not mean the memorization of names, dates, and events that characterizes so many other history classes. True, conversations during class periods are replete with names and events, but the people Price introduces are not the lifeless figures of textbooks. They are living, breathing, feeling human beings complete with idiosyncrasies and foibles. Sam Adams, while a brilliant propagandist and the "Penman of the Revolution," was a seedy dresser—so seedy that the Sons of Liberty bought him a new suit for a public appearance. John Hancock resented the Tea Act not so much because it violated his rights as a British citizen as because it threatened his livelihood as a merchant who traded in tea. Men and women in Price's class had motives—some personal, some political—and the history he teaches is viewed through the prism of these motives.

By making the characters in his lessons real, Price engages his students in thinking about the actions of those characters. Once he has introduced the people in the story, his students are eager to hear the tale of how these individuals made history. But the stories Price tells aren't finished; they are not closed books with beginnings, middles, and ends. Price emphasizes that historians present "accounts" of events, not the events themselves. Students learn about the Battle of Lexington and Concord, but they see the battle from both the British and the American perspectives. They learn about the Salem witch hunts, but they also learn that recent historiography has produced interpretations that differ from those presented by the authors of their textbook. They learn that the British viewed the Intolerable Acts as quite reasonable. Conclusions *are* exciting in Price's class, for history is not a dusty and dated collection of people and places. Instead, history is an anthology of stories, told by people with differing convictions and commitments, many of whom cannot even agree on the story line.

DIFFERENCES AND SIMILARITIES

This analysis of Price and Jensen offers a study in contrast. Watching Price, we see what Larry Cuban has called "persistent instruction"—whole-group instruction with the teacher at the center, leading discussions, calling on students, and writing key phrases on the chalkboard.[15] Jensen's classroom, on the other hand, departs from the traditional; cooperative small groups replace whole-group instruction; student debate and presentation overshadow teacher recitation; and the teacher's voice, issuing instructions and dispensing information, is largely mute.

While Jensen and Price have markedly different styles and systems of classroom organization, the students seem to be affected in ways more similar than different. In both classrooms, the issues of history spilled over the neat fifty-minute periods and continued to dominate discussions well after bells had rung. As students put away their books and left for the next class, we heard them comment, not about the Friday night dance or the basketball game, but about virtual representation and triggering events. In both rooms, the atmosphere sizzled with ideas.

What must Jensen and Price know in order to create such environments? Clearly, both teachers are skilled at organizing classrooms and conveying clear goals to students. But these two teachers are masters of their subject matter. Bacon's Rebellion, James Otis, Sam Adams, George Grenville, the Navigation Acts, the Quartering Act—these and countless other bits of information form tightly organized networks of facts stored in each teacher's mind. Both are also deeply familiar with the broader conceptual and theoretical issues of the period. They can talk at length about virtual representation, the difference between internal and external taxation, mercantilism, salutary neglect, natural rights, and so on.

But each teacher also possesses a more general body of knowledge that gives structure to this welter of information. So, for example, Price makes comparisons between colonial America and contemporary South Africa, drawing on a theoretical model of revolution borrowed from Crane Brinton. Jensen makes sense of the complex and often contradictory evidence of the colonial period through her familiarity with its historiography—the interpretations of Charles Beard, J. Franklin Jameson, Louis Hacker, Gordon Wood, and others. For both teachers, these broader and more general interpretive frameworks infuse detail with meaning. To them, history is not an endless parade of names and dates but an intriguing story filled with discernible patterns and trends.

There are striking similarities in their orientation to their subject matter. Both see history as a human construction, an enterprise in which people try to solve a puzzle even though some of the pieces are faded, some distorted beyond recognition, and some lost to the dust of time. We can know certain facts about people, events, and deeds, Jensen and Price assure their students, but as soon as we turn to questions of significance—of why something happened versus the mere fact of its happening—history becomes an act of judgment.

In many history classrooms, the textbook sifts the evidence for students, never alluding to the interpretation such sifting involves. But textbooks in these two classes played a far different role. Sometimes the textbooks entered the fray of conflicting interpretations; at other times, they acted as foils for the teachers' favored interpretations; at still other times, they served as resources to help students follow the story line of history. Viewed as "accounts" rather than facsimiles of the past, textbooks enriched but did not determine students' understanding.

Working within their visions of history and teaching, Jensen and Price rendered their knowledge into forms accessible to a diverse group of adolescents. In transforming their knowledge for teaching, Jensen and Price created a wide variety of representations of subject matter—examples, analogies, demonstrations, simulations, stories, dramatic reenactments, and debates. All of these diverse representations shared one feature: Each attempted to build a bridge between the sophisticated understanding of the teacher and the developing understanding of the student.

Creating a representation is an act of pedagogical reasoning.[16] Teachers must first turn inward to comprehend and ponder the key ideas, events, concepts, and interpretations of their discipline. But in fashioning representations, teachers must also turn outward. They must try to think themselves into the minds of students who lack the depth of understanding that they, as teachers, possess. An instructional representation emerges as the product of the teachers' comprehension of content and their understanding of the needs, motivations, and abilities of learners.

We recognize that our research marks a beginning, not an end, to thinking about the nature of expertise in the teaching of history. There is much yet to understand. What expert teachers know about history, what they know about teaching, what they know about learners—these are but pieces of a complex set of understandings that make up the professional knowledge base of teaching.

In rendering these accounts of Jensen and Price, we failed to mention several details that we see as essential in our characterization of them as experts. In focusing on Jensen's debate and Price's discussions of Lexington and Concord, we chose not to talk about other classes in which we observed them. We have not described a classroom recitation by Jensen, whose thundering voice seized the students' attention and held them spellbound for fifty minutes. Nor have we described Price's government class, run entirely by students who engaged in a six-month simulation of the U.S. Congress, each student playing the role of a legislator, proposing bills and making cloakroom deals, while Price remained invisible.

So we end on a cautionary note. Knowledge of subject matter is central to teaching, but expert knowledge of content is not the sole determinant of good teaching. Just as the history they teach is not static and dull, so Jensen and Price are not one-dimensional pedagogues who do only one thing well. Both teachers possess rich and deep understandings of many things, understandings that manifest themselves in the ability to draw from a broad range of possibilities. Indeed, it may be their very ability to alternate between different modes of teaching that earns each of them the designation "wise practitioner."

NOTES

This chapter was co-written with Suzanne Wilson and first appeared in the *Phi Delta Kappan* 70 (1988), 50–58, and in a slightly altered form in *History Teacher: Journal of the Society of History Education* 24 (1992), 395–412. The research was featured in Fred Hechinger's "On Education" column in the *New York Times* (October 12, 1988), which generated more attention to this project than to any other piece of research with which I've been involved. The Teacher Assessment Project (Lee S. Shulman, principal investigator) was funded by the Carnegie Corporation of New York. Thanks go to Louette McGraw, who helped collect the data in this report, and to Pauline Gough and Bruce Smith, whose editorial acumen ranks them among the best.

1. Diane Ravitch and Chester Finn, Jr., *What Do Our 17-Year-Olds Know? A Report on the First National Assessment of History and Literature* (New York, 1987), 194.

2. Maurice G. Baxter, Robert H. Ferrell, and John E. Wiltz, *The Teaching of American History in High Schools* (Bloomington, Ind., 1964). Compare the more recent collection by Lloyd Kramer, Donald Reid, and William L. Barney, *Learning History in America* (Minneapolis, 1994).

3. James P. Christopolous, William D. Rohwer, and John W. Thomas, "Grade Level Differences in Students' Study Activities as a Function of Course Characteristics," *Contemporary Educational Psychology* 12 (1987), 303–23; John I. Goodlad, *A Place Called School* (New York, 1984); James Howard and Thomas Mendenhall, *Making History Come Alive* (Washington, D.C., 1982); and Karen B. Wiley and Jeanne Race, *The Status of Pre-College Science, Mathematics, and Social Science Education: 1955–1975*, vol. 3: *Social Science Education* (Boulder, Colo., 1977).

4. The Teacher Assessment Project was a research and development initiative designed to generate a set of prototypes for alternative ways to assess teaching. See Chapter 8 in this volume.

5. Under the terms dictated by the school district in which this research was conducted, we used pseudonyms for both teachers in the original version of this chapter. Since the original publication, "Elizabeth Jensen" has publicly identified herself by her real name, Bonnie Taylor.

6. Thomas Bailey and David M. Kennedy, *The American Pageant: A History of the Republic*, 7th ed. (Lexington, Mass., 1983).

7. For the sake of brevity, we have excerpted students' comments. The language, however, is their own.

8. On May 30, 1765, the Virginia House of Burgesses passed a resolution stating that, while recognizing the need to pay taxes to the crown, the burgesses themselves would decide upon the appropriate methods for levying them.

9. "Virtual representation," according to Edmund Burke, its most vigorous proponent, refers to the belief that all Englishmen were represented in Parliament whether they voted for its members or not. "Parliament," declared Burke, "is a *deliberative* assembly of *one* nation, with *one* interest, that of the whole, where, not local purposes, not local prejudices ought to guide, but the general good, resulting from the general reason of the whole." See Robert A. Gross, *The Minutemen and Their World* (New York, 1976), 36.

10. The loyalists are correct here. Only 10 percent of the population of Great Britain possessed the right to vote, and many of the larger cities, including Birmingham and Manchester, sent no representatives to Parliament.

11. Louis Hacker and J. Franklin Jameson were required reading for Jensen's students.

12. Winthrop D. Jordan, Miriam Greenblatt, and John S. Bowes, *The Americans: The History of a People and a Nation* (Evanston, Ill., 1985). This was the textbook used in Price's class.

13. The term "triggering event" is drawn from Crane Brinton's model for revolution, a framework that Price introduced early in the year to help students organize the events leading to the American Revolution. See Crane C. Brinton, *The Anatomy of a Revolution* (Englewood Cliffs, N.J., 1952).

14. Ibid.

15. Larry Cuban, "Persistent Instruction: The High School Classroom, 1900–1980," *Phi Delta Kappan* 64 (1982), 113–18.

16. The act of creating "representations" of content for the purpose of instruction is at the heart of "pedagogical content knowledge." See the work of Lee S. Shulman, "Those Who Understand Teach: Knowledge Growth in Teaching," *Educational Researcher* 15 (1986), 4–14; and "Knowledge and Teaching: Foundations of the New Reform," *Harvard Educational Review* 57 (1987), 1–22.

Wrinkles in Time and Place

Using Performance Assessments to Understand the Knowledge of History Teachers

With Suzanne M. Wilson

ew topics spark as much controversy as teacher testing. And for good reason, because testing—whether to gauge basic skills or discern pedagogical expertise—makes claims about what matters most in teaching. For years, the National Teacher Examination (NTE) dominated the field. A multiple-choice test with separate sections for pedagogy and subject matter, the NTE fixed teacher knowledge as a function of right or wrong answers to questions scored with a preset answer key. Despite its limitations,[1] not the least of which were low correlations with field ratings of teaching, the NTE reigned unchallenged for decades, in part because it was easy to administer and even easier to score.

New forms of teacher tests proliferated during the 1980s.[2] These tests sprang up in contentious political environments, sometimes as devices for distributing merit pay,[3] sometimes as ways to measure teachers' basic skills.[4] Most tests followed the NTE in separating subject matter knowledge from pedagogy, despite the fusion of these spheres in teaching. Moreover, most continued to ask teachers to do something—blacken circles on a test form—far removed from daily practice.

173

Perhaps the most devastating effect of these tests was their impact on public perceptions of teaching. As arms of policy, such tests taught the public to think of teacher knowledge as something easily defined and packaged, readily decontextualized and transported. Just as tests for students stressed the "basics" over "understanding," so tests for teachers emphasized "the testable" over "the essential." Wittingly or not, these tests may have lowered the status of teaching in the eyes of the public.

Born of frustration with attempts to assess teaching through paper-and-pencil tests, the first prototypes of performance assessments emerged in the late 1980s, though they had appeared in other professions much earlier.[5] Essentially, performance assessments ask people to *do* or *produce* something. In teaching, this means asking teachers to teach a lesson to students, grade student papers, sketch out a unit plan, evaluate a textbook, watch and respond to someone else's teaching, participate in a group planning session with other teachers, and so on. Performances are scored not by their conformity to a canonical set of answers but by their reflection of the principled standards of professional thought and action.

The move toward performance assessments was not simply the advent of a new testing technology, yet another attempt to build a better mousetrap. For policymakers, it symbolized a shift from a *bureaucratic* to a *professional* view of teaching.[6] In the former view, teachers are seen as little more than functionaries who execute the mandates of higher-ups. They do not question these mandates, overrule them, or alter them in light of their own experience or circumstance. To insure that teachers conduct their work uniformly, authorities administer one-size-fits-all tests impervious to different subject matters and contexts. Teachers "do not plan or inspect their work," wrote Linda Darling-Hammond, summarizing the bureaucratic conception, "they merely perform it."[7] The alternative view depicts teachers as skilled professionals who engage in thoughtful analyses of children's needs, taking into account issues of subject matter, pedagogy, and child development. In making decisions, teachers draw on a rich knowledge base similar to the knowledge bases of professionals in other fields. In this view, teachers take responsibility for the evaluation and assessment of the field. They create, administer, and evaluate assessments of professional knowledge and skill.[8]

This shift from a bureaucratic to a professional view of teaching draws inspiration from research in cognitive psychology and parallels its rise.[9] Once seen as the arrangement of reinforcements to bring "the organism into possession of mathematical behavior," as B. F. Skinner referred to defined math instruction,[10] teaching now is viewed as a complex enterprise resistant to pat formulas. The language of behaviorism has given way to "goal and action agendas,"[11] "personal and social epistemologies,"[12] "transformation and representation of knowledge,"[13] "schema instantiations and pattern recognition capabilities,"[14] "mental scaffolding,"[15] and "cognitive apprenticeships."[16] These terms, and the conceptual systems they represent, speak to the fact that judgments of teaching have gone from noting and counting behaviors to inquiring into the meaning and appropriateness of behavior given a specific group of children, a particular piece of content, the teacher's goals and knowledge, and the demands of the larger school community. The cognitive view of teaching marries thought and action, deliberation and decision.

The findings presented in this chapter come from one of the first projects to develop and field-test performance assessments for teachers, Stanford University's Teacher Assessment Project (TAP).[17] TAP set out to develop prototypes of assessments that would inform the work of the National Board for Professional Teaching Standards (NBPTS), which has been engaged since 1987 in planning a voluntary system of national certification for teachers.[18] This certification would differ from the teacher licensure in key respects. Licensure, granted and regulated by state departments of education, represents the minimum standards in the field. Its stated purpose is to insure that people entering teaching are competent to perform the basic duties of the job. Certification goes beyond basic skills and entry-level competence. It would represent a "bold standard"[19] that would not be expected of beginning teachers, or of every experienced teacher who sought to attain it. Certification in these cases would signify accomplishment and be a mark of professional distinction.

During its four-year history, TAP developed performance exercises in secondary history/social studies and elementary mathematics, and a series of portfolio assessments in secondary biology and elementary language arts.[20] Here the focus is on three assessments TAP developed in secondary history/social studies.

BACKGROUND

Exercise Development

TAP's exercise development began with a series of "Wisdom of Practice" studies, intensive investigations of eleven history teachers nominated as "expert" by professors, school administrators, and fellow teachers.[21] Our goal at this stage of development was not to survey the entire domain of history teaching so that we could randomly sample from it, the strategy of "job analysis" commonly used by commercial test developers. More modestly, we tried to select core ideas that represented worthwhile activities that good history teachers do well.

This was obviously not a neutral process. The nine exercises in our final battery reflected an image of teaching informed by the theoretical and empirical work that preceded it. This image portrays teachers as people with deep subject matter knowledge who actively search for ways to present that subject matter to learners. It presumes that teaching is not a generic process, for good teachers must craft powerful representations (analogies, metaphors, demonstrations, examples, stories, and simulations) that bridge between what they know and what they want their students to learn. These representations look different and draw on different knowledge depending on the content of instruction—mathematics or English literature, art history or physical education. Further, the exercises in our battery assume that good teaching does not follow a set form. Depending on their goals and situations, teachers may choose to present a lecture, arrange a cooperative group activity, act as a coach and facilitator to students doing individual projects, supervise a peer tutoring activity, and so on.[22]

Research Strategy

Sample. In the summer of 1987, nineteen history teachers, representing a range of backgrounds and experiences, came to Stanford University for a three-day field test of an assessment center for history teachers. The analysis here is limited to the performances of two of these teachers. Suzanne Wilson and I participated in collecting the field-test data and in all phases of later data analysis.

The two teachers chosen displayed intriguing similarities and contrasts. In terms of the common way of measuring subject matter knowledge—the number of courses in college or graduate school[23]—both teachers would be ranked "high." One teacher majored in history, the other had a master's degree in it, and both studied at universities whose history departments ranked in the top ten in the nation. Because the majority of history/social studies teachers major in disciplines other than history,[24] their course work makes these teachers the exception, not the rule. A second similarity between the teachers is that both worked in suburban high schools in largely middle-class districts. Social studies classes in both schools are tracked, and both teachers have students from a range of ability levels. On the other hand, nearly a quarter-century of experience separated the two. Ed Barnes completed his undergraduate studies in the 1950s; Jane Kelsey completed hers in the 1980s. (Both names are pseudonyms.) The younger teacher taught for three years prior to coming to the assessment center; the older one had twenty-seven years' experience.

The analysis here is limited to three of nine exercises: (1) *Evaluations of Student Papers*, in which teachers read and responded to a set of student essays; (2) *Use of Documentary Materials*, in which teachers planned a classroom activity using primary sources; and (3) *Textbook Analysis*, in which teachers evaluated an excerpt from a widely used U.S. history textbook.[25] These three exercises provided a contrast between interactive and self-administered tasks. Together, they convey the spirit of the full assessment battery.

Data Analysis. For the purpose of this analysis, we decided not to use the formal scoring rubrics TAP had developed, though our thinking benefited from participating in their development. The goal of the scoring rubrics was data reduction; our goal in this project was to understand a smaller subset of data in greater depth than is usually possible when analyzing a larger sample of individuals and exercises. We began our analysis two years after the data were collected. Each of us independently listened to all audiotapes and reviewed all documents associated with the three exercises. As we did this, we wrote memoranda to each other about our impressions, hypotheses, questions, and concerns about the performances we reviewed. We then transcribed the audiotapes verbatim and checked each other's transcriptions for accuracy. As we proceeded from one exercise to the next, we generated a small set of hypotheses to account for the performances. We then checked these hypotheses by looking back to previous exercises and forward to the next, searching for confirmatory and disconfirmatory evidence.

During the early stages of analysis, we often had different explanations for why the teachers talked and thought as they did. Rather than push for premature consensus, we used our differences to generate multiple, sometimes competing, hypotheses. We then returned to the data to see how our hypotheses fared. With each successive pass, we added hypotheses, eliminated others, and gained or lost confidence about others.

In the following discussion, we present the hypotheses we believe best account for the differences in performance of these two teachers. This presentation draws heavily on direct quotations from teachers' spoken and written comments, as opposed to offering numerical summaries using TAP's scoring rubrics, because the questions we want to illuminate do not revolve around whether a teacher received a "4" or a "5" on an exercise. Rather, the questions we find most intriguing deal with how such judgments of quality are made, the kinds of data on which they are based, and the standards that they reflect.[26]

Instead of describing the performances and offering final judgments, we present the exercises in the order in which we reviewed them and try to recapitulate how we arrived at our final judgments. We use this rhetorical strategy for two reasons. First, we are interested in the alternative forms of argument called for in conducting and reporting a type of qualitative research not readily labeled "ethnography" or "sociolinguistics." By attempting to make our intellectual work transparent, we invite readers to judge the accuracy, reasonableness, and validity of our claims and to come to their own conclusions about the capacities and knowledge of these two teachers. Second, we believe that the thinking required to analyze performance data is complex in much the same way as the thinking entailed in accomplished teaching. It requires judgment based on multiple sources of evidence. Not readily reduced to algorithms or easily stripped of context, these judgments are an inescapable part of performance assessment. As such, they constitute an essential ingredient of the assessments we describe.

THE TWO TEACHERS

Mr. Barnes

Mr. Barnes is in his mid-fifties and has been teaching for twenty-seven years. Shortly after receiving a B.A. in speech from a prestigious West Coast university in the early 1950s, he began teaching high school social studies. In 1961, he completed an M.A. in American history at the same university. He now teaches in a suburban high school in the San Francisco Bay area. He currently teaches Advanced Placement (AP) and "regular" U.S. history to high school juniors but has also taught world geography, American government, modern European history, and social psychology.

Ms. Kelsey

Ms. Kelsey, a woman in her late twenties, graduated from an Ivy League university in 1983 with a B.A. in American history. After teaching junior high social studies in a private school for a year, she entered a fifth-year teacher education program that awards a master's degree upon completion. In her field placement, Ms. Kelsey taught in a suburban high school similar to the one in which Mr. Barnes now teaches, and became a full-fledged faculty member at the school the following year. At the time of the field test, she had taught full-time for three years—one year in a private school, two in a public school—and had teaching experience with seventh- and eleventh-grade U.S. history, eighth-grade civics, ninth-grade medieval history, and electives in psychology and art history.

EXERCISE 1: EVALUATION OF STUDENT PAPERS

Description

The Evaluation of Student Papers was a ninety-minute exercise that consisted of two parts.[27] In part 1, teachers reviewed six papers written by high school students in response to the following question: "Describe and evaluate the events and actions of people which led to the revolt of the American colonies against England." (These papers were written for a timed test as part of students' normal eleventh-grade social studies class. Although we retyped the essays, we left errors in spelling and punctuation intact.) Teachers were escorted to a quiet room and given twenty minutes to think about the criteria they would use to grade the six papers. They were also asked to think about "the level of knowledge of the group and the general misconceptions that remain." After twenty minutes, an interview took place in which teachers explained their grading criteria. In part 2, teachers were given three new essays to read and asked to "mark and make comments on each essay which will be useful to the student." Another interview followed in which teachers elaborated on their written comments. They were also asked about their strategies for helping students improve their essays.

The Teachers' Responses

Mr. Barnes. Mr. Barnes began the interview by describing his criteria for evaluating the papers. He noted that he would have first explained his expectations to students:

I would have emphasized that they should do everything that's asked for in the question in order to receive full credit and the highest grade possible. The instructions ask the students to both describe and evaluate events and actions and people which led to the revolt of the American colonies against England. So, somewhere in their essay, they should both describe events and they should evaluate their significance. And they should both mention events presumably on the part of the British government and actions or reactions on the part of the colonists. So it's really kind of a four-part essay, and they should make a very determined attempt to do all four of those things in order to receive full credit.

Mr. Barnes summarized his grading criteria as (a) a concern for the presentation of accurate facts, (b) the description of key events and individuals, (c) the evaluation of those events, and (d) the students' mode of expression. He described Essay 5, a "B" paper, as:

A pretty good essay. Toward the latter part of it, it began to get very crude in terms of the way that the ideas were expressed. There was enough factual data and enough analysis of the data to lead me to believe that the student knew what he was talking about but had some difficulty in getting it out on paper. I was particularly distressed by the substitution of the word "slowed" for "allowed" . . . also mistaking the British West India Company for the British East India Company. I'm sure to a high school student, it makes no difference at all. To a history teacher, it's all the difference in the world.

The following comment addressed Essay 2, an "A–" essay:

The student demonstrated an excellent command of the facts. There were some minor problems of sequencing, the chronology of events. He could have had a stronger topic sentence, in my opinion. To say that Britain started to become a nuisance to the colonies is rather a casual manner with which to introduce the coming of the American Revolution, especially when it's followed by such a well-organized and thoughtful elaboration of factual detail.

Mr. Barnes was consistent in his evaluation of student papers. His comments focused on students' factual and spelling errors, their mastery of historical information, their inappropriate mixture of formal and informal language, and, on occasion, their success with clever phrasing and "stirring" points.

Ms. Kelsey. Ms. Kelsey also laid out explicit criteria for evaluating the papers. She drew a chart listing the following criteria:

(a) Takes a side and tries to stick to it. (Makes an argument/states a generalization.)
(b) Uses specific facts from previous lessons to support argument.
(c) Evidence chosen supports that side or weaves story.

(d) Essay is long enough to accurately answer the question in specific detail.

(e) Essay is written with accurate grammar and spelling (that I can tell what you're talking about!). Paragraphing, structured and clear.

Ms. Kelsey began by noting that at least three of the six papers mirrored students' belief that history was a "catalogue of names and dates." She speculated that students' prior instruction had been "heavily fact-oriented" and wondered whether those essays really tapped what students knew. Her initial comments, like Mr. Barnes's, focused on how she would have prepared students for this essay:

> I would have given some more scaffolding [to the essay prompt] so that the kids understood that they were to both describe and evaluate. These appear to be average-level kids. It's really hard for them to do the two things. It's hard for a historian, and it's really, really hard for an average-level kid. So I would probably say, "Include these events and interpret these events." . . . Rules like "I want you to include at least the following or three of the following" . . . "And when you interpret, you should consider issues like 'Was this primarily political or economic?'"

In responding to Essay 2, the paper Mr. Barnes said "demonstrated an excellent command of the facts," Ms. Kelsey commented:

> This kid sounds to me like the kind of kid who's worked really hard to study. I get the impression that this kid got a message . . . that history is a catalogue of names and dates. . . . My guess is that the student walked away thinking, "I wrote a great essay. I should get an 'A.'"

In their grading criteria, both teachers focused on whether students addressed the question; both took into account students' spelling, grammar, and quality of expression. As Table 8.1 shows, the grades they awarded were almost perfectly correlated.

TABLE 8.1
Grades Assigned to Students' Essays

GRADE	ESSAY 1	ESSAY 2	ESSAY 3	ESSAY 4	ESSAY 5	ESSAY 6
Barnes	D−	A−	B+/A−	D+	B	D
Kelsey	F	B/B+	B/B+	D	B	B−/C+

Note: The Spearman rank correlation was computed by converting letter grades to a 4.0 scale, with 0.7 equal to the lowest passing grade and 4.0 to the highest, along with collapsing slashed grades into a single averaged grade, $r_s = .94, p < .001$.

But such similarities can be deceiving. Although the teachers' grades were nearly identical, the meanings they gave to these grades were not. In response to the question, "What is your general assessment of the understanding of the students in this class?" Mr. Barnes answered:

> Well, we had six essays. One A−, B+, D−, D+, B, no Cs; however, I think if one were to give those some kind of numerical coefficient and average them out, it looks like an average class to me. . . . The bell-shaped curve of distribution of abilities makes sense.

To the same question, Kelsey responded:

> I get the impression that these students think that understanding history is memorizing a mass of information, recounting a series of facts. There is not a lot of questioning going on, there isn't any interpretation—just based on what I have now.

In their responses, Mr. Barnes focused on students' ability, Ms. Kelsey on their beliefs and misconceptions. The teachers' different focuses carried over to their plans in part 2 of the exercise, which asked them to "provide remediation and enrichment" to three new students. For example, although both teachers agreed that Student B's essay was the weakest, their plans for remediation differed in tone and substance (see Table 8.2). Mr. Barnes said that he would encourage this student to read more.

> My own theory is that—it's hardly novel—today's students write so poorly, including this one . . . because they read hardly anything at all, except for what's assigned. . . . They do not read for any kind of knowledge about how to write but for remembering a few facts for a test that will get them the grade that they need to get the car for the weekend or maybe even to get into the college of their choice. But they don't pay attention to the style of the writing in the material that they're given. And this, I believe, is how people learn how to write—from reading. So remediation would be: Read more, write better. Cause and effect.

Ms. Kelsey saw things differently:

> I concentrated with this kid on . . . "giving yourself a voice" and how can you do that more effectively. . . . I would work on how to get what you know—what's here in your head—into a format. I suspect that once it was in a better format, other things would begin to fall into place better, and kids could better express what they really know. . . . Start with their own feelings, start with that because it's a great place to build a bridge between yourself and the information. . . . I might pair this kid with a more able kid sometimes, or, if I get the chance, work with the kid individually to understand how that would work. Probably do some group work with the class about outlining . . . because there's a lot of potential here that's not being realized.

TABLE 8.2
Student's Essay with Teachers' Comments

STUDENT #7 U.S. HISTORY	BARNES'S SUMMARY COMMENTS

STUDENT #7 U.S. HISTORY

When the French and Indian war ended, British expected Americans to help them pay back there wear debts. That would be a reasonable request if the war was fought for the colonies, but it was fought for English imperialism so you can't blame them for not wanting to pay. The taxes were just the start of the slow turn toward rebellion another factor was when parliament decided to forbid the colonial government to make any more money. Specie became scarcer than ever, and a lot of merchants were pushed into a "two way squeeze" and faced bankruptcy.

If I had the choice between being loyal, or rebelling and having something to eat, I know what my choice would be. The colonists who were really loyal never did rebel, and 1/3 support the revolution.

The main thing that turned most people was the amount of propaganda, speeches from people like Patrick Henry, and organizations like the "Association." After the Boston Massacre and the issuing of the Intolerable acts, people were convinced there was a conspiracy in the royal government to extinguish America's liberties.

I think alot of people also just were going with the flow, or were being pressured by the Sons of Liberty. Merchants who didn't go along with boycotts often became the victims of mob violence. Overall though, people were sick of getting overtaxed and walked on and decided let's do something about it.

BARNES'S SUMMARY COMMENTS
—your topic sentence is weak
—more factual detail would improve your essay
—note spelling and grammar corrections

C–

KELSEY'S SUMMARY COMMENTS
—The greatest strength of this essay is its outstanding effort to grapple thoughtfully with the question, why did the colonists rebel? Keep thinking personally, "What if I were here?" It is a great place to start.
—To make the essay *work*, however, you need to refine your organization strategies significantly. Remember that your reader is basically ignorant, so you need to express your views as clearly as you can. Try to form your ideas from the beginning to the middle and then an end. In the beginning, tell what side you're on: What made the colonists rebel—money, propaganda, conformity?

In the middle, justify your view. What factors support your idea and will convince your reader?

In the end, remind your reader again about your point of view.

—Go back and revise and hand this in again!

Beyond a shared concern with spelling and usage, there is little similarity in the advice provided to Student B. These different emphases were also apparent in their evaluations of the other two papers (see Table 8.3). Rather than addressing the historical content of the essays, Barnes's comments focused on generic issues of writing and expression.

TABLE 8.3
Summary of Teachers' Comments on Three Papers

STUDENT A

Assessment of student's performance

Strengths

Barnes: Has a basic understanding of what happened.

Kelsey: Student "successfully attempted to evaluate issue."

Weaknesses

Barnes: Use of street language in "formal expository writing." "Below average" knowledge of content, spelling, and grammar. Little supporting evidence.

Kelsey: "Impossible to understand what kid means." Needs work on spelling, organization, and grammar.

Strategies for remediation or enrichment

Barnes: Encourage student to read more; more reading leads to better writing.

Kelsey: Work with student to develop "voice" and "to put what he/she knows into a suitable format." Direct student to revise essay and address what made the colonists rebel. Provide group instruction on outlining.

Summary comments written on paper[a]

STUDENT B

Assessment of student's performance

Strengths

Barnes: "Better than average" comprehension of facts, events, people and actions leading to American Revolution.

Kelsey: "The information is correct and shows that the student worked hard; good grasp of events."

Weaknesses

Barnes: "Wooden" written expression lacking fluidity; tends to lapse into sentence fragments, which may be a function of running out of time.

Kelsey: "Thinks that history is a catalogue of things"; "has memorized the timeline and wrote it down." Needs work on paragraphing and capitalization.

Strategies for remediation or enrichment

Barnes: "Same remediation as Student A"; more reading; additional practice writing essays.

Kelsey: Let student know that putting down many facts will not earn high grade. Encourage student to take risks. Use small-group strategies. Pair student with a more able peer.

Summary comments written on paper

Barnes: "You recall the facts rather well but your writing could be more fluid. We will keep working on this (e.g., 'a lot' is a piece of land, not a unit of measurement)." B+[b]

Kelsey: "Evaluate what happened. This is the hard part. You need to tell me why those colonists really revolted. Why were they so angry about the acts? Political

(Continued)

TABLE 8.3 *(Continued)*

gripes? Economic ones? What held the colonists together? All of these issues beg to be explained and would definitely make this paper excellent. Also, beware of spelling and paragraphing problems. Try to break your essay into paragraphs!! And avoid abbreviations!"

STUDENT C

Assessment of student's performance

Strengths

Barnes: Excellent command of content. Impressive writing, especially use of phrases such as "audacity of the English." "Replete with all the necessary detail."

Kelsey: Good introduction and ending. Well written; "uses some neat words like 'enraged' and 'audacity.' "

Weaknesses

Barnes: "Some sentence fragments and a tendency to be imprecise."

Kelsey: Needs to ask deeper questions; needs to think harder about certain historical generalizations.

Strategies for remediation or enrichment

Barnes: "Remind him that Britain is a singular subject and 'their' is a plural adjective and you can't link the two together in the English language. . . . Remind him of some of the details that escaped him in the heat of the battle and tell him to keep up the good work."

Kelsey: [Student needs to rethink statement that Britain made a clear-cut distinction between itself and the colonies.] "During the period of Salutary Neglect the issue . . . was mercantilism. There was a clear distinction between Britain and the role of the colonies but Salutary Neglect had made it sort of this loose period when nobody had been enforcing it very much." "I would work with that kid to try and . . . push a little harder. It sounds clever but what are you really saying?"

Summary comments written on paper

Barnes: "You have an excellent command of the facts. With occasional exceptions you express yourself well. Keep up the good work." A–

Kelsey: [Student wrote, "Britain (made) a clear cut distinction between the colonies and itself."][c] "Interesting though I wonder if it's true. In fact, it strikes me that Britain had always been making that distinction especially in issues of triangular trade, but simply hadn't enforced it religiously during the period of Salutary Neglect. [Student wrote that after the French and Indian Wars, the colonists realized that Great Britain was no longer necessary for production.] "Yes it would also help to briefly explain that this was because the French threat was over, while correspondingly England was now freer to tighten hold; also England wished to use the colonies to help repay its war debts."

[a]*See Table 8.2.*

[b]*Teachers were asked to make written comments on the papers but were not explicitly asked to give them a grade. Mr. Barnes chose to do so. Ms. Kelsey chose not to after checking with the interviewer about whether assigning a grade was a required part of the exercise.*

[c]*Kelsey wrote no summary comment but made these marginal comments.*

While she did not ignore problems of composition, Kelsey focused primarily on making these better *history* essays. In this part of the exercise, teachers were not asked to assign a grade, only to offer constructive feedback to the authors. The fact that Mr. Barnes chose to grade the essays, and Ms. Kelsey did not, may indicate different orientations to this task. For Barnes, these papers may have represented finished products awaiting final evaluations, whereas for Kelsey they may have represented first drafts awaiting revision. Indeed, in two of three cases, she encouraged students to rework their essays and hand them in again.

Raising Questions About Teacher Knowledge

As windows into teacher thinking, what do these brief sketches suggest? First, there are some obvious similarities. Both teachers wanted students to present organized arguments and supported claims. Both wanted the essays to embody principles of good form. Both awarded grades that showed remarkable similarity, varying, if at all, by half-grade shades of difference. Yet when we stand back from these performances, we are struck not by their similarity, but by their difference.

Mr. Barnes approached this task with the confidence of someone who has spent twenty-seven years grading papers. He worked steadily through the papers, noting factual and spelling errors and urging students to read more so that they will write better. Indeed, Barnes's fluid approach recalls the kind of scripted processing often described in the literature on teacher expertise.[28] Ms. Kelsey, on the other hand, proceeded slowly, and her judgments carried hedges, qualifications, and alternative hypotheses: Do the papers tell us more about students' prior instruction than what they really know? Might students have written better essays with prompts and other supports? Would they have been better able to display their knowledge using other media? Indeed, Kelsey noted that in her own classroom she combines essays with other forms of assessment (such as making timelines and "learning posters") because many students "don't use words well but they really understand a lot. And obviously I want to help them use words in my class . . . but I also find other ways to help them express themselves."

With only these performances to go on, it is difficult to locate the source of these differences. Here we sketch out a series of hypotheses that might account for them.

Hypothesis A: The teachers hold different beliefs about the roles and responsibilities of students and teachers. These differences in performance may be due to teachers' different conceptions of the roles and responsibilities of teachers and students. Barnes might hold students accountable for acquiring the information teachers provide. If students pay attention, they will learn the content they need. If students pay attention to authors' styles, they will become better readers and writers. In this view, teaching follows a straight path. Direct students to good books and focus their attention on the authors' writing. Require them to demonstrate their knowledge in writing assignments. Correct errors of fact and style.

Ms. Kelsey, on the other hand, may believe that students struggle to learn and write about history. They may possess incomplete conceptions that need to be challenged. They may be unfamiliar with reading persuasive prose and composing persuasive essays. They may be uncomfortable with innovative and personal thinking. In this view, teachers are responsible for creating environments that support student experimentation with self-expression and new forms of learning.

Hypothesis B: The teachers hold different theories of learning. A related hypothesis is that the teachers hold different theories of learning. Perhaps Mr. Barnes believes that learning comes about through exposure and absorption. Provided that students are exposed to materials for sufficient periods (and encouraged to practice), they will, eventually, absorb what they need to know. Ms. Kelsey seems to believe that knowledge is constructed, not absorbed, and that students need help in constructing their historical understandings.

Hypothesis C: The teachers hold different conceptions of the history curriculum. These differences might be partially accounted for by the teachers' different conceptions of the history curriculum. Barnes corrects factual errors unlikely to cause anguish to most students, such as mixing up the British East and West India Companies, but in his opinion such errors make "all the difference in the world." Committed to insuring that students have their facts straight, he crossed out the words "a whole bunch of tea" in one essay (the student had written, "The colonists . . . pushed a whole bunch of tea off a boat") and penciled in "342 chests." Although Ms. Kelsey also corrected factual errors, she seemed more concerned with, in her words, the "big picture." She focused her comments on the lack of interpretation and analysis in these papers, rather than on their factual content. The different emphases in teachers' comments may reflect different beliefs about the kind of history that is most important for students to know.

Hypothesis D: The teachers have different underlying conceptions of historical knowledge. Hypothesis C could be viewed as a by-product of each teacher's understanding of history. What if Mr. Barnes believes that factual knowledge and detail—catalogues of interesting people and events—*are* the focal points of historical knowledge? What if Ms. Kelsey thinks more about what Joseph Schwab[29] called the "syntactical structures" of history: how historical knowledge is created and justified, the roles played by interpretation and warrant, the fallacies of evidence, and the use of evidence to craft arguments?

These four hypotheses could account in part for the differences we observed. But this exercise provides only a glimpse into the world of teacher knowledge, belief, and skill. To broaden our vision, we turn to the next exercise.

EXERCISE 2: USE OF DOCUMENTARY MATERIALS

Description

In the Use of Documentary Materials exercise,[30] teachers were given thirty minutes to review a packet of eight written and three pictorial documents about the battles of Lexington and Concord. The written materials included primary and secondary sources; the pictures showed three versions of the battles, each painted at a different time. After thirty minutes, teachers were interviewed about how they might use these materials in the classroom. They were also asked to comment on what "story [the documents] tell and how they bear on our nation's history."

The Teachers' Responses

Mr. Barnes. The interview began:

Interviewer: First, could you briefly describe some ways that you might use some of these materials in your teaching?

Mr. Barnes: Well, to begin with, I *wouldn't* use them in my regular history classes. But I could use them in my AP classes because I think the reading level is too difficult for the typical average high school student that I deal with. I know that my AP students could deal with it even though they would object to the ambiguity and to the fact that they would have to make some choices and judgments. They would rather just be told what happened and then remember it for the test.

For his able students, Mr. Barnes elaborated, documents could provide "a flavor of what historical research is all about."

I would lead off by telling them that history is not always as simple as it may seem from reading about it from a textbook in terms of what actually happened. And that the longer they stay in school and the more history classes they take, the more confused they may become as to the true nature of certain events in our history, especially events involving conflict and disagreement in terms of motive and causation and so on. This is often explored in seminars on historiography. And if they decide to become history majors, they can rest assured that this type of technique is something that they will use numerous times before they get through with their study of history. But even for those who don't go on and study history at an advanced level and take courses in historiography, there's a good lesson here in the conflict of evidence, that people have to be able to read about events, or to be able to look at pictures about events and make choices as to the validity, the relative weight or merit, of certain kinds of events.

When asked about classroom activities he would plan, Barnes focused on the question of who fired the first shot at Lexington:

All of the students could read all of the written documents and the pictorial documents during a class period or as a homework assignment. And then, the following day, we could have a discussion about them. . . . Which [side] fired first? Did the colonists fire first or was it impossible to know? . . . There's all kinds of other ways. You could use a jigsaw activity[31] . . . you could simply have kids read these and give them a test as to what were the two basic points of view, the two basic differences. Or you could have oral reports, individualized oral reports from kids who have read all of these, what they think happened and why they think it happened. You could have a paper, like a seminar paper . . . trying to reach some kind of conclusion as to what evidence seems more valid and why and their conclusion about the nature of events as near as they can determine. . . . So basically it's either break it up into component parts with individual students taking documents and reporting either to groups or to the whole class, or all students reading all documents and then a generalized dissection of each one during class time. Just start with one and go through the rest of them. I think they both have merit.

When asked what he would do if some students didn't understand the main points of the documents, Mr. Barnes said he would use the "good old didactic approach. If they can't guess, I'll tell them."

Ms. Kelsey. Mr. Barnes focused on his most able students. Ms. Kelsey generated multiple uses of these documents for learners at various ability levels. She said that the documents offer

a fabulous way to get the kids to start to think historically about what really happened. . . . It's a good exercise in precision and certainly in point of view on how our interpretations of history would be altered by our points of view upon it. [It would] be a great way to get kids to work with the language of the time and the perceptions that people had. To really get down and mess with it, and start working on some critical skills in determining what really happened. But also how each account might vary and why. [One purpose] that just jumps out at me is the question of historical interpretation and bias that appears in our interpretations over time. . . . I'd start with the points of view and how each point of view uses bias to make its case. . . . There's an affective goal there, too, that the students should really get in and really experience that as well. . . . I would encourage kids to do that, to think about their own perceptions of reality in the world they experience. It could be a wonderful tie-in to the contemporary bias in journalism. It could also be an exercise in recording precisely what they have experienced. . . . If I were going to think about a hierarchy of skill, I think it's a little lower on the hierarchy than trying to assess bias, and it would depend on the level of my kids where I'd start working. For a lot of them, their sense of language is so fuzzy and imprecise, something that you can slide past the teacher and get an okay grade on, rather than giv[ing] people a juicy sense of what happened. With a lower level set of kids, I might just let them think for awhile. Which [document] really tells you with the most detail what really happened. . . . I could couple that with an exercise where they build an explanation of something. And then with very able students—no, actually, I could do this in a variety of ways and make the assignment in a couple of tiers—I might encourage kids to then quote from documents and try to develop an argument. It would be a great DBQ [Document-Based Question] if it were AP kids.

To Ms. Kelsey, these documents presented a range of curricular and pedagogic possibilities (see Table 8.4). She agreed with Mr. Barnes that original documents challenge most students but disagreed about the instructional implications of this challenge. The problems posed by documents would deter Mr. Barnes from using them except with his most able students. Ms. Kelsey, on the other hand, would use them with all students, but would craft activities at different "tiers" for students of varied abilities, experiences, and interests. She held no illusions about the difficulties documents pose for lower-level students, higher-level students, and even teachers (as her comments below attest). But she believed that students can overcome these difficulties if teachers first "build bridges" that allow learners to engage with the raw material of history:

The very first day I would start with an exercise that does talk about precise observation. . . . I would start by building a kind of a bridge and I would talk about something in contemporary events. . . . [I'd] work with [students'] own personal experience: What happened this morning when you got out of bed? When we had the assembly last week that we all went to? Something like that, something that we could discuss. Other kids read the newspaper or watch the news. . . . I'd use that as my bridge and I'd go back to this episode where we have these eyewitness accounts, and I would start by looking at what each account said and I would probably have them go through something like [the exercise] I just went through. I would have them talk about what the documents said. They have to summarize the facts that they know for sure. That's pretty hard work there, the difference between a fact and an inference. . . . I was in a seminar where I saw a bunch of teachers stumbling over that, and if we stumble, I know that the kids will. . . . I would have them cooperate . . . partners, perhaps, comes to mind. Three at the most. This is . . . pretty intense, and certain kids are going to have trouble summarizing what the document said. But just about everybody I think can usually ask a question or two, and they're pretty fun. So I would go through that, and I would really build that with the kids and have them build a kind of chart. Then I would analyze who can you trust more. I would add some more documents from the British point of view and then you could really get in and re-experience that some more. You could have the kids enact them. . . . I would culminate the activity with an essay of some kind.

DOCUMENTS STUDIED, HYPOTHESES REVISITED

In both teachers' plans, students would read and discuss documents. They might engage in debate and would do some kind of writing. Mr. Barnes planned to send students off to work with documents as homework, or perhaps use them during an in-class reading assignment. After students read the documents they would discuss them in class or report back to each other.

Ms. Kelsey began with a different set of premises. The Battle of Lexington took place a long time ago, and students might have difficulty

TABLE 8.4
Summary of Teachers' Purposes for Using Documents

BARNES'S USES	KELSEY'S USES
1. historiography	1. historiography
2. conflict in evidence	2. contrasting documentary evidence with textbook explanations
3. lesson in how bias influences the observation of reality	3. recording and observation skills
	4. point of view and bias
	5. language and perceptions of a different era
	6. thinking about why different accounts vary
	7. exploring students' perceptions of reality
	8. contemporary bias in journalism
	9. using persuasive language
	10. building an explanation or an argument with quotations
	11. preparing for the AP examination's Document-Based Question

making personal connections to the past. Perhaps she would need to begin with something more immediate—either students' own experiences or something they have seen on television. Moreover, students, like adults, have trouble distinguishing fact from inference and may need to examine their assumptions. They might need practice in asking questions about the trustworthiness of evidence. Because of the complexity of these materials, she would put students into small groups and provide them with a range of tasks so that all students could participate.

Both teachers thought hard about using documents in their classrooms. Both took into account student abilities and subject matter. Why, then, did they think so differently about the purposes of these documents and the kinds of activities they might use?

After the first exercise, we speculated that the two teachers might hold different conceptions of historical knowledge (Hypothesis D), with Mr. Barnes seeing history as primarily about facts and Ms. Kelsey seeing it as interpretative and perspectival. But here the two teachers sounded alike. At one point, Mr. Barnes remarked that history "involves a lot of sifting of facts, a lot of interpretation of data, and then making the best educated guess possible," likening the process to a "fascinating detective story." These comments shed new light on Hypothesis D. It seems that both teachers recognize the interpretative nature of historical knowledge, the centrality of evidence, and the influence of point of view. In this sense there is greater similarity in the teachers' views than we originally thought.

Although Barnes and Kelsey may hold parallel views about the complexity of historical knowledge, they differ in their beliefs about the nature of school history (Hypothesis C). Mr. Barnes seems to think of school history in two ways: a history of facts and events for average students; and a history of facts and events, with some understanding of the interpretative aspects of historical knowledge, for the college-bound. Instructional planning, then, becomes a matching process in which teachers make judgments about students' ability and then locate materials students can handle. Knowledge of history comes in blocks of facts and interpretations. Factual knowledge precedes knowledge of interpretation, and less able students, according to Mr. Barnes, may never reach the interpretative side of the subject.

Though her high school also tracks by ability, Ms. Kelsey embraces a different view of the history curriculum. She sees a close connection between the history she studied as an undergraduate and the history she teaches adolescents. In her view, factual knowledge and interpretation are bound together, so interwoven that it is impossible to disentangle the two. To be sure, Kelsey modifies her assignments and activities according to her students' ability, but these variations serve a common goal—engaging *all* students in the process of interpreting the past.

We see further support in this exercise for Hypothesis B (learning theories). As in the previous exercise, Mr. Barnes made numerous references to an exposure/absorption theory of learning. Students learn if they listen and pay attention to the topics teachers "present," "get across," and "tell." Ms. Kelsey, on the other hand, repeatedly emphasized the building of connections between history and students' lives, and the need to create situations that help students see the relevance of past to present. Yet it is difficult to say whether these differences stem from teachers' beliefs about learning or conceptualizations of historical knowledge (Hypothesis D), for the two go hand-in-hand. If knowledge comes prepackaged, teaching is straightforward: Just deliver the packages. But if knowledge is dynamic, teachers cannot simply hand over prepackaged facts, for understanding these "facts" rests in no small measure on understanding the ever-shifting interpretative frameworks in which they are embedded.

Data from this exercise also help us to expand Hypothesis A (roles and responsibilities). In analyzing Ms. Kelsey's plans, we noted that her students would also read documentary materials, but first she would model for them how she might question the documents. She would lead them through the tangle of historiography, knowing full well how easily they can lose the trail. Barnes's students, on the other hand, might read documents for homework or use them during class, but either way, they would receive little preparation for the assignment. Mr. Barnes assumes that students will navigate their own way through the documents; Ms. Kelsey assumes that it is her responsibility to provide stepping-stones along the route.

Still another hypothesis emerges from these data. The differences we found in this exercise might have less to do with theories of learning or conceptions of role than with differences in teachers' pedagogical content knowledge, the intersection of subject matter knowledge and knowledge of learners that Lee Shulman[32] characterized as the "unique province of teachers." (We refer to this possibility as Hypothesis E.) The essence of pedagogical content knowledge is transformation, the process by which teachers turn their subject matter knowledge into representations that bridge the chasm between what they know and what they want their students to learn. We noted only a few transformations in Mr. Barnes's plan. Ms. Kelsey's plans, on the other hand, displayed varied transformations of content.

Pedagogical content knowledge also embraces teachers' ability to anticipate content likely to prove difficult or easy for learners. Aware of the difficulty of these materials, Mr. Barnes restricted their use to AP students, but he showed little awareness of the formidable challenges these documents present to able students—even those with high SAT scores, good grades, and high scores on subject matter achievement tests. In contrast, Ms. Kelsey noted that even teachers can have trouble with documents. To simplify the task, she would eliminate redundant documents and arrange students into pairs or trios to work collaboratively.[33]

We wonder whether the focus on pedagogical content knowledge is itself a manifestation of something still deeper. And so, we revisit and recast Hypothesis D (historical knowledge). Is it possible that Barnes did not plan preparatory activities because he was not aware of the intellectual challenges they presented? Correspondingly, did Kelsey craft activities on slanted language, bias, and perspective-taking because she was more attuned to these aspects, qua historian, than Barnes? Indeed, whereas Kelsey corroborated evidence, speculated about the origins of documents, raised multiple competing hypotheses, and generated themes that captured patterns in the evidence, Mr. Barnes talked only of a single dimension in the documents: the dispute over who fired the first shot. Although Barnes and Kelsey may both view history as "detective work," Kelsey appears—at least in this exercise—to be the shrewder detective.

We recognize that there are other ways to account for these differences. Perhaps Ms. Kelsey tried harder. Perhaps Mr. Barnes skimmed documents instead of reading them carefully. We cannot know this from our data. And so we bring our set of hypotheses to the third and final exercise.

EXERCISE 3: TEXTBOOK ANALYSIS

Description

During the three hours of the Textbook Analysis Exercise,[34] teachers evaluated a selection from Paul Todd and Merle Curti's widely used *Rise of the American Nation*.[35] We asked them to imagine that the book was being considered for adoption by an urban school district and that their task was to

> provide a *candid review*. . . . Think about such aspects as the soundness of the history the textbook presents, the book's appeal to students, the quality of the writing, the book's potential as a tool for enhancing social studies skills, the book's appropriateness for different kinds of students, its general strengths and weaknesses, and any other information relevant to its possible adoption.

To provide a focus for the analysis, teachers were asked to give special consideration to three subtopics of the American Revolution: (a) the role of minorities and women; (b) the Boston Massacre; and (c) the issue of taxation and representation. Teachers received the text selection, a short excerpt from the accompanying teacher's manual (including examples of ready-made worksheets and tests), and a response form with questions and ample space to write answers. Sample questions included the following: "How does the text measure up with regard to recent scholarship in history?" "How might students of different reading levels react to the text?" "How appropriate is the text for the different types of teaching styles used in history/social studies classrooms?" A series of shorter questions directed teachers to specific sections of the text. This exercise did not include an interview component.

The Teachers' Responses

At the most basic level, the two teachers differed in how much they wrote: 1,892 words for Ms. Kelsey, 1,001 words for Mr. Barnes. We were aware, however, that length of response is not equivalent to depth or breadth of response.[36] In analyzing the teachers' responses, we found that they disagreed on (a) the soundness of the history presented by the text, (b) the book's effect on student understanding, and (c) the pedagogical usefulness of the worksheets and activities in the teacher's manual.

Historical soundness of the text. In evaluating the historical soundness of the text, particularly as it applied to the history of women and minorities, Mr. Barnes wrote:

> I believe that the text presents sound history concerning the role of minorities and women in the Revolution, surpassing the texts I currently use in the amount of attention devoted to these two groups. No text I have used before devoted as much as the two entire paragraphs in *Rise* allotted to "Women in the Revolution." . . . I know of no recent scholarship which is neglected in *Rise* concerning the three subtopics.

Ms. Kelsey disagreed:

> This is standard rah-rah stuff, with the bias one generally sees toward white, male, political history. It's upsetting to see so little mention of recent work, especially stuff like Nancy Cott[37] on colonial women or various historians' work on minorities. The illustration [of a slave ship] on page 97, for example, is well-known and I've seen it elsewhere, but it's not true that it's the "only picture drawn from life"—check out slave trading manuals from the period, which show how bodies could be packed most efficiently and subdued—they have detailed drawings of manacles and whips. *That* generally sets the kids thinking—this illustration, by comparison, is like a cruise ship. Also, despite the token reference to Crispus Attucks, the slave trade and Afro-American contributions to the economy and culture of the colonies are glossed over, and women, too, are relegated to cameo appearances.

These differences were thrown into relief by the teachers' responses to the textbook's account of Pontiac's Rebellion. The passage read:

> Under the able leadership of Pontiac, an Ottawa chief, the Indians joined forces to prevent any further invasion of their lands. For nearly a year, the Indians and whites were locked in a desperate struggle. The Indians destroyed most of the British forts west of Niagara. Death and destruction raged along the length of the western frontier. Finally, British and colonial troops recaptured the forts. The Indians accepted generous peace terms. Pontiac declared, "We shall reject everything that tends to evil, and strive with each other to see who shall be of the most service in keeping up that friendship that is so happily established between us."[38]

Mr. Barnes characterized this explanation as "clear, accurate, and grade-appropriate." Again, Ms. Kelsey disagreed:

> Uh-oh. I have a hard time believing things were this rosy and, unfortunately, my students will be all too slow to question a passage like this. The vague passages in paragraphs 2–4 make it sound like only the British and colonial troops were the repositories of order (and by implication virtue). And the Pontiac quote is nauseating, isolated as it is from the appropriate context of his plight. Works like Morgan's *American Slavery, American Freedom* [1975] clearly indicate the cruelty which colonists in fact inflicted. (By the way, what *were* those "generous peace terms"? Also, these early land conflicts neatly presage later pushes for "manifest destiny"—a conceptual opportunity the author ignores.)

Effects on students' understanding. The teachers also disagreed about the book's effects on student understanding. In response to a question about the text's effectiveness in "addressing the historical misconceptions that many students possess," Mr. Barnes thought the book was "especially effective" in two places: first, in a caption to a picture of the Boston Tea Party, which has the raid taking place during daylight, the text warns readers that "actually the raiders sneaked on board the ship at night";[39] and second, in a caption for an engraving of the Boston Massacre, the text alerts readers that "actually there were only ten soldiers and about sixty protesters who clashed on that March day in 1770."[40] Ms. Kelsey, on the other hand, interpreted "student misconceptions" as the broad, entrenched beliefs about history she referred to in Exercise 1. She saw the text as "reinforcing misconceptions, hardly ameliorating them," because "the poor treatment accorded women, Blacks, and Native American cultures will tend to reinforce students' despairing conviction that history is all politics, wars, and the deeds of white men."

Pedagogical usefulness of supplementary materials. These divergent views carried over to the teachers' evaluations of the text's supplementary materials. Mr. Barnes wrote that these materials contained "*many* excellent skill building activities and ideas." His sole objection was that a suggested essay question might have been better asked in an "objective format."

Ms. Kelsey was less positive. For example, both teachers responded to a worksheet on mapping skills.[41] Entitled "Completing a Map: Western Lands," this worksheet asked students to "label the 13 colonies," identify "the southern boundary of western territory added to Quebec by the Quebec Act of 1774," and name "the five colonies [that] did not claim land west of the Proclamation Line of 1763." Mr. Barnes listed the worksheet among the six "excellent skill building activities" he would use. Ms. Kelsey was less enthusiastic:

> The map worksheet gives kids *no chance* to get creative, whether with color, symbols, or interpretation. The map is also too sketchy to give anything but political information and thus leaves out critical information like the South's main waterways, the importance of the Appalachians, the position of the Adirondacks and Green Mountains. It fails to show either Boston or Charleston. And it thus severely hampers students' embryonic perceptions of *both* diversity and unity in the colonies.

TAKING STOCK

The Textbook Analysis exercise clarified some of our earlier hunches and deepened others. Comments such as "I know of no recent scholarship which is neglected" show that Mr. Barnes has not followed developments in American history since the sixties. He seems to have extensive knowledge of "textbook history," the factual and chronological content found in school textbooks, but seems less knowledgeable about the interpretive frameworks historians use to bring meaning to the past. It appears, then, that there are *substantive* differences in the subject matter knowledge of the two teachers, an extension of Hypothesis D (historical knowledge).

Perhaps the teachers' sharpest disagreement concerned the book's treatment of women and minorities. We speculate that this disagreement stemmed from the qualitatively different touchstones each teacher used to judge the book's soundness. Mr. Barnes compared the book with other textbooks, especially the two he uses. Ms. Kelsey held the text to a different standard—works by Nancy Cott in women's history or Edmund Morgan on slavery. Using this standard, the treatment of women and minorities in sidebars and end-of-the-chapter sections seemed shabby indeed. After Exercise 1, we speculated that Barnes and Kelsey hold different conceptions of their roles and responsibilities (Hypothesis A). Here we find further evidence for that assertion but with particular reference to the teachers' perception of their role vis-à-vis curricular materials. For Mr. Barnes, teacher decision making took on a binary quality. When he evaluated some aspect of the book, he either said it was excellent or, as in the case of the essay question, that it should be replaced. In his view, teachers accept or reject curricular materials but do little to adapt and modify them. This view sheds light on Barnes's responses in the previous exercise, when he was adamant that primary documents could be used with AP but not with average students.

Ms. Kelsey sees curricular materials as something to adapt and transform. We saw this in the previous exercise when she described her plans to modify the set of documents. In this exercise, she described how she would mold suggested activities and ready-made worksheets. For example, she saw value in Worksheet 22, an eyewitness account of the conditions at Valley Forge that "starts to get at some serious issues like 'Do you think it is a reliable source?' " But she recognized that a question of this magnitude needed to be adapted before it could be given to students.

Perhaps these different approaches are best exemplified in the teachers' summary comments about the "benefits and drawbacks of adopting this book." For Mr. Barnes, the chief benefit of adoption would be to "put a well-written, up-to-date, grade-level-appropriate textbook into the hands of students and a fine set of accompanying materials into the hands of each teacher." The chief drawback would be the expense: spending so much money on books that "students might still refuse to read . . . because it is, after all, only a textbook." Mr. Barnes tended to cast educational decisions in black and white: The book should be adopted but students wouldn't read it.

One might imagine that Ms. Kelsey would find few benefits in adoption. On the contrary, she found a way to turn the book's shortcomings into pedagogical opportunities: "[The text could] be adapted in many different ways by a creative teacher. The reading level is reasonable, and glitches in information could be valuable critical thinking exercises, especially with supplementary materials." Different premises, it seems, motivate each teacher's stance toward curriculum. For Mr. Barnes, curricular materials present fixed options. For Ms. Kelsey, they present potentialities to be shaped to fit particular contexts and goals.

Still other differences echo between the lines in the teachers' written comments. Ms. Kelsey's sensitivity and attention to the relationship between history and student motivation surfaced again in this exercise, supporting Hypothesis E (pedagogical content knowledge). In evaluating a suggestion in the teacher's manual that students conduct research projects on Mary Warren, John Hancock, Joseph Warren, Samuel Adams, and other figures from the Revolution, she commented, "My kids are about as interested in researching Sam Adams as I am in hearing Twisted Sister [a 1980s rock group]. The activity badly needs some spark." Similarly, in Exercise 2, she referred several times to the affective experience of reading original sources, how reading the words of the people who made history can be exciting for adolescents, a "fabulous way to get the kids to start to think historically."[42]

These comments suggest a way of thinking about history that never loses sight of the interests and dispositions of adolescents. They suggest that Ms. Kelsey believes that historical materials, carefully selected and thoughtfully presented, can excite and motivate students. In contrast, we found little in Mr. Barnes's responses that spoke to student motivation. If anything, we found evidence that Barnes thinks students are unmotivated and find little in the history curriculum that excites them. When reviewing the "A–" essay in Exercise 1, he assumed that the student was writing "about a topic he might not have any personal interest in." In the same exercise, he remarked that "today's students don't read" except to get a good grade or to "get the car for the weekend or maybe even to get into the college of their choice." In Exercise 2, he believed that even his AP students would balk at a document exercise: "They would rather just be told what happened and then remember it for the test." Here he assumed that students would not read textbooks, no matter how interesting or well-written. We could find no instance in which he spoke about historical content that excites, challenges, or unsettles students, nothing analogous to Ms. Kelsey's memory of presenting students with pictures of manacles and whips, about which she remarked: "*That* generally sets the kids thinking."

THE CONTEXTS OF JUDGMENT: WRINKLES IN TIME AND PLACE

We value professional judgment, yet this analysis reminds us of its complexity. On one level, we feel confident in saying there were real differences in the performances of Barnes and Kelsey, and that these differences are significant in a number of ways. Moreover, data from six additional exercises, which we reviewed prior to completing this article, provide support for the hypotheses we lay out here, but not without added qualifications and expansions.[43] Yet taking the next step, moving from observations of differences to making decisions on their basis, raises questions about how teachers will be judged—and by whom. We now turn to some of these issues, beginning with concerns we encountered as "judges" ourselves.

It would be dishonest for us to claim that we did not find ourselves favoring Kelsey's responses over Barnes's. Nor would we suggest that our affirmation of one teacher over the other was a coincidence or historical accident. Indeed, the differences we found between these two teachers represent major shifts in how we, as individuals and as members of academic communities, conceptualize teaching, learning, and the discipline of history. Ms. Kelsey studied to be a teacher at a time, 1984, and a place, a prestigious research university, where the effects of the cognitive revolution were being felt as never before. In her course work she encountered Vygotskian notions of mediated learning and studied various strategies—cooperative group work, cross-ability tutoring, dyadic learning—for applying them. A class on literacy introduced her to Linda Flower and John Hayes's model of composition, with its strong emphasis on preparing multiple drafts of written work.[44] And the social milieu of her education program included a commitment to the learning of sophisticated content by *all* students, as well as an emphasis on the scaffolding of instruction that might allow this to come about.[45]

Similarly, her understanding of history reflected recent developments in that discipline. History has undergone dramatic changes in the past few decades[46] as traditional political and economic history have been joined (some would say supplanted) by forms of history unheard of in previous eras. A review of these developments noted:

> The new social history, the new working class history, the new educational history, as well as black history, native history, feminist history, and ethnic history encompass only a few of the topic areas and methodologies which emerged to challenge the traditional historical synthesis in the late 1960s and 1970s.[47]

The single narrative heralding the accomplishments of great, mostly white, men gave way to a panoply of competing voices. Not only have the previously powerless been enfranchised, but the previously enfranchised have been transformed.[48]

More than simply being a new set of topics, these changes cut to the epistemological core of the discipline. The notion of historians discovering the official story of the past faded by the early 1980s as history, along with practically every other discipline, reeled from the impact of the linguistic turn. No longer were historical narratives simply written—they were *constructed*;[49] and a disinterested history isolated from the commitments of its authors, a view that held sway as recently as the mid-1960s,[50] yielded to a history that bore, even celebrated, the imprint of those who composed it.[51] In short, it would have been remarkable for someone like Mr. Barnes, trained when he was, to emerge with the kinds of knowledge and the *view* of that knowledge that Ms. Kelsey displayed. Likewise, as someone who received her B.A. from a prestigious history department in the mid-1980s, had Ms. Kelsey *not* possessed these understandings she would have been seen as having missed the whole point.[52]

As researchers with roots in the educational, psychological, and historical communities, both of us learned to frame our thinking in ways similar to those we lay out in the preceding paragraphs. Moreover, we are not unique in holding these perspectives, but espouse them as members of discourse communities that construct and share these commitments. In one important respect, we found favor with Ms. Kelsey's performances because her views on learning and teaching were in close alignment with our own. Indeed, we could not have imagined a better match.

This brief effort to place ourselves, our performance exercises, and the responses of these two teachers in context casts a different light on these data. Teaching cannot be judged apart from the time and place in which it is situated. Had these exercises been field-tested in 1957, not the late 1980s, many of Mr. Barnes's observations would not have been questioned. Few people, for example, would have challenged his belief that teaching history consisted of imparting a set of facts about economic and political history; few would have been surprised at his citing as an example of a student misconception the false belief that the Boston Tea Party took place during daylight. Many would have agreed that primary documents are more appropriate for AP students than those in the "regular" or "remedial" tracks.[53] Likewise, the belief that a set of essays reflected the normal distribution of students' abilities—not their prior instruction, their motivation to succeed, or the conditions of the test's administration—would have found a receptive audience, as would the notion that practice makes perfect in essay writing. Finally, Barnes's reliance on what he called the "old didactic approach" found much support in the education research literature of the 1960s and 1970s, a literature dedicated to establishing the most effective ways to deliver verbal information so that students could remember it on achievement tests.[54]

To be sure, we can place Mr. Barnes's ideas into a context that renders them less problematic than an assessment designed in the late 1980s. Moreover, we need not enter a time machine to find such contexts today. Although scholars and reformers might call for the abolition of tracking[55] and alternatives to frontal instruction,[56] most schools remain tracked, and most teaching remains didactic. Much as reformers and academics might argue for alternative images of schooling,[57] teaching looks eerily the same as it has looked for most of this century.[58]

Even if we were to implement change, diversity of belief, knowledge, experience, and disposition among teachers would, and should, remain. The old would still dwell alongside the new, the liberal alongside the conservative. This mixture leaves the question of judgment forever difficult and uncompromisingly complex. In the final section, we again offer a set of possibilities and ask the reader to consider each in turn.

ALTERNATIVE ASSESSMENTS, ALTERNATIVE ACTIONS

Several possible courses of action arise from our descriptions of Kelsey and Barnes. Our goal is to describe some options and explore their implications, to pose but not answer dilemmas of interpretation and action. By sketching out different ways these data can be acted on, we hope to highlight the slippery nature of using such assessments to set standards of teacher excellence.

For simplicity's sake, we resort to several rhetorical fictions. First, we pretend that we would act only on the data presented here, not the additional six exercises in the battery, the direct observations in the field, and other sources of information that would be assembled in a real assessment. Second, we cast the courses of action as simply as possible—a binary decision of pass or fail—though any performance system will surely present its results on a continuum of low to medium to high. Third, we play devil's advocate in this discussion, stating possibilities in terms uncomfortably stark, hoping that such starkness better reveals the implications of each possibility.

Possibility 1: Mr. Barnes passes the assessment, Ms. Kelsey fails. It is easy to get swept up in the youthful idealism that permeates Ms. Kelsey's responses. While many might applaud her commitment to helping all students learn things she deems important, others would have reservations. For example, her focus on "history as perspective" deemphasizes the knowledge that binds us together, the shared knowledge of history that many commentators believe is necessary for informed citizenship. Mr. Barnes's focus on "342 chests" of tea, although easy to parody when ripped from context, represents a view of learning that has the weight of tradition behind it. When two-thirds of seventeen-year-olds cannot date the Civil War within fifty years, when nearly a third do not know what countries the United States fought in World War II,[59] how can we justify devoting a week of instruction, as Kelsey would do, to "recording and observation skills"? History *is* interpretation, but interpretation must be backed by solid knowledge of facts. Kelsey's deemphasis of facts might suggest that she needs to work with experienced teachers to develop a more balanced perspective on the nature of historical knowledge.

Nor is Barnes's lack of expertise in feminist or minority history a fault. The history classroom needs generalists, not people who can illuminate a single corner of our past. The explosion of new types of historical research has imperiled our ability to provide a "big picture" of the American past. A spirit of "every man his own specialist" has led to the fragmentation of knowledge and spawned legions of brick-makers with no builders in sight.[60] The social studies had already witnessed this kind of fragmentation in the 1960s, when a welter of "mini-courses" littered the curriculum. Ms. Kelsey's tendency to give in-depth treatment to issues such as women's history or social history might result in similar confusion in students' minds.

It is clear from Ms. Kelsey's words that she prefers depth over coverage. Yet U.S. history teachers are charged with covering our entire past, and her plans for one unit are unrealistic if extended across an entire year.[61] One cannot cover all topics in equal depth, and Kelsey's responses provide us with little insight into whether she acknowledges this or—more important—possesses the skills to deal with it. The brand of teaching she espouses has shown remarkably little staying power in schools. If predictive of anything, her idealism forecasts early flight from the profession. Barnes's approach, on the other hand, represents the quick processing of an expert, someone who has learned to cope with huge amounts of information in an instant. His method and outlook exemplify tried and true pedagogy, an approach to teaching that has withstood the test of time. We are quick in this age of reform to dismiss these traditions, sneering at the kind of experiences they provide for students. As an editorial in the *Social Studies Review* lamented, "Rigorous techniques such as drill and recitation have fallen into ignominy. Forward-thinking courses seek to liberate students from old attitudes, as though from Dickensian prisons."[62]

Ms. Kelsey says things that sound good to ears trained on the rhetoric of current reforms. Barnes, on the other hand, practices a solid pedagogy that has weathered torrents of reform. And so these questions arise: Should our standard of teaching excellence consider the long view, taking into account venerable ways of conceptualizing good teaching? Or should our approach be unabashedly presentist, borne by the hope that what we offer today is not merely new but better? Or should we make some attempt to do both, grafting old onto new in the belief that eclecticism will lead not to confusion, but to strength?

Possibility 2: Mr. Barnes fails the assessment, Ms. Kelsey passes. Stated in the starkest of terms, one might argue that teaching carries an ethical responsibility to insure that *all* students have access to important knowledge and the opportunity to use it in ways that stretch their minds. According to this argument, Mr. Barnes made a fatal error when he flatly rejected the use of primary documents for anyone but his top students. He believes that students of different abilities should be provided with different curricula and different goals. Yet the notion that only elite students should be provided access to specialized knowledge or given the opportunity to interact with stimulating curricula is being challenged by today's reform efforts.[63] It is not that Mr. Barnes would disagree with the idea that "all students can learn." He believes they can. But he would disagree with the claim that all students can learn complex subject matter and think about it in sophisticated ways. His words suggest that he does not question the labels students bring with them to class. Moreover, there is little evidence that his pedagogical practices would lead him to reconsider these labels.

By denying certification to Mr. Barnes, Possibility 2 takes a stand on what teachers ought to know, think, and believe about teaching and learning. But despite this stand—and the statements of reformers, policymakers, and scholars that it represents—there are many schools in which Mr. Barnes would be a valued staff member. We would go so far as to say that the notion that "all students can learn sophisticated content" is a normative ideal not yet supported by empirical evidence. We know of no studies that demonstrate that remedial students can successfully interpret difficult historical sources, no studies that systematically document teachers' success helping *all* students learn to identify, explore, and solve historical problems. We believe—indeed, we hope—that such studies will be forthcoming. But in the meantime, can we penalize Barnes for not embracing a hope that has yet to be realized empirically?

To what extent, then, should the historical, intellectual, and social contexts in which teachers practice be factored into the outcome of an assessment? Should Barnes and Kelsey be judged by the same standards? Or should these standards take into account each teacher's intellectual and personal history or even the norms of the schools in which they work?

Possibility 3: Both teachers pass. If a group of experienced history teachers reviewed Mr. Barnes's performance, they would likely agree that he is a competent professional who deserves to pass the assessment. They would note that he could justify his answers, discuss teaching in a way consistent with their own understanding, and demonstrate deep knowledge of the history contained in textbooks. They would note that he is a thoughtful and deliberate thinker. The fact that the two teachers differ in several areas—their conceptions of history, their substantive knowledge of history, their beliefs about the goals of history/social studies education—should not be held up for question. Rather, according to this view, these differences should be accepted as inherent in the work of teaching, perhaps even celebrated. After all, historians do not agree about the nature of historical scholarship, nor do policymakers and parents agree on educational goals or curriculum. And psychologists and anthropologists have not reached agreement on the nature of learning. No one holds the definite answer to such questions as: What should students know about history? How should teachers teach? What differences among students matter? Mr. Barnes and Ms. Kelsey would answer these questions differently—our data bear witness to that. And in a democracy, we would hope to create communities that nurtured and supported diversity of thought and opinion.

Yet there is something unsettling here. The diversity we seek to celebrate is rooted in knowledge. For example, we value diverse historical views when they engage each other in ways that enrich the totality of our understanding. But the intellectual diversity in schools often has roots elsewhere. Schools are diverse because the closed-door norms of teaching support isolationism and privatism. Physically and intellectually separated from each other, teachers grow apart and often have little idea how a colleague teaching the same topic to similar students might go about it. The opportunities to talk about teaching are few; the opportunities to watch other adults doing it, even fewer. Consequently, students experience a haphazard diversity, a hodgepodge of different views that they, as novices, are expected to synthesize. A diversity built on acknowledged differences of knowledge, background, and opinion is laudable; but one that results from isolation and ignorance benefits no one, least of all students.

Moreover, we wonder whether some forms of diversity are of limited value. For example, should we celebrate a diversity of "anything goes"? Or should diversity be held accountable to standards grounded in knowledge and principles?

Possibility 4: Both teachers pass provisionally and are provided opportunities to improve their skills and knowledge. Perhaps the problems of context raised above could be addressed by ongoing professional development for both teachers. Mr. Barnes has been in schools for close to 30 years and has had little opportunity to experience the intellectual shifts that have occurred outside them. Yet these shifts have implications for how one thinks about teaching. Fundamental shifts in how we view knowledge, equity, democracy, history, and education—shifts that historians and psychologists, philosophers and political activists are well aware of—are just now trickling down as school reforms. If Mr. Barnes were a member of the communities of discourse that spurred these shifts or if he were provided with easy access to them, he, too, might have come to think in different ways about teaching, students, and history. Rather than being limited by the intellectual currents of the decade when he completed his master's degree, he would have grown as knowledge grew, changed as perspectives changed.

Ms. Kelsey is likewise a child of her time. She seems enamored of ideas we also find appealing: voice in writing; constructivism in learning; and helping all students, not just the brightest, learn challenging content. She seems blessed with the idealism and romanticism of many young teachers who have not experienced the clashes of educational theory and practice that come with years of experience. Discussing her assumptions and beliefs with other teachers would undoubtedly help her, either by clarifying and sharpening her knowledge and beliefs or by altering and amending them.

CONCLUSION

In sketching out these different possibilities, we may have tried some readers' patience. Offering alternative scenarios may be taken as a sign of indecision. Maybe our time would be better spent designing exercises that can be acted upon with certainty. If an instrument allows multiple decisions—decisions differing not only in degree but in direction— what can be said about its validity? Indeed, how can the process of validation begin?

Ironically, we view these different scenarios as a start. Each speaks to the "explanatory perspective" on validity sketched out by Lee J. Cronbach,[64] a perspective that pursues validation by formulating alternative ways to view accumulated findings. Validity, to paraphrase Cronbach, is not a property of instruments but a property of arguments. Each scenario, or argument, uses our data differently and leads to different decisions. Each offers us the chance to play devil's advocate by raising questions, questioning assumptions, and making us rethink things we prize so dearly that we forget they are hopes and aspirations, not documented truths.

No doubt we could have developed a single scenario consistent with our beliefs about good teaching. But this is a perilous way to proceed. As convincing to us as such a scenario might be, it would still be one way among many to view teaching. By sketching out different ways to attach significance to the same data, we call attention to the fact that competing images of teaching always vie for our allegiance. Choosing among them reflects what we value, what we want for our teachers and our children.

Although we embrace many of the commitments enunciated by organizations like the National Board for Professional Teaching Standards— commitments to multiple images of good teaching, to teaching as an enterprise informed by knowledge and skill, to using performance assessments as more accurate proxies of teaching—we leave this analysis cautious about what happens after the data are in. Teaching, like the history that Kelsey and Barnes encountered in these exercises, is bound by place and time. Judges will be hard-pressed to make high-stakes decisions about "better" and "worse" teaching even from the rich data generated by exercises like these. We offer this observation not as condemnation but as warning. Just as it is difficult to communicate the complexities of teaching to the lay public, so it will be difficult to communicate to policymakers how full of conflict, how rife with contradictions, their decisions about accomplished teaching will be.

A POSTSCRIPT

We bring this exploration to a close with a scenario fundamentally different from those that precede it. All the previous scenarios draw on an assumption so basic it almost goes unnoticed: Each assumes that the best way to assess teaching is to assess the individual teacher. This assumption is a pillar of modern psychometrics, and there is little in the emerging literature on performance assessment that challenges it.[65]

But the more we think about individual teacher assessment, the more questions we have. For example, what interests us most are the cumulative effects of teaching, not what students learn after a single course. After four years of high school, have students developed a historical cast of mind? Are they acquainted with different ways of viewing the past, and can they use them to think about the present? Do curriculum divisions become walled off in students' minds, or do teachers help students forge connections between developments in America and events beyond its shores?[66] These questions all go beyond a single course. In other words, students' educational experience is not the summative value of each teacher's efforts, but rather what happens when these efforts come together and coalesce into something larger. If the *sine qua non* of historical understanding is the integration of multiple perspectives, the coordination of different kinds and forms of knowledge, shouldn't we look to assessments that capture what *groups* of teachers can do together rather than what each can do apart?

In this image of education, classes would engage each other in ways that expand and amplify some perspectives, balance and temper others, and challenge and confront still others. We would not leave it up to students to sort out their teachers' different perspectives but would highlight these differences and use them to teach students about intellectual difference and reasoned debate. The success of such a curriculum would rest on the ability of a group of adults to join together and pool their talents. Teaching would be a fundamentally social enterprise and would demand a set of assessments, and an accompanying psychometric theory, that would capture the totality of experiences that these individuals, a *faculty*, create for students.

If schools were so structured, if the image of the individual file cabinet gave way to the image—and metaphor—of an electronic file share, we believe that the prevailing intellectual diversity among teachers would yield to a diversity based on engagement and knowledge. If Barnes and Kelsey were to teach in such a school, we might not expect Barnes to embrace the perspectives of feminist historians nor expect Kelsey to begin penciling "342 chests" on students' essays about the Boston Tea Party. But we would expect a healthy exchange of ideas, not only about the nature of historical knowledge but also about how to engage students who might otherwise be cast as unmotivated or, worse, unable. In such a school, these two teachers might better understand why they hold the views that they do. And we would expect that over time they would discover ways to exploit their differing views for pedagogical purposes.

Setting new standards for teachers is one thing; providing the conditions for their attainment quite another. For teachers to attain such standards on a vast scale, schools as we know them would have to change. Yet we wonder, for example, how many policymakers would endorse a school day in which a third of the teacher's time was devoted to reflection on and ongoing study of the discipline he or she teaches? A school building that provided teachers with carrels of their own, removed from the hubbub of ringing bells and other demands? An approach to teacher in-service that looked less like an EST seminar and more like the sustained learning activities that characterize true professional development?

Schools like these are few, but they do exist.[67] If they were to become the norm, we might even find individually administered assessments playing a role that thwarted change. Our hope, then, is that these assessments will become a way station in school reform, not its terminus. Acting as a catalyst, performance assessments might lead us to focus on *communities* in which teachers learn and benefit from each other. When this happens, individual assessments will have outlived their purpose and will be swept up in the changes that are our future.

NOTES

This chapter represents the final piece I wrote with Suzanne Wilson based on our joint research experience at Stanford University. It appeared in the Winter 1993 issue of the *American Educational Research Journal* (vol. 30, pp. 729–70). Many people commented on previous drafts of this article: Hilda Borko, Jere Brophy, Earl Butterfield, Larry Cuban, Janice Fournier, Pam Grossman, Mary Kennedy, Gaea Leinhardt, Dan Perlstein, Deborah McCutchen, Sue Nolen, Peter Seixas, and Roger Soder. Because we heeded only some of their suggestions, we alone are responsible for the content. We also thank Lee Shulman, whose enduring intellectual company inspired us to finish this analysis. Several years after this article appeared, I published a second article on the social uses of performance assessments. See Samuel Wineburg, "T. S. Eliot, Collaboration, and the Quandaries of Assessment in a Rapidly Changing World," *Phi Delta Kappan* 79 (1997), 59–65 (http://www.pdkintl.org/kappan/kwin9709.htm).

1. Edward H. Haertel, "Assessing the Teaching Function," *Applied Measurement in Education* 1 (1988), 99–107; T. J. Quirk, B. J. Witten, and S. F. Weinberg, "Review of Studies of the Concurrent and Predictive Validity of the National Teacher Examination," *Review of Educational Research* 43 (1974), 89–113; Linda Darling-Hammond, "Mad Hatter Tests of Teaching," in B. Gross and R. Gross, eds., *The Great School Debate* (New York, 1985).

2. Edward H. Haertel, "New Forms of Teacher Assessment," in Gerald Grant, ed., *Review of Research in Education*, vol. 17 (Washington, D.C., 1991), 3–29.

3. See B. Berry and R. Ginsberg, "Creating Lead Teachers: From Policy to Implementation," *Phi Delta Kappan* 71 (1990), 616–21.

4. Lorrie A. Shepard and A. E. Kreitzer, "The Texas Teacher Test," *Educational Researcher* 16 (1987), 22–31.

5. See B. Davey, "Evaluating Teacher Competence Through the Use of Performance Assessment Tasks: An Overview," *Journal of Personnel Evaluation in Education* 5 (1991), 121–32; Barbara W. Grover, "The Teacher Assessment Dilemma: What Is Versus What Ought To Be!" *Journal of Personnel Evaluation in Education* 5 (1991), 103–19.

6. Darling-Hammond, "Mad Hatter."

7. Ibid., 532.

8. National Board for Professional Teaching Standards, *Toward High and Rigorous Standards for the Teaching Profession: Initial Policies and Perspectives of the National Board for Professional Teaching Standards* (Detroit, 1989).

9. See Holmes Group, *Tomorrow's Schools: Principles for the Design of Professional Development Schools* (East Lansing, Mich., 1990); Carnegie Forum on Education and the Economy, *A Nation Prepared: Teachers for the 21st Century* (New York, 1986); Nel Noddings, "Feminist Critiques in the Professions," in C. B. Cazden, ed., *Review of Research in Education*, vol. 16 (Washington, D.C., 1990), 393–424.

10. B. F. Skinner, "The Science of Learning and the Art of Teaching," *Harvard Educational Review* 24 (1954), 91.

11. Gaea Leinhardt, "Expertise in Mathematics Teaching," *Educational Leadership* 43 (1986), 28–33.

12. James C. Greeno, "A Perspective on Thinking," *American Psychologist* 44 (1989), 134–41.

13. Lee S. Shulman, "Those Who Understand Teach: Knowledge Growth in Teaching," *Educational Researcher* 15 (1986), 4–14.

14. David C. Berliner, "In Search of the Expert Pedagogue," *Educational Researcher* 15, no. 7 (1986), 5–13.

15. Annemarie Palincsar and Ann Brown, "Reciprocal Teaching of Comprehension-Fostering and Comprehension-Monitoring Activities," *Cognition and Instruction* 1 (1984), 117–75.

16. Allan Collins, Jan Hawkins, and Sharon M. Carver, "A Cognitive Apprenticeship for Disadvantaged Students," in Barbara Means, Carol Chelemer, and Michael Knapp, eds., *Teaching Advanced Skills to At-Risk Students* (San Francisco, 1991), 216–43.

17. The principal investigator for TAP was Lee S. Shulman. During its four-year history, TAP issued over a hundred articles, technical reports, and other documents. Each of the exercises described here is described more fully in a TAP technical report, which includes a full scoring guide, instructions to administrators, instructions to candidates, and copies of exercise materials.

18. See Joan Baratz-Snowden, "Performance Assessment for Identifying Excellent Teachers: The National Board for Professional Teaching Standards Charts Its Research and Development Course," *Journal of Personnel Evaluation in Education* 5 (1991), 133–45; National Board for Professional Teaching Standards, *High and Rigorous Standards*.

19. Lee S. Shulman and Gary Sykes, "A National Board for Teaching: In Search of a Bold Standard," paper prepared for the Task Force on Teaching as a Profession (Hyattsville, Md.: Carnegie Forum on Education and the Economy, May 1986).

20. See Angelo Collins, "Portfolios for Biology Teacher Assessment," *Journal of Personnel Evaluation in Education* 5 (1991), 147–67; Rick Marks, "Pedagogical Content Knowledge: From a Mathematical Case to a Modified Conception," *Journal of Teacher Education* 41 (1990), 3–11; Kenneth Wolf, "The Schoolteacher's Portfolio: Issues in Design, Implementation, and Evaluation," *Phi Delta Kappan* 73 (1991), 129–36.

21. See Chapter 7 in this volume.

22. See Shulman, "Those Who Understand," 4–14, and Lee Shulman, "Knowledge and Teaching: Foundations of the New Reform," *Harvard Educational Review*

57 (1987), 1–22; Pamela L. Grossman, Suzanne M. Wilson, and Lee S. Shulman, "Teachers of Substance: Subject Matter Knowledge for Teaching," in M. C. Reynolds, ed., *Knowledge Base for the Beginning Teacher* (New York, 1989), 23–36; Suzanne M. Wilson, Lee Shulman, and Anna E. Richert, " '150 Different Ways' of Knowing: Representations of Knowledge in Teaching," in James Calderhead, ed., *Exploring Teachers' Thinking* (London, 1987), 104–24.

23. See National Center for History in the Schools, "Teachers' Academic Preparation in History," *National Center for History in the Schools Newsletter* 1 (1991), 4, 10.

24. Ibid.

25. See Lee Shulman, Edward H. Haertel, and Tom Bird, *Toward Alternative Assessments of Teaching: A Report of Work in Progress* (Palo Alto, Calif., 1988), for a description of the other six exercises in history and the nine exercises in elementary math.

26. Likewise, we have not calculated an interrater agreement or Cohen's *Kappa* for our judgments because they were not comparisons of codes or ratings but comparisons of interpretations. In this sense, we concur with Donna S. Sabers, K. S. Cushing, and David C. Berliner, "Differences Among Teachers in a Task Characterized by Simultaneity, Multidimensionality, and Immediacy," *American Educational Research Journal* 28 (1991), 70, who argue that "agreement in assigning numbers is no less subjective than agreement of researchers about propositions that faithfully describe the data."

27. Suzanne M. Wilson and Louette McGraw, *Evaluation of Student Papers, History*, Tech. Rep. No. H-3 (Palo Alto, Calif., 1989).

28. See, for example, Berliner, "Expert Pedagogue"; Gaea Leinhardt and James G. Greeno, "The Cognitive Skill of Teaching," *Journal of Educational Psychology* 78 (1986), 75–95; Ralph T. Putnam, "Structuring and Adjusting Content for Students: A Study of Live and Simulated Tutoring Addition," *American Educational Research Journal* 24 (1987), 13–48; Sabers, Cushing, and Berliner, "Differences Among Teachers."

29. Joseph J. Schwab, "Enquiry and the Reading Process," in Ian Westbury and Neil J. Wilkof, eds., *Science, Curriculum, and Liberal Education* (1958; reprint ed., Chicago, 1978), 149–63.

30. John McGreevy and Lawrence Hyink, *Documentary History Exercise*, Tech. Rep. No. H-1 (Palo Alto, Calif., 1989).

31. Until he came to the assessment center and experienced the "Cooperative Small Groups" exercise, Barnes had not heard of Aronson's "jigsaw technique," as his comments elsewhere attest: "A secondary way, which I would not have thought of until I came here, would be to use this jigsaw technique." Briefly, this is a strategy in which individuals learn different content and pool their learning in a group setting. See Elliot Aronson, *The Jigsaw Classroom* (Beverly Hills, Calif., 1978).

32. Shulman, "Those Who Understand."

33. Turning the lens of pedagogical content knowledge back on Exercise 1 provides another perspective on that exercise. An important aspect of teaching is knowing how to provide feedback that leads to improvements in students' work. Specificity is often viewed as key, and knowing how to "provide feedback" goes from

general pedagogical knowledge to pedagogical *content* knowledge when the question moves from "how can you make this a better essay" to "how can you make this a better piece of *historical* writing." We noted a dramatic difference between the two teachers when it came to the specificity of their written comments on students' papers, particularly with respect to issues of historical content.

34. Samuel Wineburg and Deborah Kerdeman, *Textbook Analysis, History* (Tech. Rep. No. H-7, (Palo Alto, Calif., 1989).

35. Paul Todd and Merle Curti, *Rise of the American Nation* (Orlando, Fla., 1982).

36. Suzanne M. Wilson, *Understanding Historical Understanding: Subject Matter Knowledge and the Teaching of U.S. History* (Ph.D. diss., Stanford University, 1988).

37. Here Kelsey refers to the Americanist Nancy Cott, author of such works as *Bonds of Womanhood* (New Haven, 1977) and *Root of Bitterness* (New York, 1975).

38. Todd and Curti, *Rise*, 98–99.

39. Ibid., 109.

40. Ibid., 106.

41. The questions on the form allowed for some leeway in response, and the teachers' responses overlapped at some points but not others. For example, the prompt under "The text and social studies skills" was phrased: "Does the text and accompanying teachers' guides (including the worksheets) help or hinder the development of social studies skills (e.g., map reading, understanding of charts and figures, evaluating data, primary sources, original art work, etc.)? [cite page numbers when appropriate]." Teachers were free to respond to any or all of the supplementary materials, but in some cases they were directed to specific pages and examples.

42. See John A. Scott, "Historical Literature and Democratic Education," *History Teacher* 25 (1992), 153–73.

43. See Suzanne M. Wilson and Samuel S. Wineburg, "Using Performance-Based Exercises to Measure the Pedagogical Content Knowledge of History Teachers," paper presented at the Annual Meeting of the American Educational Research Association, Chicago, April 1991; Samuel S. Wineburg, *A Candidate-Centered Approach to the Assessment of Teaching*, Tech. Rep. No. H-15 (Palo Alto, Calif., 1989); and Samuel S. Wineburg, "Unanswered Questions About Performance-Based Assessments of Teaching: A Case Study," paper presented at the Annual Meeting of the American Educational Research Association, Chicago, April 1991.

44. See Linda Flower, *Problem Solving Strategies in Writing* (New York, 1981).

45. Palincsar and Brown, "Reciprocal Teaching"; David J. Wood, Jerome S. Bruner, and G. Ross, "The Role of Tutoring in Problem Solving," *Journal of Child Psychology and Psychiatry* 17 (1976), 89–100.

46. See Michael Kammen, *The Past Before Us: Contemporary Historical Writing in the United States* (Ithaca, 1980); Peter Novick, *That Noble Dream: The "Objectivity Question" and the American Historical Profession* (Cambridge, England, 1988).

47. Peter Seixas, "Parallel Crises: History and the Social Studies Curriculum," *Journal of Curriculum Studies* 25(1993), 235–50, quotation from pp. 237–38.

48. See Robert F. Berkhofer, "The Challenge of Poetics to (Normal) Historical Practice," *Poetics Today* 9 (1988), 435–52; William Cronon, "A Place for Stories: Nature, History, and Narrative," *Journal of American History* 78 (1992), 1347–76.

49. Cronon, "A Place for Stories."

50. See for example Henry Steele Commager, "Should the Historian Make Moral Judgments?" *American Heritage* 17 (1966), 92–93.

51 Kammen, *Past Before Us.*

52. We thank Peter Seixas for helping us understand the importance of this point.

53. Such curriculum differentiation formed the basis of James B. Conant's plan to reform American education. See James B. Conant, *The Education of American Teachers* (New York, 1963); and see Robert L. Hampel's keen analysis of the "Conant Plan" in *The Last Little Citadel* (Boston, 1986), especially chap. 3.

54. J. H. Hiller, "Verbal Response Indicators of Conceptual Vagueness," *American Educational Research Journal* 8 (1971), 151–61.

55. See for example Jeannie Oakes, *Keeping Track: How Schools Structure Inequality* (New Haven, 1985).

56. Roland G. Tharp and Ronald Gallimore, "Rousing Schools to Life," *American Educator* 13 (1989), 20–25, 46–52.

57. California State Department of Education, *Mathematics Curriculum Framework for California Public Schools, K–12* (Sacramento, 1985), and *History–Social Science Framework for California Public Schools, K–12* (Sacramento, 1988); Holmes Group, *Tomorrow's Schools;* National Council of Teachers of Mathematics, *Curriculum and Evaluation Standards for School Mathematics* (Reston, Va., 1989); Theodore R. Sizer, *Horace's School: Redesigning the American High School* (Boston, 1992).

58. Larry Cuban, "Persistent Instruction: The High School Classroom 1900–1980," *Phi Delta Kappan* 64 (1982), 113–18; John I. Goodlad, *A Place Called School* (New York, 1984).

59. Diane R. Ravitch and Chester E. Finn, Jr., *What Do Our 17-Year-Olds Know? A Report on the First National Assessment of History and Literature* (New York, 1987).

60. See T. S. Hamerow, *Reflections on History and Historians* (Madison, 1987); Gertrude Himmelfarb, *The New History and the Old* (New York, 1987).

61. I thank Jere Brophy for bringing this point to our attention.

62. "Europe Reconsidered," *Social Studies Review* 2 (Fall 1992).

63. See Lauren B. Resnick and Daniel P. Resnick, "Assessing the Thinking Curriculum: New Tools for Educational Reform" in Bernard R. Gifford and Mary C. O'Connor, eds., *Changing Assessments: Alternative Views of Aptitude, Achievement and Instruction* (Boston, 1991), 37–75.

64. Lee J. Cronbach, "Five Perspectives on the Validity Argument," in Howard Wainer and Henry I. Braun, eds., *Test Validity* (Hillside, N.J., 1988), 3–18.

65. See Richard J. Stiggins and Barbara Plake, eds., "Performance Assessment" [special issue], *Applied Measurement in Education* 4, no. 4 (1991).

66. See Paul Gagnon, "Why Study History?" *Atlantic Monthly*, no. 176 (1988), 43–66.

67. See Deborah Meier, "Reinventing Teaching," *Teachers College Record* 93 (1992), 594–609; Sizer, *Horace's School.* For an example of teacher professional development in the workplace, see Sam Wineburg and Pam Grossman, *Interdisciplinary Curriculum: Challenges to Implementation* (New York, 2000); and Pam Grossman, Sam Wineburg, and Steve Woolworth, "In Pursuit of Teacher Community," *Teachers College Record* (in press).

IV

HISTORY AS
NATIONAL MEMORY

9

Lost in Words

Moral Ambiguity in the History Classroom

Popular culture provides us with stock images of mind-numbing history classrooms. The teacher in *Ferris Bueller's Day Off*, an adolescent movie released in 1986, begins his tortoise-paced lecture with the following soliloquy:

> In 1930, the Republican-controlled House of Representatives
> endeavored to alleviate the effects of the—anyone? anyone?—
> Great Depression. Pass the—anyone? anyone?—the tariff bill.
> The Hawley-Smoot Tariff Act, which—anyone? raised or
> lowered?—raised tariffs in an effort to collect more revenues for
> the federal government. Did it work? Anyone? Anyone know
> the effects? It did not work and the United States sank deeply
> into the Great Depression. Today we have a similar debate over
> this? Anyone know what this is? Class? Anyone? Anyone?
> Anyone seen this before, the Laffer Curve?

This brief excerpt illustrates all of the features of society's bad (cynics might claim "typical") history teacher. The monotone presentation. The forced march through the past. The bespectacled Caspar Milquetoast figure delivering a Socratic monologue. The blackboard teeming with inconsequential notes—all facts to be briefly committed to memory and expunged with the same haste. The students, for their part, sit mute and glassy-eyed, a few scribbling notes but most yawning in boredom. However this image got there—through bitter experience or sheer media repetition—it is clearly part of society's collective imagination.

No doubt there are teachers who resemble Ferris Bueller's history instructor.[1] But there are other teachers, perhaps in places we might overlook, who provide a striking contrast to the caricature. Such is the case with Richard Stinson.[2] None of the conditions in his high school, from the uninspired state-mandated curriculum, to the drab industrial-green walls of his classroom, to the mixture of "regular" and vocational ed youth who are his students, to the location of the school in a run-down working class neighborhood south of San Francisco would earmark his class as one that departs from the ordinary. Indeed, in terms of its outward characteristics it matches the attributes of low-aspiration, low-expectation venues recognizable from the popular as well as the scholarly literatures.[3]

But Richard Stinson is not the ordinary pedagogue. With seventeen years teaching experience, he has traveled a long path from his college history major to his stewardship as chair of the Social Studies Department at Thurmund High School. Along the way he came to understand that the past would not grip students in the same way that it had gripped him, growing up as the son of missionaries and traveling to remote corners of the globe. He knew that before he could thrust students into complicated issues of constitutional law or states rights, he would first have to capture their attention. He would have to help them see the remoteness of the past as an outer shell beneath which lay enduring issues of burning importance. This belief was more than a pedagogic creed or an abstract teaching philosophy. Stinson had earned a reputation at Thurmund as a break-the-mold teacher, willing to do the unconventional to inspire student interest in eleventh-grade U.S. history, a subject that typically aroused little interest even among other teachers at the same school.

The following class session took place during a two-week observational sequence in Stinson's classroom in December 1986, at the time when Ronald Reagan's secret funneling of money to the Nicaraguan Contras was being revealed. Stinson was a participant in a research project aimed at understanding the expertise of skilled practitioners; he had been nominated by peers, administrators, district personnel, and students themselves. The following case study highlights the fact that even in the hands of an exemplary teacher, the issues at the heart of history teaching can easily take on a life of their own, defying our best and most valiant attempts to fix their course.

THE CONFRONTATION

Nothing in Richard Stinson's seventeen-year teaching career prepared him for class that Wednesday morning—certainly not the two previous lessons in the sequence, which had gone pretty much as planned. This lesson, the third in the opening unit on the formation of the American government, was usually the most straightforward of the three. As in the past, Stinson planned to discuss yesterday's activity, a game conceived by his eleventh-graders two days before and played by them the previous day. He planned to help students think about the parallels between this game—especially the power struggles and compromises that characterized it—and similar forces at work in American society. He would also help them think about an essay due at the end of the week on the question "What are the parallels between the game we created and people living together in U.S. society?"

He had taught this unit many times before and found that even when it "bombed" it worked. Although he had seen many changes during his years in Garden Ridge, watching it turn from a stable bedroom community of white, middle-class families to an ethnically diverse community in which renters outnumbered homeowners, this assignment remained a constant. From past experience he knew that it provided students with a powerful metaphor for understanding the turbulence of the "Critical Period," that tense and uncertain time between the colonists' victory at Yorktown and the drafting of the Constitution in Philadelphia.

Stinson's plan for this Wednesday was to ask his second-period "generals" class to review yesterday's session, easily the most unusual fifty minutes of the school year. When they came to class on Tuesday, students placed their books on their desks, put on their jackets, and went outside to the school tennis courts. There he gave each side a bag of equipment—two badminton racquets, a Frisbee, a Nerf ball, and several ping pong balls along with chalk and a blackboard—and repeated the only rule they had to keep: They could do anything they wanted with this equipment as long as they found some way to use *every* piece of it.

What happened during this class recapitulated what had happened many times before: a group of highly energetic adolescents, thrilled about abandoning the classroom, burst on to the tennis court ready to play. They quickly reviewed the rules from the previous day and began. But before long they found these rules insufficient and started making adjustments. Most students were left without racquets or balls and stood aimlessly on the sidelines watching their peers have all the fun. These bystanders started negotiating with the more active players, suggesting adaptations and introducing new rules, all in an attempt to find a way for more people to be involved.

Standing over six feet tall, Stinson assumed a commanding presence on the sidelines, but he did little except remind students of the rules they had agreed upon the previous day. He became directive only in the last two minutes of the hour, when he told students to "think hard about what this game means because you'll have an essay due on Friday." But Stinson knew that he had to do more than that to prepare students for this essay. Left to their own devices, students would have a hard time connecting the concrete experience of the game with an abstract debate over the Constitution. So, for class the following day he scheduled a discussion to debrief this experience, a time when he could help students see the parallels between the compromises they made with rackets and balls and those made by the nation's founders in the eighteenth century.

Class began on Wednesday with a brief discussion of current events, dominated by the fast-breaking Iran/Contra scandal. Stinson directed students' attention to a newspaper article taped to the board, "Poll Indicates Reagan's Approval Rating Down 15 Points." "Yo, he is still my main man," said Donnie, tall and ungainly and sporting a black Mack Truck cap. Other students joined in to support President Reagan. Many of the more vocal students were wearing caps with the logos of Allied Van Lines and United Cargo, the freight companies that employed their parents. Others wore military jackets with names like Subic Bay and Okinawa embroidered on the back. In this environment, at least, President Reagan's reputation was unscathed by the day's news.

Students quieted down as Stinson moved to the center of the class: "For your essay due on Friday, I want you to think about the parallels you see between the game you came up with and people living in American society today. A couple of people said before class that they were having trouble seeing connections. I hope that possibly, as we discuss this, we can get a few ideas going." Stinson then went to the board and divided it into two sections: "The Game" and "U.S.A." "Okay, James," he began, "any parallels?" James, a slightly built boy who had arranged the notebooks on his desk into a symmetrical pile, seemed puzzled. Hesitating, he said, "Well, . . . we had to change the rules."

"Exactly," boomed Stinson. "We changed the rules, especially in how we scored. Can you think of any basic rules or laws in American society that have been changed?" James looked stumped, as did the rest of the class. This was no surprise to Stinson. He knew that it would take time for students to understand that America's system of laws was created through debate and compromise, an insight absolutely essential to students' understanding of the formation of American government. While some students may have sensed the connection between the game and American legislative processes, Stinson wanted it to be crystal clear.

"Well," he continued, "if we have changed the rules of the game, then the parallel is that we've made alterations or changes in the way we live in America, no?" This prompt gave students the structure they needed. Immediately Ellen suggested, "Yeh, like the Depression and all those social programs." John added, "And what about all those constitutional amendments." Stinson pressed him to be more specific. "Like not being able to drink." "Yes," Stinson nodded. "Good!"

The discussion started to take off, and Stinson, now smiling and animated, darted from the center of the classroom to the side and back to the board. When Nicole commented that the game was "all confused," Stinson used her response to explain how the period they were about to study, from the end of the Revolutionary War to the drafting of the Constitution, was known as the "Critical Period," a time marked by indecision, inaction, and growing discontent—the very qualities that characterized Tuesday's game. When Stacy observed that not everyone participated in playing the game, or even in making the rules, Stinson pushed her to make the connection to U.S. society. "Well, in society some people vote and some don't, but even if you don't vote you're still going to have to abide by those rules." Before long the discussion was running by itself, every teacher's dream. When one student recalled a feature of the game, another generated its analogue in American society. As students assumed more responsibility for the discussion, Stinson receded into the background. He listened hard to students' comments and quietly filled in the chart on the blackboard.

It all began innocently enough, and no one could have predicted that this one comment would lead where it did. Donnie's question set off a chain of events that challenged Stinson's ability to manage the intellectual and moral climate of his classroom as few other challenges in his seventeen years of teaching had.

"Mr. S.," Donnie began, "you were watching over us in the game, kind of like the government or something, and when we made up a rule you had your little say in it too."

"I only set the parameters of the game, Donnie. What would be the parallel? What agency or institution in America sets the parameters on us?"

"You mean like the Supreme Court?" Donnie asked.

"Well," Stinson crunched up his forehead, "would the chief justice say that he puts parameters around us?"

Donnie seemed to be following Stinson's lead. "Okay," Donnie paused to gather his thoughts, "let's say that you were the equivalent of the Supreme Court or say the Constitution, and then there was somebody, like the principal, watching over us, taking notes. Would that be a higher form of government?"

Stinson's satisfaction was written all over his face. Again he seized the opportunity to make Donnie and the rest of the class think harder: "Is there any government or legal force in the world today that can tell the U.S. what to do?"

Some students answered, "No way!" A few others laughed derisively at the thought.

"You may laugh," Stinson said, moving from the side of the class to the front, "but did you know that the World Court, which is an agency of the United Nations, has felt that the U.S. has operated in violation of international law in Nicaragua? By mining its harbors and taking overt military action against Nicaragua, we have been found in violation of international law. But the question I'm aiming at is this: Is there any authority that transcends the Constitution?"

Students fidgeted at their desks, but no one uttered a word.

"Well," Stinson continued, "What about moral authority or religious authority?"

The mere mention of religion set off a flurry of "oohs" and "ahs," the students' signal that a taboo had been broached. Paul, sitting in the front row, seemed to initiate a script that had been played many times before. "So, Mr. S., are you saying there is a God?"

Stinson hesitated. "Come on, Mr. S.," students chided, but Stinson, seeming to enact a part in a well-worn script, refused to take the bait.

"Okay, let me ask you this, Donnie: What was the defense at Nuremberg of the Nazi officials in the dock?"

"Obeying a superior," Cindy piped up.

"Yes, Cindy, they were following orders from their superiors, and they weren't in a position to disobey because they were being told what to do. Did that defense get them off the . . ."

Before Stinson could complete his sentence, Chris interrupted, "You know, Mr. S., thirty-two Nazis were acquitted."

Yes, Stinson did know. He also knew that Chris would know, since Chris, Donnie, and Dave, the three members of the Wednesday after-school "War Club," knew practically every detail of World War II, from the number of casualties at Midway to the extent of damage in the firebombing of Dresden. But the comment left Stinson unfazed.

"Did it get Herman Goering off the hook? Albert Speer off the hook? More important, should it have gotten them off the hook?"

Stinson's question ignited a minor explosion in the class, a cacophony of "yesses," "no ways," and "of courses." Students were engaged and passionate, arguing with each other as much as responding to Stinson's query. He pressed on with this topic because it was important for students to understand that Americans have always assumed that a larger moral force buttressed their legal system. Through a series of questions, he hoped to get students to see what they had already intuited.

"Say there was incontrovertible evidence that I had been involved in the extermination of innocent people," Stinson continued. "I didn't like it but I had been given orders to do it. Let me ask you," he said, his voice rising to a mock crescendo, "would you do it?"

Donnie was the first to answer. "Well, let me ask you, Mr. S. What would happen if you refused orders?"

"I would be punished, I would be . . ."

But before he could finish, Tim broke in: "You probably would have gotten shot and thrown in a pit!"

"So," Stinson paused, his six-foot-two-inch frame hovering above Tim's slight build, "does that mean I'm justified in doing it?"

Again the class erupted into an free-for-all, with nos and yesses, charges and countercharges flying everywhere. Above it all, Chris's baritone voice made itself heard: "Tell me, what is more important: self-survival or survival of the masses you don't really care about anyway?

"You tell me, Chris," Stinson replied, staring squarely at him, waiting for an answer. For a moment, the atmosphere turned tense and silent, but Chris did not back down: "I'd save my own skin."

At that moment, the game, the chart, and even the essay students had to write for Friday were far from Stinson's mind. To leave such attitudes unchallenged would have violated everything Stinson believed about teaching. Didn't students have a unit on the Holocaust in tenth grade?

Had it made no impression on them? Didn't they realize the implications of what they were saying?

All eyes were on Stinson, who for the first time in the class period looked rattled.

"Okay, let's see," he said, "so . . . if I understand you, Chris, you're saying I'm justified in killing innocent people. Does having orders get me off the hook? What do you think, Cindy?" Cindy, one of the most articulate students in the class, had been oddly silent during this discussion, and calling on her was a calculated guess that she would help turn the tide. "I think that it just means," Cindy stated forcefully, "that you are participating in the illegal acts your superiors are doing."

Thank goodness, Stinson thought to himself, a small dose of reason in this moral quagmire. This comment, he hoped, would put the discussion back on track and help him get back to his point about a higher law that transcends laws enacted by human beings. All he had to do was make this point explicit. "So," he said building on Cindy's comment, "if you are going to disobey the governmental structure above you, then what law or principles are you following?" Surely this more directed question would help students see the point behind the question that started all this. But that was not in the cards for today. Debby responded, "You're not—you're not obeying any principle or law!"

Stinson's eyes darted to the clock. Fifteen minutes left before the bell. He had to bring this discussion to a close, to return to the essays due on Friday. Yet how could he leave these issues out in the open, without an appropriate response? Again, before Stinson could catch his breath, Donnie responded to Debby's claim.

"Yes, you are. You *are* obeying a principle. In the case of the Nazis, to disobey orders would also be disobeying religious laws, since the SS really believed—a lot of them did at least—that Hitler was their God-given leader, their messiah. And one more thing. Back in the Second World War, our men were killing their men; they were killing ours, just because those guys were told to do it, and they were doing it on a bigger scale, that's no worse than what our men did. Isn't it the same thing? They were told to do it or they'd be court-martialed."

Stinson looked incredulous. "Are you equating a soldier fighting in war with a guard exterminating innocent people?"

"Well, it's still soldier versus soldier." Chris's comment evoked a round of raucous applause. The students' excitement, or at least the excitement on the faces of Chris, Donnie, and Dave, clashed with Stinson's ashen expression.

"Even if a guy wipes out forty thousand people over a four-year period," Chris continued, "and if he didn't do it he would have gotten court-martialed, and if one of our guys didn't shoot one of their guys or went AWOL or whatever, he would have gotten court-martialed."

"So what you're saying, Chris," asked Stinson, "is that an SS guard who exterminates people is justified because he was doing what everybody else in the Second World War was doing? Following orders?"

Chris seemed to back down, or at least to regroup. "Well, let's talk about Vietnam. In World War II, at least, you were fighting an army. But in Vietnam, hey, it was different. The enemy was all over, hiding in bushes, the enemy was everywhere."

Vietnam. At least the word had finally been uttered. Throughout this discussion, Stinson's mind had raced to My Lai, particularly to an image fixed in his mind of a little boy, not more than five years old, lying face down next to his murdered father. Stinson also knew that Vietnam was very much on the minds of Chris and Donnie, both of whom had fathers wounded in Vietnam. He hesitated momentarily but decided to pursue an example that had occurred to him earlier. It was risky, but he needed some way to jar these kids out of their moral complacency.

"Okay. Let's say that you're with a squad in Vietnam, and you guys come into a village and this village has been giving you guys a lot of problems, a lot of sniping, and the lieutenant in charge of the squad is pissed off." Stinson's language set off another flurry of "oohs" and "ahs." But for the first time in minutes, the room fell silent.

"And so he orders you," Stinson continued, "to bring out all the villagers, and there are women, children, and old men; a lot of the older boys and men are not there, and he says to you, 'Hey I'm sick and tired of this damn village, we're going to take care of it right now. Round them up and shoot them, we are just going to wipe them out; they are not going to give us any problems any more.'" Stinson paused. Deliberately, methodically, he turned to face his students. As if speaking directly to every one of them, he asked, "Would you do it?"

No one said a word. Some fidgeted nervously, folding pieces of paper into tiny triangles or tapping their pencils on their desk. Maybe he was finally getting through. He decided to take it one step further.

Without breaking role, he glared at Chris, Donnie, and Dave. "I'm telling you right now," his voice amplified, "take 'em out and shoot 'em. What would you do?" he pressed. "Would you say yes or no?"

The boys averted their eyes from Stinson's. It was Cindy who spoke—Cindy, who had been the lone voice of morality earlier in the hour. "Listen," she began, her voice sympathetic and apologetic. "When you make a commitment to do something, you're going to do things you don't like."

Alex, who had said nothing during the period, muttered loud enough for all to hear, "How do you know you *don't* like it?"

Stinson's head was spinning. Alex's bravado, the desire of a sixteen-year-old boy-man to shock his peers, he could understand. But Cindy? If she felt this way, what did the others think? There were five minutes left in the period when Stinson slumped down in a chair in front of his desk. After what seemed an interminable pause, he faced the class somberly.

"I will try not to inject my own personal feelings into this. But I am really disturbed by what I'm hearing here. This incident occurred in 1968 at My Lai, and the person involved, William Calley, the person who pulled the trigger, and his commanding officer, Captain Medina, were court-martialed, not for *not* doing it, but for *doing* it. The army itself found this to be an unconscionable action. Why do you think so?" Stinson asked, his question as much accusation as query. "The army itself said that this is not what Americans do; even though an order was given, this was beyond the pale, a violation against humanity."

Stinson's timing was impeccable. The clock began to hum as it did right before the bell was about to ring. There was a minute left to go, and this comment seemed to bring closure to this difficult discussion. But Donnie wouldn't have it. His quivering voice conveyed a mixture of passion and anger.

"Mr. S., it's like the Revolutionary War; a farmer picks up a gun and shoots and then goes back to the field, same thing. People in Vietnam, you could never tell who your friend was, you didn't know—your buddy could be a Viet Cong soldier, you just didn't know."

Donnie spoke from his heart, drawing on the experience of his dad, who lost his left leg to a land mine near Da Nang.

Stinson felt for Donnie but could not tolerate the implications of his comment. "So what do you do, Donnie? Are you saying that we must shoot first and ask questions later?"

"That's right," said Dave, coming to his friend's defense. "You never knew who was right; they shot at us; people make a lot of bad judgments."

Chris joined in. "You have to take actions like that. Because the only way you win a war like that is to exterminate the whole population."

Stinson was visibly flustered. He sat at his desk, cradling his head between his two muscular arms. "There are some really disturbing implications in what you just said, Chris. That the only way to win is to wipe out everybody. I ask you," Stinson sighed deeply, "what kind of victory would that be?"

Chris responded without flinching, "A complete victory!"

Students' laughter, raucous and nervous, almost drowned out the bell signaling the end of the period.

THE AFTERMATH

It is easy to second-guess the pedagogical decisions Stinson made in the heat of the moment, but we should not lose sight of the striking difference between his history class and those that have been caricatured by the media and bemoaned in the scholarly literature. Stinson has succeeded where many fail. His classroom seethes with energy, becoming a crucible where issues of history mix with issues of cultural memory. For Stinson's students, "school knowledge" and knowledge from their everyday experience are not separate categories, at least as far as the past is concerned. It is because Stinson has succeeded in creating an atmosphere where education is not "academic" but instead is a process of debate, discussion, and questioning that these adolescents go from "playing school" to putting their own views and selves on the line.

Whether in the classroom, the newsroom, or the streets of the inner city, whenever the past meets the present over issues of contested memory, the ingredients are present for a conflagration that can rage out of control. During these fifty minutes the classroom becomes a battleground, pitting student and parent against teacher and curriculum in a contest over how the past will be remembered. "Curriculum" here refers not just to the mandated U.S. history curriculum Stinson teaches but also to the largely tacit but deeply felt "hidden curriculum" of his classroom—his belief that history should be a humanizing experience that makes students' thinking more nuanced, while cultivating in them a distaste for easy answers. Though never enunciated in such formulaic terms, this goal motivated all that Stinson did. It was with this goal that Stinson faced his greatest challenge: how to move a group of adolescents to consider the dark side of social life, the notion that goes back to the second book of the *Republic* that might does not make right.

As this discussion careened out of control, knocking down distinctions between combatants and civilians, Allied military campaigns of World War II and the Einsatzgruppen's murder of Jews on the Polish front, Stinson raced against the clock, that ubiquitous arbiter of intellectual life in the place we call school. Though sharing the fifty-minute format with the geometry or chemistry classroom down the hall, the history classroom differs in profound ways. While discussions on solving equations with two unknowns or the foundations of Avogado's number may provoke teachers to ask themselves deep questions about learning and pedagogy, they rarely raise questions about what it means to be human, what it means to answer to powers that dwarf the self. Moreover, the geometry or chemistry teacher does not have to contend with cultural forces that feed young people a steady diet of images and narratives that often seek to anesthetize rather than cultivate thought. Particularly when the history classroom ventures into the terrain of "lived history," events still active in social memory and kept alive by those who experienced them, the history teacher is just one voice, and often a muted voice, in a cacophonous marketplace of MTV, movies, disc jockeys, parents, neighbors, peers, and others.

Add to this cauldron the ethos of adolescent culture, particularly the testosterone-fueled bravado of sixteen- and seventeen-year-old boy-men and one starts to see the challenges faced by Stinson and others like him. We might attribute some of Donnie's and Chris's brashness to a "boys-will-be-boys" desire to shock, as well as to the resurgence of militarism that characterized the Reagan administration. At the same time, it is hard to listen to their words, their wave-of-the-hand dismissals of the rawest of violence and not hear echoes of contemporary violence, particularly violence that has occurred within school walls.

In thinking about what Stinson might do after a discussion like this, there is a tendency to seek a right course of action, as if some formula existed for teaching young people how to make meaning from the past and live their lives with a sense of decency. It is a strategy I reject here. Instead, I want to bring this chapter to a close by opening it up further— by suggesting that the reader put herself or himself in Stinson's shoes and ask what the next day's class might look like. In this spirit I offer the following three scenarios.

Scenario A: A Man of Faith

When questioned about his own religious beliefs, Stinson hedged. He is in actuality the son of a minister and a devout Christian who was involved in Christian youth movements prior to his decision to enter teaching. In reflecting on this class later in the day, Stinson wondered whether one can have a serious discussion about morality without invoking God. After replaying the discussion in his mind, he returned to the classroom and shared, in a more direct way than ever before, his own view on the issues of the discussion. At the beginning of next class he looked Donnie squarely in the eyes and said:

> Donnie, you said that killing innocent women and children may be a "complete victory." Perhaps in your eyes, but I have to be honest with you. The thought disturbs me greatly. For me, such an action is the epitome of sin and must ultimately be judged in the eyes of God. I'm sorry, Donnie, but I can no longer restrain myself. You see, I believe that we will be held accountable for our actions on a day of judgment. On that day, we will not be evaluated by whether we obeyed the will of our staff sergeant but whether we obeyed the will of the Divine. In the final result, I believe, we answer to God, not man. And believe it or not, this principle was a motivating force behind the Constitution that we will study this year. Teachers are not allowed to use the podium of the public school to promote a particular religious belief, but neither can we pretend that our actions, our social commitments, and the way we navigate the world are unaffected by our beliefs. In this case, I am not only your teacher but a fellow human being. And it is in that capacity that I must address the implications of what you said in class.

Scenario B: History Class as Town Meeting

Stinson thought hard about what had transpired, but he could not fathom Donnie's response. What could motivate such beliefs? He decided to call Donnie's father and talk to him about the boy's behavior in class. During this phone call, Stinson decided to ask the father to come and speak to his history class about his experiences in Vietnam. The next morning students entered the second-period U.S. history class to find Donnie's dad sitting in the place reserved for Stinson. This vet began his talk with this question:

> Why did I lose my leg in Vietnam? I'll tell you why: Because we were double-crossed by our "friends." We were told to fight a war but to fight it with one hand tied behind our backs. I'll tell you this, no matter what your history books tell you, we could have won that war if we had been allowed to fight it the way we knew how. Did civilians get killed in Vietnam? Of course they did. You show me one war in the history of mankind where civilians did not get killed. I'm sorry, but that's war. If we weren't prepared for that to happen, we should have never got into it in the first place. Once we did, we made a mistake by handcuffing our troops the way we did. A lot of our best and brightest came home in body bags because some paper pusher in D.C. thought he knew what was right. A lot of kids your age are walking around with crippled dads because so-called Americans supported the enemy and burned the American flag while we risked our lives.

Scenario C: My Lai

As Stinson thought about things his students said—the notion that killing children is justified because you were ordered to do it—his mind flashed to the first article he had read about the My Lai massacre. After class he went to his files to retrieve it. The *Life* magazine article, "The Massacre at My Lai," featured eyewitness accounts and photographs of the American soldiers killing women and children in that Vietnamese village.[4] He would have students read the article in class tomorrow, talk about Calley's trial on Thursday, and have students write an essay on Calley's plea and the verdict of the military court for Friday. The "Critical Period" and the Articles of Confederation were important, but there were more pressing issues that had to be dealt with now, while students' interest was high. The "Critical Period" would have to wait.

CONCLUSION

As society continues to be wracked by social problems, the place of history in the curriculum remains precarious. History is always being called on to justify itself amidst calls to teach "environmental education," "service education," "peace education," and a host of other competitors. Of late the rising violence in American schools has increased calls for "character education," courses and curricula designed to instill values among American youth.

Many of these attempts have been criticized as conservative attempts to lobotomize inner-city rage and dilute an already watered-down curriculum. But Stinson's classroom shows us that when history is approached courageously and at its deepest levels, no new curriculum is needed to engage enduring questions of values. In classrooms like his, history cannot avoid issues of character. Teachers like Stinson allow adolescents to break out of the mode of playing school and put themselves on the line. Discussions in such classrooms will inevitably boil over into the contentious issues of judgment, conflict, and tension that characterize a free society. This is what Dewey meant when he wrote that schools are not training grounds for democracy but the places where democracy is enacted. Either the classroom becomes a site where we learn to talk to one another, or we will suffer the enduring consequences of never having learned to do so.

NOTES

This case study is based on an actual discussion in the history class of a participant in the Teacher Assessment Project at Stanford University, which was directed
by Lee S. Shulman, and funded by the Carnegie Corporation of New York. I have
edited some quotations from the discussion but have made every effort to retain the
original meaning. The writing of this case study was stimulated by conversations
with Judy Kleinfeld of the University of Alaska, Fairbanks; it originally appeared in
a series she edited, "Teaching Cases in Cross-Cultural Education," published by the
University of Alaska Press (Fairbanks, 1993). It has been substantially revised and
updated for this volume.

1. Empirical evidence on history teaching does little to challenge this image,
particularly when addressing "typical" or garden-variety instruction. There are
many explanations for lackluster history instruction. Some focus on teachers who
feel compelled to cover a mandated curriculum at the expense of the content that
most concerns students: See Roy Rosenzweig and David Thelen, *The Presence of the
Past* (New York, 1998). Other explanations focus on teachers' inadequate subject
matter preparation: See Diane Ravitch, "The Education of History Teachers," in
Peter Stearns, Peter Seixas, and Sam Wineburg, eds., *Knowing, Teaching, and Learning History: National and International Perspectives* (New York, 2000). The research
described in this chapter, as well as that described in Chapter 7, explicitly sought
out the "nontypical" and nonrepresentative classroom.

2. This name and all others are pseudonyms.

3. Reba N. Page, *Lower-track Classrooms* (New York, 1991).

4. *Life* (December 5, 1969), 36–45.

10

Making (Historical) Sense in the New Millennium

ear the end of an interview about the Vietnam War, Fred Lewis expressed concern about how little his sixteen-year-old daughter, Anita, knew about the war. As the interview came to a close, Fred speculated about how he might teach Anita about this period.

Fred Lewis's response to his daughter's ignorance speaks volumes about how we become historical in the new millennium, about how ordinary people think about the transmission of historical knowledge in the modern age. He does not suggest taking his daughter to the library. Nor sitting down with her and looking up Vietnam in an encyclopedia. No mention of Encarta™ or the Internet. Although Fred worked with a Vietnam vet, he never suggested the possibility of arranging a meeting. Instead, he formulated the following plan for teaching his daughter about Vietnam:

> I was thinking maybe we could—we'll have to get a copy of *The Green Berets*, you know, with John Wayne or something like that, so she's a little bit more aware of what was going on. I don't know how accurate all that is, but at least it would bring up some questions.

Fred Lewis faced a dilemma familiar to many parents. It is hard for one generation to get used to the idea that their own children have no sense of what happened a few short years ago. Like many parents, Fred wants his daughter to be "a little bit more aware" of what went on before her birth. To create this awareness, he responds as any good teacher would: He thinks about curriculum. In fact, given his own political and ideological leanings, Fred has a clear idea of what materials to look for and where to find them. It's not to his neighborhood library that he turns, but to his neighborhood Blockbuster.

THINKING ABOUT THE PAST

In 1996, with a grant from the Spencer Foundation, I embarked on a longitudinal study of how ordinary people like Fred and Anita conceptualize their lives as historical beings. I focused on the lives of fifteen adolescents and their parents. The young people attended three high schools in the Seattle area. One was a meandering inner-city complex, with a tracked and differentiated curriculum, large classes, and students who spoke twenty-three different native languages. A second school was at the opposite end of the spectrum: With tuition set at over $10,000 per year, this private preparatory academy had classes of ten to twelve students who would sit around a table with their history teacher, who held a Ph.D., to discuss the day's assignment. The third school, the one Anita Lewis attended, was dedicated to "furthering God's Kingdom" by helping students understand and apply "principles of scripture" in a way "which pleases God." Students attending this school were mostly white and middle-class, from a range of Christian denominations.

In each of the three schools, I selected five students as they embarked on their state-mandated eleventh-grade U.S. history course. I wanted to understand how these young people thought of themselves as historical beings prior to starting eleventh grade, their last formal exposure to U.S. history in high school. I wanted to know what the experience of learning U.S. history meant to them during the year, and how they remembered the content of instruction a year later, as they completed high school and prepared for the future. For a year, I, along with my team of graduate students,[1] spent countless hours in these three schools, watching history classes, audiotaping lectures, touching base with our fifteen participants, all the while collecting, cataloguing, and sorting their assignments, tests, class notes, and term papers.

Our interests went beyond the classroom. We wanted to understand how these fifteen teenagers understood their *own* pasts, including the histories of their families and communities. This meant interviewing them in the context of their homes, typically in their living rooms, and asking them to tell us the stories of their own births (an event that they had heard about entirely from others), and to narrate the most important events in their lives. From here, we asked them to "draw a map"[2] of the most important events in the life of the nation, offering a look at how a diverse cross-section of adolescents conceptualized history from their own perspective. This initial interview, which in some cases ran as long as three hours, was one of eight formal interviews over the course of two and a half years.[3]

Each of these students grew up in a family, and we wanted to capture this aspect of their experience as well. The educational literature is filled with claims about the "family as educator," but the meaning of this phrase is anything but clear. To better understand students' contexts for developing a historical self, we subjected parents to the same grueling life history interviews that students engaged in, and over the course of the study we interviewed or surveyed parents twice more.[4] Finally, each of the three teachers participated in the same life history interview, along with several other interviews along the lines of those completed by students.

THE VIETNAM INTERVIEW

It is impossible to do more than convey a sense of the findings that have emerged from our nearly 150 formal interviews with students, parents, and teachers; 130 hours of direct classroom observation; and our analyses of over 2,000 pages of written documents. In the spirit of economy, I focus here on the richest and certainly the most memorable data-gathering activity across the two years of data collection: our joint parent–child interview about the Vietnam War and the meaning of the 1960s.

In studying Vietnam, we wanted to examine a historical event that was experienced by parents in their own lifetimes but had already become "history" for their children—the difference, if you will, between *lived memory* and *learned memory*. We were faced with many dilemmas in examining this issue. The last thing we wanted to do was create a setting that seemed like a test; our primary goal was to get one generation to talk to the other about an issue of historical significance. To reduce the pressure and create a somewhat natural setting, we decided to focus on pictures and song.[5]

We built our interview around a series of six iconic pictures and a two-minute presentation of a song. The pictures included the *Life* magazine picture of a nine-year-old Phan Thi Kim Phuc running naked after a napalm bomb attack; an ambiguous picture in which a GI, holding two Vietnamese children under his arm, appears to be fleeing a battlefield;

construction workers at a pro-war rally in front of Manhattan's City Hall in May 1970; a flower child placing a daisy into the gun barrel of a National Guardsman during the March on the Pentagon in October 1967; a Vietnam vet, chalk in hand, tracing the name of a fallen comrade at the Vietnam War Memorial; and a cartoon from 1968 in which the Angel of Death, standing against a background of tombstones, asks Uncle Sam: "What should I put down as the reason for dying?" The song we played was "Woodstock," written by Joni Mitchell and performed by Crosby, Stills, Nash, and Young. ("Who are they?" wondered nearly half of the teens.) The interview took the form of free-response: Parents and children wrote down their reactions to the pictures and song without revealing them to each other, and then shared these responses with us in discussion. We made sure that children spoke first about each picture so that their responses would not be biased by those of their parents.

After the first few interviews, it became clear that we had stumbled upon a format more powerful than we had imagined. Tissues joined the list of required supplies in the interview room. For many parents, Vietnam inhabited and continues to inhabit their present, and does so with an intensity that spills over with little provocation. Their responses to this interview captured the contemporary political spectrum in microcosm, from those people who mark Vietnam as the beginning of the fall, the event that launched America into its current abyss of crime, sex, and lawlessness, to the mother who wistfully turned to her sixteen-year-old and sighed, "It's not like now, where everybody is out for himself. Back then we had a *purpose*."

The interview with the Delaney family—sixteen-year-old John, his mother, Karen, and his father, Ken—represents the potential of this approach to shed light on the larger questions of historical consciousness that motivated our work. The Delaneys are white, middle-class, and devoutly Christian. John attends the Christian high school described earlier. He is an intelligent, outgoing student, active in the school drama society, articulate in his responses, and well-spoken about his beliefs. In his history class of twenty-two students, he was consistently among the most vocal participants. The Delaneys live in a modern two-story house in a picturesque suburb of Seattle, with quiet cul-de-sacs, well-tended lawns, and children riding their bikes on the sidewalks.

Ken and Karen are in their mid-forties. Both were in high school during the last years of the draft, and neither had siblings or close relatives who served in Vietnam. But this fact did not dull the emotion both mother and father displayed. Like many respondents in our sample, the Delaneys regarded the Vietnam experience not as a distant event that had brushed against their lives, but as a core moment that continues to shape their present. Indeed, the intensity of their emotion provided a point of contrast with sixteen-year-old John. On viewing the Pulitzer–prize winning picture of Kim Phuc in *Life*, Karen, sobbing, turned to John (who did not recognize the picture) and explained its origin. Ken, his voice shaking as well, picked up her sentence, using language that blurred past and present: "What are we accomplishing, why are we doing this? And who's profiting by all this show of force? That doesn't look like a very substantial army they're fighting there."

After a silence during which the parents regained their composure, I turned to John and asked if there was anything he wanted to ask his parents, anything that aroused his curiosity. John's answer touched on the role of emotion in understanding history. Because of his distance from Vietnam, John claimed that he was "more objective" than either parent and, consequently, could offer a better historical account.

John: I think I have more of an objective view because I didn't live through it, I don't know people who went to Vietnam and didn't come back, or anything . . . I didn't live through it, I never had to look at our government and go, "Why are they in there?" I can look back more than, I think, than [my parents] can. . . .

Interviewer: Do you think the fact that you have less emotion with it helps or hinders you in understanding what went on?

John: [Having less emotion] helps, but I think if I was dealing with someone who'd gone through it [having less emotion] wouldn't [help] at all. I think it would dampen me because I wouldn't be able to relate as much if I was talking to someone who'd gone through it and all of a sudden was just kind of feeling sad about what went on, I would be like—I wouldn't have much response for them. But I think in a logical scholarly way—I'm not a scholar or anything—but I guess in a logical Vulcan kind of response [laughs]—I can go, "Well, this is what happened, these things happened and these things happened and this is the"—I think I can probably weigh the pros and the cons more objectively.

Here, then, is a rough epistemology of historical understanding, according to a bright sixteen-year-old participant in American culture. For John, emotion threatens historical objectivity, yet it is the very ingredient that would help him were he to "deal with someone" who had experienced the trauma of war. However, this emotion, which John viewed as the foundation for empathy, remained outside the purview of legitimate historical understanding. For John, historical understanding is best captured by Mr. Spock, the Vulcan character from *Star Trek*, whose most striking characteristic (besides his pointed ears) was the inability to feel.

John's views need to be taken seriously, for they were not unique among our participants, and surely they contain a grain of truth. Unbridled passion poses a threat to historical understanding, especially when the forces of emotion cause the historian to skew or suppress data or to hold on to cherished beliefs in the face of evidence to the contrary. Yet it is hard to imagine serious historical work in which emotion plays no role—if not in the historians' passion for the subject (which allows scholars to spend endless hours slogging through documents, often in dark and poorly heated archives), then at least in historians' ability to empathize with the people they seek to understand. John, a serious and intelligent high school junior, has an image of historical scholarship carried out by emotionless drones alienated from their human origins. At the base of this epistemology is a contradictory implicit logic: Historians are most objective when they are not personally connected to their subject; however, it is precisely one's personal connection that generates interest and passion. Oddly, for John, those best suited to carry out historical work are those least motivated to do it.

John's response is consistent with the instruction we observed at Revelations High School, where his history teacher marched the class in a straight line through the U.S. history curriculum. His class was characterized by heavy doses of minute historical facts, and weekly objective tests in preparation for the Advanced Placement exam. We noted a wide chasm between the Biblical posters lining the room (on the largest, neatly printed letters read: "What would Jesus have done?") and the generic "anywhere any time" quality of instruction. If one factor gave shape to this history curriculum, it was not the testaments of Mark and Matthew but the policy decisions of the Educational Testing Service in New Jersey.[6]

In light of what we observed in John's classroom it is tempting to connect his views to the kind of history to which he had been exposed. There is surely a connection, but we believe it goes far beyond the influence of a single teacher plowing determinedly through the curriculum. Indeed, John's views about what makes good history were shared, for the most part, by his parents. History, for John's dad, was about "analysis," and he even expressed concern that the emotion he displayed in our interview might introduce unwanted "bias" into our study. In this regard, father and son were of like mind.

At work here, we believe, are powerful and relatively stable ideas about everyday criteria for sound historical judgment and the day-to-day work of the historian. To some extent, the Delaneys' views reflect notions prevalent soon after history's arrival in the modern research university, but by the 1930s such views were already being questioned by two presidents of the American Historical Association, Carl Becker and Charles Beard. Also notable is the chasm between these ideas and those expressed by contemporary historians about their work. One might even claim that in our postmodern age, historical works that abjure emotion are themselves suspect, viewed as devices that mask, through rhetorical means, the underlying polemical nature of their arguments. As the profession celebrates subjectivity and positionality, two cardinal virtues of postmodernity, notions of objectivity and its attainability live on in the Delaney household.

John may feel that he is more objective and less emotional about Vietnam than his parents, but at points in the interview he displayed clear and strong reactions and looked to bolster his claims by appealing to sources that were hardly dispassionate or objective. An example was John's response to the picture of the GI leaving a battle scene with a young child tucked under each arm. The picture is itself ambiguous and was variously interpreted by our respondents. Some viewed the GI as a kidnapper; others (including John and his parents) viewed him as a rescuer. Indeed, it was John's interpretation of the subject as a soldier saving lives in the midst of the horrors of war that led to the following response:

> Here's this guy running, and maybe that's not what he was doing, but it looks like he's running out and he's got these two kids under his arms, kind of ironic that we think of Vietnam, you always hear someone say, "Oh, baby killers." So here's this guy running out, and he's got these two kids, it's like he's saving them from the disaster that's going on behind him. I thought it was a well-taken photo.

John's language merits attention. First, it was a rare moment in our interviews when an adolescent so clearly reported an instance of the past intruding into the present. John reports that he hears the epithet "baby killer" aimed at Vietnam vets not once or twice but "always." Where, then, might John hear this? From our observations and documentation in his classroom, we know that Vietnam figured hardly at all there, beyond a single sixty-minute discussion in this U.S. history course. Nor was this the type of thing that either his mother or his father would likely say. The historical basis for the image of the "spat-upon" veteran is weak, to say the least, and certainly not documented to a point that would warrant, some thirty years later, the strength of John's everyday recollection.[7] In fact, as

Eric Dean notes in *Shook Over Hell: Post-traumatic Stress, Vietnam, and the Civil War*, the first American troops withdrawn from Vietnam were greeted in John's backyard, downtown Seattle, by a crowd that cheered, "Thank you, thank you": "Flags waved, ticker tape showered down on the troopers, and pretty girls pressed red roses into the men's hands."[8]

Where, then, might John hear such epithets? Or, more generally, what sources of information contribute to John's understanding of Vietnam? In the course of this interview, John mentioned several. One was a report he completed on Richard Nixon, in which he set out to prove that "Nixon was a good president based on his accomplishments in foreign affairs." In researching this report, John read "some biographies and autobiographies," but he did not note the names of any. (Nor did we have the presence of mind to probe him.) Indeed, the only point in the interview where John provided a specific reference for a historical claim came in response to his statement that "war was good for the economy."

Interviewer: Okay, so help me get a little bit better understanding for a second. One person might say that the war was a very costly effort. We are expending all of these armaments and we're losing our planes and we're losing young people and it's the sheer cost of transporting [troops] there, so, so, how does, from your understanding, how does profit enter into it?

John: Oh, because you—any point in history you look at, war builds up an economy. It's like in *Schindler's List*—Schindler said, I tried all these businesses and they never worked because I never had one thing. What changed his luck? War. And it's, because with war there's a higher demand for metal works because you're losing your planes and your equipment and your helicopters and tanks and what not, you need to make those, and you have to have someone back in the U.S. to make those things.

Asked to elaborate on a claim about the benefits of war, John turned neither to something learned in school nor to formal knowledge about economics. His proof text came from Steven Spielberg's *Schindler's List*, a movie based not on a piece of history but on a piece of historical fiction by Thomas Keneally. John's claim about the relationship between war and profit may have some basis, but this is surely beside the point. Important here is the specificity of his reference, compared with his earlier vague statements about "some books and autobiographies" consulted for his report on Nixon. His language in this instance is direct and comes with no introduction, qualification, or preface such as, "It's like, I saw *in the movie, Schindler's List*." John works on the assumption that he and the interviewer share cultural knowledge (in this case, a correct assumption!), and that he can draw on a facet of this shared knowledge using shorthand. In making his claim about war, John calls upon the past, but it is a filmic past that he remembers, a past that blurs fact and fiction, and that ultimately, in John's reasoning, provides warrant for a historical claim.

This was not an isolated instance, either in John's interview or in our other interviews. Indeed, another movie played an even greater role in John's understanding—in this case, a movie that integrated actual historical footage into the visual flow of fictional events. *Forrest Gump* served, and apparently continues to serve, as an occasion for the Delaney family to sit together and discuss the past.[9] The family owns a copy of the film and has watched it together repeatedly. John: "We talk about Vietnam and I guess the family, *Forrest Gump* always brings up something along those lines. You know, they always mention the money and the greed and I understand where they're coming from." The movie also served as a meeting point between the Delaneys and close family friends—for example, Don Waverly, a Vietnam vet. John: "Don doesn't talk about Vietnam. Doesn't really say anything about it. . . . Don watched [*Forrest Gump*] with us once, and he was real quiet during the Vietnam scenes."

Forrest Gump served as the starting point in the Delaneys' discussions of the sixties. Unlike other families in our sample, who made a pilgrimage to the Vietnam Veterans Memorial, the Delaneys' point of reference was a videocassette. The only specific source of information about Vietnam that John quoted verbatim came not from parents, teachers, ministers, or any of the books he had read; it was a snippet of dialogue from *Forrest Gump*.

> Interviewer: You mentioned *Forrest Gump* in the beginning of the interview.
> John: Good movie.
> Interviewer: And you mentioned it in reference to what?
> John: Oh, that movie really just centers around the sixties. It's a story of the baby boomer generation, from 1950 something to 1980 something. It's their life. My parents I think related to it in a totally different way than I did. I have friends who say it was one of the most boring movies they've ever seen. Now I disagree with that statement, I thought it was a really good movie. That it had a lot to say, could learn a lot from it—attitudes. But you watch Vietnam and the guy says to Forrest Gump, one of the hippies looks at Forrest Gump in his military uniform, and he goes, "Who's the baby killer?"

It was this very scenario, in which an SDS look-alike taunts the uniformed Gump by calling him a "baby killer," that John claimed to "always hear" in his daily life. This celluloid image was the clearest and sharpest recollection John had of the entire Vietnam era.

It is tempting to characterize John's comments here as just another instance of how contemporary film influences our understanding of the past, a phenomenon that has become a cottage industry for scholars in cultural studies.[10] Obviously, John is influenced by a film—several films, to be exact. But that observation only scratches the surface. A film, or in this case a home video, has become an occasion for the Delaney family to revisit the past. They convene in their living room, take a cassette from their shelves, and insert it into a VCR. Unlike a pilgrimage to a historical site or a trip to a history museum, the videos in our home entertainment centers speak to the American imperative of convenience. While we may "go out" to the movies to see the past, in the video age the past becomes something we possess. The usable past on video is, above all, the *always available past.*

Like our other possessions, the videocassette is available to us when the need arises. In this interview alone there were three specific references to watching *Forrest Gump* as a family activity, including one time when the Delaneys watched with their friend, the Vietnam vet Don Waverly. We can even imagine that the Delaneys watched the tape at other times as well. Through this repeated viewing, the video comes to function in a role not unlike that of cherished writings and sacred texts in earlier times. Snippets of video dialogue offer convenient metonymies—their invocation calls up a flood of feelings, values, and associations. Because the human mind remembers detail far better than its provenance, the detail remains but its source falls away.[11] So John is correct when he says that he always hears "baby killers," but it's likely that he hears it most often from a character whose lines were written by the screenwriter Robert Zemeckis. In other words, the fictionalized past, not the historical event, becomes John's frame of reference for the present.

The Delaneys' viewing habits give a new twist to the notion of the family as educator. The family still educates, to be sure, but not in some stylized Norman Rockwell way. It's not the kitchen table where stories are transmitted from generation to generation, but the living room couch, once the VCR starts to play. The family serves as the context for this video history lesson; the family mediates the larger cultural narrative that Hollywood provides. Whereas in traditional societies the family would travel to sites of memory—battlefields, shrines of saints, or other commemorative locales—here the *"lieux de mémoire,"* to invoke Pierre Nora, is not a site *per se* but an object.[12] The videocassette obviates the need for pilgrimage and conforms to the imperatives of modernity. It permits ritual without pilgrimage by putting the past at the touch of a button.

COLLECTIVE MEMORY AND COLLECTIVE OCCLUSION

The findings from the Delaney interview provide a glimpse of what our approach has elicited. The Delaneys are one of fifteen families. In this section, I survey trends in the full sample of parents and adolescents.

Like John Delaney, the other teenagers in this study possessed rich narratives about Vietnam, and each student easily identified the picture of a man standing in front of a wall of chiseled names as a "vet standing before the Vietnam War memorial" in Washington, D.C.[13] On viewing this picture, many of the youths and many of their parents narrated a story of today's Vietnam vet, ill-treated upon his return to American soil. While individuals limned this story in greater or lesser detail— sometimes depicting a "spat-upon" vet, hitchhiking futilely by the side of the road, his life embittered by hippies and society at large—the over- all effect was the same. Not the instigator of atrocities in a far-off land, as the vet was viewed in wake of the My Lai massacre, today's Vietnam vet is remembered as a victim of, not a perpetrator in, Vietnam.[14]

The images shared by our participants illustrate some of the differ- ences between *collective* and *historical* memory.[15] For example, scholars across the disciplines have examined the question of whether it was com- mon for veterans to be "spat upon" on their return to the United States.[16] The literature, from Jerry Lembcke's sociology to Bob Green's journal- ism to archival research examining 380 newspaper reports of "home- comings" by Thomas Beamish, Harvey Molotch, and Richard Flacks at the University of California, Santa Barbara,[17] suggests that this collective image has little basis other than its crystallization in the media. An exam- ination of the historical record shows a stronger documentary basis for remembering veterans' ill-treatment at the hands of *other veterans* than their abuse by raging hippies.[18] But stories of veteran-to-veteran abuse never made it into our interviews. Such stories, and the larger sets of issues they represent, have blurred from memory. Over time, these sto- ries have been collectively *occluded* from popular memory.

Collective occlusion is the flip side of collective memory. It speaks to that which is no longer common knowledge, no longer easily retrieved or taken for granted. Collective occlusion asks us to think about the sto- ries, images, and cultural codes that become blocked in the transmission process from one generation to the next. Archived in historical memory and present in lived memory, occluded stories are at risk of being lost in the everyday processes of how societies remember and transmit their pasts to a new generation.[19]

I prefer the term "occlusion" to the more widely used "amnesia" for several reasons. First, "occlusion" conveys a sense of blockage; it is not that these memories are erased or forgotten, but that they are not salient and not easily seen. Second, even when memories are occluded, they are, in historical and archival cultures, available in books, on the Web, and often in specialized university seminars. Finally, "amnesia" misrepresents the complexity of social memory by conveying monolithic, socially uniform processes. "Occlusion," with its connotations of partiality and opacity, tries to convey this complexity more authentically.

The intergenerational aspect of our study illuminates what gets lost in the transmission from lived memory to learned memory. For example, all the American-born parents in our study quickly established a context for the picture of the young man standing in front of the outstretched gun barrels of a ring of National Guardsmen, placing a pink carnation in the barrel of one of the guns (Photo 10.1). Even if parents were not able to fix the exact location of this event (the "March on the Pentagon" in October 21–23, 1967, which drew 50,000 protestors to

Photo 10.1 March on the Pentagon, October 21, 1967 (© Bernie Boston Photography, reprinted with permission)

Washington, D.C.) they understood its larger meaning: a hippie, representing peace and nonviolence, confronting police, national guardsmen, or possibly members of the state militia, during some kind of civil disturbance over the war. But the codes parents took for granted were anything but self-evident to their children. Consider, for example, the following sequence in the interview with Jacob Curfman, sixteen, a classmate of John Delaney's at Revelations High School:

Jacob: I didn't totally understand what it was I'm looking at, but it looked like—it looked like this guy's being held at gunpoint, with the bayonets, and he's putting flowers in the bayonets or something, I can't make it out. But it looks just kind of like a gesture of peace in the midst of all the ugliness that's going on. Like this guy's just trying to make a statement about the war, that he wants peace. That's kind of what it looked like.

Interviewer: Any thoughts as to how [this man] might have gotten in front of the bayonets?

Jacob: Not really. I'm not sure. Unless he's like maybe aiding U.S. soldiers or something, I don't know. But doing something they didn't like, maybe just being held prisoner or something.

Interviewer: Held prisoner by whom?

Jacob: The North Vietnamese or whatever.

Or consider the response of Claudine Serber, a student at the elite college preparatory school:

Claudine: I said it's a eulogy given at a funeral. And it shows the numerous people who died during this time period.

Interviewer: What makes you think it's a eulogy at a funeral?

Claudine: Because he's holding little flowers. . . . It just seems like he's saying the . . . eulogy. Saying, you know, "This person was killed or he was a brave person." . . . It's a formal ceremony and the person who's standing seems to be like a relative of the man who died. And they're all standing around like protecting his grave sort of. You know, they're gathering around to remember him for the last time.

Jacob Curfman, who believed the flower bearer was being held captive by the North Vietnamese, and Claudine Serber, who thought that he was eulogizing a fallen American soldier, dramatize the difficulty many students had in decoding the cultural messages embedded in this picture. Nearly half (or seven out of fifteen students) failed to provide an appropriate context. At the same time, students clearly knew what a "hippie" was, knew that hippies protested against the war in Vietnam, even knew what hippies looked like: long hair to the middle of their backs, John

Lennon glasses, headbands, tie-dyed tee shirts, and peace signs. Judged against this standard, the young man in the "March on the Pentagon" picture was clearly *not* a "hippie" as defined by the canonical texts and images of the cultural curriculum on Vietnam (see Photo 10.2).

A related process of simplification was apparent in the way adolescents set the stage of the Vietnam conflict. In the abbreviated narrative of many (but not all) students, the players in the Vietnam drama were stark and distinct: soldiers fighting in Vietnam and hippies protesting at home. Hippies constituted a negative element in American society, not because they were wrong in opposing the war but because they went overboard in blaming the soldiers.[20] Americans who did not march on Washington marched in silent protest at home. In a curious twist of historical revision,

Photo 10.2. Contemporary image of the Hippie. (Courtesy of MicroSolutions)

we all voted McGovern. Vietnam, as remembered by these youths, was a war waged without supporters.[21]

What happens, then, when adolescents confront evidence that directly challenges their memory: a flag-waving *rally* in support of President Nixon, during which 100,000 hard-hat wearing construction workers jammed Manhattan's City Hall (May 20, 1970) with signs like, "WE HARD HAT MEN ARE BUILDING AMERICA, NOT DESTROYING IT: GOD BLESS AMERICA," "THIS COUNTRY ISN'T PERFECT BUT IT'S THE BEST ON THE FACE OF THIS EARTH," "MR. PRESIDENT: AS COMMANDER IN-CHIEF WE SUPPORT YOU"?[22] (See Photo 10.3.) Eleven of twelve American-born parents, whether supporters of the war or not, easily identified this as a pro-war rally. Fred Lewis, Anita's father, responded this way to the picture:

> Many men and women did demonstrate patriotism even though there was confusion about the purpose of the war. . . . They were going to support the government even though they didn't necessarily know all the reasons why. I

Photo 10.3. Hardhat demonstration, Manhattan City Hall, May 20, 1970 (© AP/Wide World Photos, reprinted with permission)

saw these people as the typical blue-collar workers. . . . The guys that are just out there sweating everyday, and they're, they're saying: "Well, we're not the intellectual elite here, but we're going to give you our support."

For Ellen Oshansky, the mother of one of the students at the private preparatory academy, this picture evoked a dramatically different response.

[The men in the picture] are a bunch of assholes—they're chauvinistic, ill-informed, nonthinking men guided by their penises who are into being powerful, into feeling important through putting other people down. . . . I find them to be mostly ill-informed and non-informed. They don't think, they don't analyze. These are people who today probably listen to Rush Limbaugh and want to hear what is going to make them comfortable. . . . It's "my country right or wrong."

Lacking the concept of "rally" and possessing only that of "protest against the war," adolescents who viewed this picture did not revise their beliefs based on new evidence. Rather, these young people squeezed this visual image into their existing understanding of the Vietnam era. Sixty percent of students turned the picture of flag-waving hardhats into a protest *against* the war. Jacob Curfman expressed the confusion of many students:

Jacob: [This picture] just seems kind of out of place with the rest, because most of the people we see in pictures like this are protesting, not waving flags. . . . So I'm not really sure what to think. . . . And the sign, "We hard hat men are building America, not destroying it," like maybe kind of held the war in contempt, but they were trying to show that they were still trying to keep the country going, I guess.

Interviewer: Why do you say maybe they held the war in contempt?

Jacob: Just, well, that *sign.* I mean the whole attitude of the thing looks like it might be pretty patriotic, but this one sign caught my attention. It says, you know, "We're building America not destroying it," like the soldiers were. Or the government was, or whatever.

For Jacob, the agents of destruction referred to in the sign are American soldiers or the American government.[23] Andrea Clarke, a public high school student whose father served in the Navy during the war, was more certain about her interpretation.

Andrea: I put that this was a protest against the war.

Interviewer: [Surprised] *Against?*

Andrea: Against, yes. It looks like it might have been a certain group. All these people, they look like they're construction people or something like that, with their hats on, and it looks like lots of different ethnicities in here. It says, "We hard hat men," so, obviously, they're

> doing something with their hands or something like that. So they
> didn't want to—obviously these people felt like the war was destroy-
> ing their jobs, their homes, destroying the country as whole.

Gloria Lawrence, a student at the private preparatory academy,
interpreted the picture as a "strike by construction workers":

> They want the soldiers to be brought home. . . . That these men are going on
> strike and risking their jobs to protest the soldiers in Vietnam, and they want
> them brought home, because they are their family members and their brothers,
> cousins, sons. I'm sure this was part of the protest that was going on.

LANDSCAPES OF MEMORY

In contrast to the diversity of views displayed by parents in this study, students' understanding of Vietnam occupied a narrow bandwidth. The history instruction we watched in these three classrooms was quite varied, but
we would not know it from the uniformity of the adolescents' responses.
Despite the various political, ethnic, racial, religious, and ideological sub-
groups they represented, their collective responses attest to the power and
sweep of the cultural curriculum that hovers above such groups.

We have embarked in this work on an empirical journey into the col-
liding worlds of history and memory, of knowing the past using the ordinary sense-making capacities we use to know most things, and knowing
it as the result of disciplined habits of mind. In analyzing our data, we are
less concerned with whether people's understanding corresponds to some
canonical body of information than we are with trying to generate
topographies of historical memory, rough maps of how ordinary people
think about the past and use it to understand the present. At present, those
who design textbooks and curricula for teaching school history neither
acknowledge nor recognize collective memory as a significant force—
indeed, as *the* force—to be reckoned with in teaching and learning. But it
is the substance of collective memory, I would claim, that serves as the
framework for what we attempt to teach kids in school.[24]

Roy Rosenzweig and David Thelen[25] recently undertook a telephone
survey of over a thousand Americans to understand how the past is used
in everyday life. Such an approach allows these researchers to generate a
broad image of the incidence of everyday activities related to the past (and
the meanings people attach to these activities), such as pursuing family
genealogies or visiting historical museums. As valuable as such information may be, it does not allow us to locate individual responses in the con-

text of the family, the school, the church, and the community. Nor does it provide the detailed portraits of understanding that would allow educators access to the nooks and crannies of students' cognitive landscapes.

The approach taken here involves a narrower sample, and the resulting generalizations are, by necessity, more modest. Such generalizations point us to an emerging theory of everyday historical understanding rather than to any direct statement of incidence and frequency beyond the participants in our study. Nonetheless, commonalties across these diverse participants, with different educational backgrounds, religious views, and ways of seeing the world, give us confidence that trends we see in this sample are more than idiosyncratic.

Collective memory acts as a filter.[26] Not only do the details of historical events become less vivid as time passes, but what is remembered or occluded from the past is constantly being reshaped by contemporary social processes: acts of state that commemorate certain events and not others, decisions by novelists and filmmakers to tell one story and not another, and an amorphous set of social needs that draw on some elements from the past while leaving others dormant.

Indeed, it was this last aspect—the demands that the present places on the past—that led the French sociologist Maurice Halbwachs to claim that collective memory was not about the past at all, but was entirely a reflection of contemporary social needs and the contemporary social condition. The onset of modernity and rapid social change, according to Halbwachs, created an abyss between the present and the past, akin to "two tree stumps that touch at their extremities but do not form one plant because they are not otherwise connected."[27]

The neo-Halbwachians, sociologists Barry Schwartz and Yael Zerubavel, take a less extreme stance and see a dialectic between historical memory and the historical record (as represented in the work of historians).[28] Like Pierre Nora, these scholars focus their attention on sites of memory—battlefields, monuments, museums—as well as on the production of cultural materials related to the past: novels, popular books, films, and essays. To date, however, there have been few if any attempts to track how the processes of historical memory play out in the lives of ordinary people: how it is that the proverbial person-on-the-street embodies (or doesn't) the broad social processes posited by the theorists of collective memory.

Without this perspective, we open ourselves to the criticism noted by James Wertsch of conflating the production of cultural products with their consumption.[29] Individuals are influenced by, and also act upon, the products of elites. Attempts to arrive at a conception of collective memory that bypasses the individual (a collective memory curiously held by no one in particular)[30] will run aground on the banks of reductionism and essentialism. To understand how societies remember, we need both macro- and micro-analyses of cultural transmission, adaptation, and reformulation.

We are clearly in the earliest stages of trying to understand our data. Our hope, ultimately, is that by shedding light on how adolescents make sense of the past, we can learn how to better engage their historical beliefs, stretch them, and call them, when necessary, into question. In that sense, our investigation is more than a foray into cultural studies. As a cognitive scientist in the original sense of that term—a worker in an interdisciplinary field that draws on anthropology, sociology, and psychology in an effort to understand the phenomena of consciousness[31]—I am also a meliorist. Given these images of adolescent understanding, and continued support for them in other studies, what direction should new curricula take? How would we design effective education for new teachers of history? What software might we design, and what on-line questions would we ask, based on these and similar findings? In designing new educational interventions, who, exactly, are we designing them for? And what do we actually know about the existing understandings and beliefs of the "end users" of our educational innovations?

I recently described these findings to a friend, a longtime veteran of the high school history classroom. Chagrined, he pointed out that history teachers themselves depend heavily on videos and other products of the cultural curriculum, and should remove them from the classroom. But this, I believe, won't help. The calculus classroom may be the site where we learn advanced mathematics, but we learn history everywhere—school hardly possesses a monopoly. Removing videos from the classroom leaves them intact in the home, on the DVD, on cable and DirecTV, and practically everywhere else. Rather than pretending that we can do away with popular culture—confiscate videos, banish rap music, magnetize Nintendo games, and unplug MTV and the Movie Channel—we might try instead to understand how these forces shape historical consciousness, and how they might be used, rather than spurned or, worse, simply ignored, to advance students' historical understanding.

NOTES

This chapter was written especially for this volume. Sections have appeared, in slightly altered forms, in Peter N. Stearns, Peter Seixas, and Sam Wineburg, eds., *Knowing, Teaching, and Learning History: National and International Perspectives* (New York, 2000). I also presented an early version of this chapter at a working conference on "Transmission of Tradition," held in Hanover, Germany, in September 1999. I thank Professor Harald Welzer for inviting me and for his encouragement of this work. I also thank my collaborators in this project, Susan Mosborg and Dan Porat, with whom the ideas here were developed and refined. Finally, I have benefited much from on-going conversations with Reed Stevens about this work.

1. These interviews were conducted by myself, Alex Shih, Diana Hess, and Susan Mosborg.

2. I drew on Peter Seixas's formulation of this task. See his "Mapping the Terrain of Historical Significance," *Social Education* 61 (1997), 22–27.

3. Our research tasks and interviews ranged from an interview in which students read the daily newspaper (to see how they connected past and present) to an interview asking them to narrate the struggle for Civil Rights in American history to another interview in which they explained to us what they thought their teachers meant by comments written on their term papers.

4. We also asked parents to complete a 30-item multiple-choice test on historical facts. Parents' responses allowed us to compare their scores with those earned by their children on the same test. Contrary to conservatives' claims of an "erosion of memory" across generations, we found no statistically significant difference between the parents' and students' scores, with a slight advantage going to the students.

5. Photo elicitation is a technique developed by the anthropologists Margaret Mead and Gregory Bateson. For an overview of more recent uses, see Douglas Harper, "On the Authority of the Image: Visual Methods at the Crossroads," in Norman K. Denzin and Yvonna S. Lincoln, eds., *Handbook of Qualitative Research* (Thousand Oaks, Calif., 1994), 403–12.

6. This, however, is only a partial picture, for history was also taught in religion classes at this school. In our interview focusing on reading the daily news, we asked students to review a recent Mississippi court case about prayer in school. Four of five students from Revelations, independently of one another, drew on Thomas Jefferson's letter to the Danbury Baptists, a primary source document taught in religion class. See Susan Mosborg, "Assessing Historical Significance," manuscript (University of Washington, 2000).

7. See Jerry Lembcke, *The Spitting Image: Myth, Memory, and the Legacy of Vietnam* (New York, 1998).

8. Eric Dean, *Shook Over Hell: Post-traumatic Stress, Vietnam, and the Civil War* (Cambridge, Mass., 1997). Dean's source is "Joy in Seattle; Troops Withdrawn from Viet Nam," *Time* (July 18, 1969), 5.

9. *Forrest Gump* played a major role in adolescents' reconstructions of the Vietnam era, more than any other single source—including parents, teachers, or text-

books. Other movies spontaneously discussed by adolescents included *Rambo, Dazed and Confused, Platoon,* and *Apocalypse Now.* References to *Forrest Gump* were made across all three schools; it was the only "text," visual or otherwise, that united both generations. The movie was mentioned in 60 percent of the interviews on Vietnam. No other text even came close.

10. See, for example, William Adams, "War Stories: Movies, Memory, and the Vietnam War," *Comparative Social Research* 11 (1989), 165–83. The literature is voluminous. For overviews see Keith Beattie, *The Scar That Binds: American Culture and the Vietnam War* (New York, 1998); Linda Dittmar and Gene Michaud, *From Hanoi to Hollywood: The Vietnam War in American Film* (New Brunswick, N.J., 1990); and John Hellmann, *American Myth and the Legacy of Vietnam* (New York, 1986).

11. Colleen M. Seifert, Robert B. Abelson, and Gail McKoon, "The Role of Thematic Knowledge Structures," in John A. Galambos, Robert B. Abelson, and John B. Black, eds., *Knowledge Structures* (Hillsdale, N.J., 1986).

12. Pierre Nora, "Between History and Memory: Les Lieux de Mémoire," *Representations* 26 (1989), 1–15.

13. The picture of the Vietnam Veterans Memorial was by far the most identifiable of the six we presented to adolescents, exemplifying Nora's point that it is how we commemorate past events, not the events themselves, that is remembered by future generations. Over a million and a half people file by the Vietnam memorial each year, leaving over 25,000 mementos. In nine of the fifteen families, a parent, a child, or both have made a pilgrimage to the wall. For a recent study of such pilgrimages, see Kristin Ann Hass, *Carried to the Wall* (Berkeley, 1998).

14. Telford Taylor, the presiding attorney at the Nuremberg trials, issued this indictment in his 1970 book, *Nuremberg and Vietnam: An American Tragedy* (Chicago): "We have smashed the country [of Vietnam] to bits and will not even take the trouble to clean up the blood and rubble. . . . Somehow we failed ourselves to learn the lessons we undertook to teach at Nuremberg, and that failure is today's American tragedy" (p. 207). The act of transforming our self-image from perpetrator to victim began during the latter part of the war, according to H. Bruce Franklin. "The actual photographs and TV footage of massacred villagers, napalmed children, Vietnamese prisoners being tortured and murdered, wounded GIs screaming in agony, and body bags being loaded by the dozen for shipment back home were being replaced by simulated images of American POWs in the savage hands of Asian communists" (*M.I.A., or Mythmaking in America* [Brooklyn, 1992], 54). Asks Fred Turner, in *Echoes of Combat: the Vietnam War in American Memory* (New York, 1996), 11, "How is it then, that in twenty years, the image of the American soldier as executioner should have vanished and that of the American soldier as victim should have taken its place? Why do so many Americans cling as tenaciously now to the image of the veteran-as-survivor as they once did to the notion of the GI-as-stone-cold-killer?"

15. I recognize the conceptual problems related to "collectivizing" memory, an act that is often regarded as an individual process. As Amos Funkenstein noted in "Collective Memory and Historical Consciousness," *History and Memory* 1 (1989), 5–26, just as a nation cannot mourn or celebrate, it cannot, properly speaking, remember. On the other hand, at least since Hegel, there has been an awareness that social processes are always implicated in acts of individual remembering.

Among psychologists, Vygotsky articulated this view most clearly. For an overview of these issues, see Patrick H. Hutton, *History as an Act of Memory* (Hanover, N.H., 1993), as well as the insightful review of Hutton by David Gordon in *History and Theory* 34 (1995), 340–54.

16. In contrast to the multiple stories we heard of ill-treatment of Vietnam veterans, domestic support for the Vietnam War was rarely mentioned in our interviews. However, a Harris poll in 1966 noted that 73 percent of Americans said they were "deeply concerned" about the war, and 61 percent said that they were "personally involved." See Turner, *Echoes of Combat*, 127.

17. Lembcke, *Spitting Image;* Bob Green, *Homecoming: When the Soldiers Returned from Vietnam* (New York, 1989); Thomas D. Beamish, Harvey Molotch, and Richard Flacks, "Who Supports the Troops?" *Social Problems* 42 (1995), 344–60.

18. See in particular David E. Bonior, Steven M. Champlin, and Timothy S. Kolly, *The Vietnam Veteran: A History of Neglect* (New York, 1984), 99–118. Bonior and his colleagues note that well into the 1980s, established veterans groups opposed spending new federal dollars on programs for Vietnam veterans, such as the one proposed by Jimmy Carter in 1977 to upgrade dishonorable discharges that had been unfairly meted out during the war. Bonior and colleagues write: "The problem for major organizations ran deeper than money. It had emotional roots. The president's program had captured all of their ambivalence about these strange, new, sometimes long-haired veterans, some of whom had thrown their medals away and seemed to hold nothing sacred. Vietnam veterans with less than Honorable Discharges were the loser veterans who had lost the 'little war' in distant Vietnam. Somehow, their attitude toward Vietnam veterans led to a change in their long history of concern over the discharge system" (p. 108). The authors note that by 1977 not one of the major veterans' organizations had elected a Vietnam veteran to its top post, and as late as 1981 the Veterans of Foreign Wars did not have a single Vietnam veteran in any of its senior staff positions.

19. See Paul Connerton, *How Societies Remember* (Cambridge, England, 1989), for a related argument. Connerton's thesis about the bodily enactment of memory is provocative but I find it outdated in an increasingly information-rich, technologically sophisticated global society.

20. Consider the words of seventeen-year-old Luis Fara, a student at the public high school: "Hippies [were] the type of people who made it real difficult for the soldiers who came back . . . these kinds of people were the ones that didn't support the soldiers. Because after all, [the soldiers] weren't the ones that were in charge, they were just doing their job, and I think [hippies] made it really difficult for the soldiers really afterwards even to cope with what they had to go through. . . . I think it's alright to be against a war, but I don't think it's right to blame actual soldiers for some of that, because they don't have a real big say in the issue."

21. Compare this memory to surveys of attitudes taken at the time, even during the latter years of the war. For example, after Richard Nixon ordered the mining of Haiphong harbor and escalated the war by extending it into Cambodia and Laos, *Time* commissioned Daniel Yankelovich Inc. to engage a group of 200 Americans, from a cross-sample of 2,000, in extensive interviews. "Seven out of ten express a renewed confidence in the President's conduct of the war. Only three of ten give

him a vote of no confidence." "Time Citizens Panel: The President Buys More Time—and Some Hope—on the War," *Time* (June 12, 1972), 16–17. Several themes stand out in the *Time* survey. First, support for Nixon was spread across Democrats and Republicans, and there were voters from both parties who strongly felt that the war needed to be escalated (recall that the date was June 1972!). "Fight it and get it over with," says Mrs. Wilma ("Billie") Renner, a Lawrenceburg, Ind., housewife and a Republican. "We're being pushed around overseas and at home. I'm disgusted with people not backing President Nixon." Or this: "Walter Glamp, a Dublin, Md., high school counselor who voted for Edmund Muskie in his state's primary, feels that the President's advisers would have voted against the mining if they thought it was unduly risky. 'I believe,' he says, 'that the North Vietnamese now will watch their step before taking any escalatory actions of their own.'" Several other themes were noteworthy: that the mining of North Vietnamese harbors was "risky but worth it"; that the mining of harbors differed from the bombing campaign and would prove to be more effective; and that the attitude of supporters was a hawkish "we won't be bullied." Recall that George McGovern, who ran on a platform of immediate withdrawal from Vietnam and amnesty for draft dodgers, was defeated in the biggest landslide in American presidential history. McGovern's statement "If Americans themselves were not criminals then at least they supported a government run by criminals" was clearly not how Americans saw themselves then, or, judging by the responses of families in our sample, how they see themselves now. See Theodore White, *The Making of a President, 1972* (New York, 1973), 116.

22. This rally was held on Armed Forces Day. Other signs at the rally (not visible in the photo presented to parents and students) read "Stop Leftwing TV" and "Impeach the Red Mayor," a reference to New York's John V. Lindsay, an opponent of the war. See R. M. Fried, *The Russians Are Coming! The Russians Are Coming!* (New York, 1998).

23. The idea that the American *government* was the agent of destruction in Vietnam, not soldiers or even the citizens who supported them domestically, was a theme that echoed in these interviews, even by parents with avowedly conservative positions. In this respect, these interviews provide a different sense of how Americans view the culpability of the American government than the one depicted by Michael G. Kammen. See his *Mystic Chords of Memory: The Transformation of Tradition in American Culture* (New York, 1991), 657, in which he claims that the "U.S. government disappears as a devastating force" in the current mythology of Vietnam. The ordinary people interviewed in this study clearly disagree.

24. One would be hard-pressed to find in the *National Standards for United States History*, published by the National Center for History in the Schools, University of California (Los Angeles, 1995), any serious examination of how contemporary culture shapes modern historical consciousness. Framers of the standards, unburdened by empirical data, operated largely on the fantasy that by changing textbooks they could change how history is taught and understood. An ethnographic study of classroom instruction by John Wills showed that even in a classroom that used new materials on Native Americans, and in which the teacher clearly supported the new approach, culturally encoded beliefs, enshrined in the texts of the larger culture, ultimately triumphed over new textbook narratives. See John Wills, "Popular Cul-

ture, Curriculum, and Historical Representation: The Situation of Native Americans in American History and the Perpetuation of Stereotypes," *Journal of Narrative and Life History* 4 (1994), 277–94.

25. Roy Rosenzweig and David Thelen, *The Presence of the Past* (New York, 1998).

26. See Nora, "Between History and Memory," 1–15.

27. The source of this citation from Halbwachs is Barry Schwartz, "The Reconstruction of Abraham Lincoln," in David Middleton and Derek Edwards, eds., *Collective Remembering* (London, 1991), 104.

28. See Schwartz, "The Reconstruction," and Yael Zerubavel, "New Beginning, Old Past: The Collective Memory of Pioneering in Israeli Culture," in Laurence J. Silberstein, ed., *New Perspectives on Israeli History: The Early Years of the State* (New York, 1990).

29. See James V. Wertsch, "Can We Teach Knowledge and Belief at the Same Time?" in Peter N. Stearns, Peter Seixas, and Sam Wineburg, eds., *Knowing, Teaching, and Learning History: National and International Perspectives* (New York, 2000).

30. For a related point see James Fentress and Chris Wickham, *Social Memory* (Cambridge, Mass., 1992).

31. On the difference between current fashions in cognitive science and its earlier interdisciplinary roots, see Jerome Bruner, *Acts of Meaning* (Cambridge, Mass., 1990).